Principles of EDP Management

Principles of
EDP Management

Alexander
Gaydasch, Jr

Reston Publishing Company, Inc.
A Prentice-Hall Company
Reston, Virginia

Library of Congress Cataloging in Publication Data

Gaydasch, Alexander.
  Principles of EDP management.

  Includes index.
  1. Electronic data processing – Management.
I. Title.
QA76.9.M3G39   658'.054   81-12001
ISBN 0-8359-5604-0   AACR2

  Copyright 1982 by
  Reston Publishing Company, Inc.
  A Prentice-Hall Company
  Reston, Virginia 22090

To CLAIRE
For her patience and encouragement

Contents

Preface

Several years ago I was asked by Roosevelt University in Chicago to develop and teach a course in data-processing management. A list of appropriate topics was suggested and I began to search the literature for a suitable textbook. I found none. I was astonished to discover that, despite the thousands of EDP books on the market, no single text attempts to cover the body of knowledge required to manage a data-processing organization. Considering the awesome turnover of EDP managers and the general disaffection of top management with same, it is curious that more books have not been written on the subject. Data-processing management is a challenging, exhausting, rewarding, frustrating, exciting, important job. It deserves all the support it can get from computer science curriculums and from textbooks.

This book is intended to be the primary text for a survey course in EDP management. In addition, it may be of interest to programmers, systems analysts, and non-EDP executives who need an overview of the EDP management function. Checklists that are provided can also be useful as "memory joggers" for people writing documentation, conducting walkthroughs, preparing a long-range plan, or performing other EDP tasks.

To understand the subject matter covered in the book, the reader should have some experience in applications programming and systems analysis, as well as familiarity with basic operating systems, hardware, telecommunications, and project management concepts. Computer science students should have successfully completed course work in these areas.

The book is organized into a series of topics that are related, but that need not be read in any particular sequence. However, if the reader plans to use the entire book, I suggest starting with Chapter 1 and ending with Chapter 15. This most successfully imparts the panorama intended by the author.

The level of detail in each chapter is generally geared to a presentation of concepts rather than "how-to" material. The reason for this is that most of the topics are covered in great detail in many specialized textbooks. Any attempt on my part to provide a competing level of detail would doom the purpose of this work as a survey text.

This book is intended as a blend of theory and practice. Theories are presented when a theoretical framework is useful in understanding reality. However, I avoid theories when they do not adequately explain reality. I try not to compromise my perceptions of how EDP is or should be managed by advocating universal principles. Rather, I present explanations, guidelines, and suggestions based on my 15 years of experience in the field and on my understanding of other people's experience.

Following are some notes on the terminology used in the book.

- I frequently refer to the EDP manager. By this, I mean the highest-ranking data-processing executive, the person charged with developing, maintaining, and operating the major application systems for the host organization. In today's distributed data-processing environment, and, indeed, under the old-style policies of decentralization, the EDP manager does not necessarily control *all* EDP resources. But someone clearly has major responsibility. He or she is the focus of this book.

- Firm, company, host organization, and organization are used more or less interchangeably. All these terms refer generically to the entity using computers, be it a university, a government agency, a private company, or other institution.

- Hardware model numbers and other vendor-specific terminology are avoided in favor of generic product names and descriptions.

- A Glossary is provided at the end of the book. It is by no means comprehensive and is not intended to serve as a dictionary of data-processing terms. Rather, it covers specific usages in the book.

Acknowledgments

Special thanks go to Claire Gaydasch for her suggestions and comments; to Jack Turner for his insightful technical review; to Firouz Tehrani for his critique of the auditing chapter; and to Teri Nelson for an excellent job of typing my sometimes illegible manuscript.

Naturally, I take full responsibility for the accuracy and quality of the book's contents.

1

HISTORICAL CONTEXT

Today's problems are clearly more important than what happened 20 years ago, so why should an EDP manager, confronted by problems requiring immediate attention, be interested in the history of the profession? There are two very practical answers to this question.

First, history can sometimes arm her students with the ability to make predictions about the future that could not be made without a knowledge of the past. This predictive capacity enables us to anticipate events instead of merely reacting to them. It enables us to avoid some of the mistakes of the past; "He who does not learn from history is forever condemned to repeat it."

Second, long-range planning, an indispensable part of the modern EDP manager's job, is impossible without an understanding of the historical context. The context is important because it provides insight into the direction a firm's EDP activities are headed, based on the general experience of the industry.

Although written almost a decade ago, two *Harvard Business Review*[1] articles accurately delineate the salient characteristics of EDP history since the 1950s. The analysis in this chapter is, in large measure, based on this work. Our analysis examines major hardware, software, and applications development trends, the impact of EDP on the host organization, and the evolving styles of EDP management.

THE 1950s: THE "GEE WHIZ" ERA

The first computers used in the private sector were acquired on faith. The technology was new and expensive, and its success was prob-

---

[1]Frederic G., Withington, *Five Generations of Computers, Harvard Business Review,* July-August, 1974, pp. 99–108; Cyrus F. Gibson, and Richard L. Nolan, *Managing the Four Stages of EDP Growth, Harvard Business Review,* January-February, 1974, pp. 76–88.

lematic. The impact of computers on people and organizations was not known. By today's standards computer systems of the 1950s and early 1960s were primitive: vacuum-tube technology; unit record equipment; slow tape drives using huge, bulky magnetic tapes; rudimentary load-and-run operating systems; and tedious machine-language programming now seem to belong to a distant stone age. However, during the infancy of EDP it was all startling and exotic.

The first computer applications were scientific and military. Soon, however, the U.S. Census Bureau and other large government agencies began to use computers to process vast amounts of paperwork. Giant corporations in the private sector quickly followed suit.

Repetitive, well-defined accounting applications were the first candidates for automation. Thus, the first organizational impact of computers was felt by the clerical staff. The widespread belief at that time was that the computer would cause serious unemployment among clerks, bookkeepers, and other white-collar office workers. Unemployment did, in fact, occur. However, some of the displaced were absorbed into the data-processing function as keypunch operators and control clerks; thanks to the booming economy of the 1950s, others found employment in companies that had not yet automated.

Despite the high prices of early hardware, some cost savings were achieved through clerical reductions. Evidence suggests, however, that management's preoccupation with justifying EDP on the basis of job elimination began to wane by the end of the "Gee Whiz" era. Except in the earliest days of data processing, cost savings, where it has occurred, has tended to take the form of cost avoidance, that is, the ability to slow the growth of clerical staff rather than to reduce the number of clerks. When the history of EDP is finally written, the contribution of computers to reducing cost will be dwarfed by their other benefits.

THE 1960s: THE PAPER PUSHERS

The decade of the 1960s was a tremendous growth period for the computer industry, which doubled in size several times over. It was the heyday of batch applications. Huge volumes of data were processed, but processing was done in a very routine fashion. Every company wanted a computer, and every data-processing manager was obliged to produce bills, payroll checks, and reports on everything from yesterday's sales to the status of accounts receivable.

Applications continued to be heavily concentrated in well-defined functions that were once performed manually. However, accounting applications, payroll, and billing systems were no longer the end-all of the technology. The development of inventory control, personnel, and manufacturing systems also took place. Firms began to explore the computerization of processes that were not as well defined as the earlier financial applications. Teleprocessing was also widely introduced by the late 1960s. However, it was not to permeate the industry until the 1970s.

In addition, some very exotic airline reservation, credit-card processing, and securities tracking systems were implemented. Without these "new business opportunity" systems, the widespread use of credit cards, efficient air travel, and many other aspects of modern life would not be possible.

As expected, the brunt of change was still absorbed by clerks and other office workers. However, as EDP applications became more ambitious, people outside the office became increasingly involved: stock clerks feeding the computer information on withdrawals and additions to inventory, shop foremen using bills of material explosions and computer-generated production schedules, sales managers examining the impact of marketing campaigns, and production managers evaluating the costs of producing various product lines.

The 1960s were also years of great technological change. Transistors replaced vacuum tubes. Magnetic tapes and disks replaced card files as storage media. Compilers and assemblers virtually eliminated machine-language programming. Extensive macro and subroutine libraries reduced the non-application-specific coding programmers were once burdened with. Operating systems became complex and resulted in higher throughput, but at the cost of an ever-increasing need for large amounts of core storage.

The technology spawned a number of new job functions. The most notable of these was system programmer, the individual charged with generating the complex operating system and making it work properly. A greater degree of job specialization took place. The "Renaissance man," who could "do everything," was overwhelmed by the technology and replaced by the specialist. But some things remained the same: in spite of the proliferation of nonfinancial applications, the data-processing manager still reported to the controller.

Organizationally, the decade began with a high degree of centralized control over the EDP function. However, the demand for computer services caused substantial decentralization. As the decade drew to a close, the pendulum swung back to tighter central control. Project control was not highly stressed during the 1960s. This resulted in a very high incidence of development schedules that were not met. The EDP manager earned a reputation for failing to apply sound business practices to his or her area of responsibility.

The "Paper Pusher" era was also a time when even the toughest, most demanding managers meekly submitted to the technicians who made the computer work. Therefore, a high degree of mismanagement and folly was tolerated. Although some retrenchment and control began to take place, dramatic change was not to occur until the 1970s.

THE 1970s: THE COMMUNICATORS

The period of the late 1960s and early 1970s was characterized by the widespread introduction and use of teleprocessing (TP). The continuing drop in hardware costs coupled with increased TP capabilities resulted in the proliferation of sophisticated on-line and real-time applications.

Complex management information systems (MIS), whose main function was to provide data for decision making (as opposed to transaction processing systems, which produce a "product" such as a payroll check) were attempted by many large organizations. These systems were frequently developed to provide data and perform functions that were not possible before the advent of the computer.

A widespread but somewhat optimistic belief was that timely, accurate information produced by the computer would make a dramatic difference in management effectiveness. Unfortunately, this was to prove untrue. Data collection problems caused serious inaccuracies. Many managers steadfastly refused to use computer-generated information, even when it was accurate. Long development cycles, lack of tangible system results, and nebulous paybacks tried the patience of upper management. This resulted in the cancellation of many MIS projects.

Despite the disappointing results achieved by many MIS systems, more and more decision-making information became available to management as a by-product of traditional transaction processing systems. Hence, an increasing impact was felt by middle management. Clerical personnel and bookkeepers were no longer the only "victims" of automation. The practical result was not the thinning of middle management ranks, as had sometimes happened with the clerical function a decade earlier. Rather, the manager's job changed. She or he was expected to learn to use the computer, since some operational data needed to perform a job were now easily available. This removed the tedium of manually compiling needed information from mounds of data but it also removed the control. The middle manager now had to rely more and more on the vicissitudes of computer processing.

Key technological changes that had a wide impact during the 1970s were the following:

- Large scale and very large scale integration (LSI and VLSI) and other component miniaturization, which increased the speed and reliability of hardware.
- Virtual storage, which reduced the importance of program size as related to considerations of readability and maintainability.
- Minicomputers, which precipitated the trend toward distributed processing.
- Intelligent interactive terminals, which changed the complexion of program development work and user access to central files.
- Data base management systems (DBMS), which contributed to increased file integration and precipitated ambitious plans for the central stewardship of corporate data.
- Large-capacity peripheral and main memory storage, which increased the range of applications that could be developed by placing greater amounts of data on line.
- Proliferation of commercially available application packages, which reduced development time for many systems.

Organizationally, the 1970s were characterized by tighter management control of the EDP function and by a reevaluation of the computer's capabilities and limitations. This frequently resulted in a retrenchment that caused cancellation of marginal projects and the reduction of overly ambitious plans. EDP managers, responding to top management's increasing caution and skepticism, began to run a tighter ship. Project-management controls, standards, and efficiency tools were improved or, in some cases, introduced. More attention was paid to end users in order to gain their support and to discourage them from acquiring their own computing resources.

By the middle of the 1970s the typical large, geographically dispersed organization had the following features:

- One or more large-scale computers at corporate headquarters processing the bulk of the firm's applications.
- A full central staff of programmers, analysts, software specialists, and the like.
- Terminals in distant locations used to feed the central facility and to access central data.
- A few pioneering minicomputers processing some applications independently of the central computer and others in conjunction with the corporate mainframe.
- A few "holdover" general-purpose computers at remote locations or divisions. For political reasons or because of the nature of their applications, these computers could not be eliminated as part of the

firm's centralization efforts. These older, second- or third-generation systems have the following characteristics:

—They are used to process applications that cannot be transferred to the central facility or reprogrammed at a reasonable cost.

—They have limited communications capabilities and are used to pass data from the field to the central site.

—They are maintained and operated by a skeleton staff that is discouraged from making any but the most critical changes to the systems.

THE PRESENT

Perhaps the most distinguishing feature of the environment of the late 1970s and early 1980s is the proliferation of mini- and microcomputers, the increasing computing power and control available to end users, and the dramatic progress that has been made in computer technology.

The patterns of EDP resource distribution and control have altered drastically in the last 10 years. High-level languages and inexpensive minicomputer systems that are easy to use and make few demands on the physical environment have, for the first time, given end users a large measure of control over their own systems. Unfortunately, this has frequently resulted in data redundancy and inconsistency between users, equipment incompatibilities, lack of standardization, and the needless duplication of hardware, software, and staff. These problems are being addressed through the increasing flexibility of distributed processing systems.

The emergence of distributed data bases is one example of this flexibility. End users have access to their own data through the use of partitioned or replicated data bases provided by the central facility. Partitioned data bases are subsets of the central data base; replicated data bases are copies thereof. These subsets or copies are available to different processors for inquiry purposes but not for updating. The central facility retains control of data updates. However, the end user can access his own data by writing programs in high-level, user-oriented languages and executing them via interactive facilities.

Another example of control over distributed systems is the ability of various components in a network to "talk" to each other and to the central computer. This reduces hardware incompatibilities and provides the central facility with greater control over the network. In addition, the importance of controlling corporate data and of enforcing standards across data-processing fiefdoms is being recognized.

This will serve to place organizational curbs on the untrammeled acquisition and use of computing power by different locations, divisions, and departments.

The computer now permeates every level of the organization. It affects both the head of the organization and the lowliest clerk. The flow of information is increasingly bidirectional. That is, data are being returned to their original providers in a useful form. This exchange enables logistical decisions to be more centralized, while decentralizing tactical decisions to "where the action is." There is a continuing emphasis on nonfinancial applications. Systems are being developed for less structured functions and for applications that were previously not cost justified. An increase in computer modeling is also taking place. In addition, many small companies can now cost-justify owning computers.

The MIS mistakes of the 1970s are being rectified by arranging the implementation of MIS systems into more modest components that require shorter development cycles. The goals of these systems have also become more realistic.

Organizationally, the EDP function now rarely reports to the controller in large organizations. It may report to the president, a senior vice-president, or an officer who oversees several areas, such as administration, finance, and information services.

Another new aspect is the increasing attention legislatures are paying to the potential privacy abuses posed by the computer. Although current state and federal laws are generally directed at government agencies and, in some cases, at large financial institutions, the private sector will be subject to greater coverage in future legislation. Therefore, firms must pay increasing attention to the impact their application systems may have on privacy.

Table 1–1 summarizes the major impacts of the last 30 years on hardware, software, application systems, and EDP organizations.

LESSONS OF THE PAST

The following lessons drawn from the EDP history of the 1950s, 1960s, and 1970s should be of particular interest to the EDP manager.

- Different firms are at different stages in the use of computers. Although we can generally relate various computing trends to specific time periods, some firms are considerably ahead of their time, while others are still in the 1960s. Adventurous companies took the plunge into teleprocessing, data-base management software, and primitive forms of distributed processing at a time when these were

TABLE 1–1. Historical Context of Electronic Data Processing

Stage	Summary	Hardware	Software	Applications	Impact on Organization
The 1950s: The "Gee Whiz" Era	First halting steps	Vacuum tubes; unit record equipment; first tape drives	Rudimentary load and run operating systems; few utilities	Scientific and military; also simple, repetitive accounting functions; programming is done in machine language	First appearance of exotic computer technicians; first fears of automation among employees
The 1960s: The Paper Pushers	Tremendous growth; large quantities of information processed in a routine manner producing vast quantities of paper	Transistors; random-access, mass-storage devices; fast tape drives and printers; disappearance of much EAM equipment	Compilers, I/O control systems; advent of complex operating systems; greatly expanded use of macro and subroutine libraries; much greater availability of utilities	Proliferation of applications, mostly batch, for well-defined procedures; beginning of "new business opportunity" type applications, such as airline reservations systems	EDP reports to controller; centralization of EDP followed by decentralization; poor project control; heavy impact on clerical staff (some layoffs, transfers, and retraining); end of the computer "Renaissance man"
The 1970s: The Communicators	Advent of widespread teleprocessing	Large-scale integrated circuits; interactive terminals; virtual storage, minicomputers and relatively cheap hardware	Complex operating systems; DBMS software; use of productivity aids such as interactive programming	Teleprocessing applications; development of first MIS systems; development of systems performing functions that had not been done before; greater use of application packages	Centralization; beginning of distributed processing; greater impact on middle management; tighter management control of EDP

Present	Easier user access to data; expanded distributed processing (DDP); increased user control of EDP	Very large file storage; miniaturization; micro- and miniprocessors; very small companies buying computers; Advent of personal computing	Interactive languages; user-oriented English language processors; widespread use of DBMS	Interconnection of systems; emphasis on corporate data and the reduction of data redundancy Nonfinancial applications; Computerization of less structured functions	Combination of centralized, decentralized, and distributed processing; impact on middle and upper management EDP reports to higher-level management; government intervention (privacy legislation)
Summary of trends since the 1950s		Cheaper, faster hardware	More elaborate, more complex, more expensive software	Less structured functions, less emphasis on direct cost savings	Centralization to decentralization to centralization to distributed processing; greater people versus hardware costs, greater management versus clerical impact; more user involvement

still novel, untested technologies. Conversely, some firms still do little teleprocessing and continue to maintain a totally centralized environment. It is, therefore, always necessary to learn the specifics of a situation before making assumptions based on broad historical trends.

- No firm can long remain totally immune from technological trends and the attitudes those trends inspire. For example, the use of "tried and true" second- or third-generation computer systems may be highly cost effective for a specific company; but the scarcity of programmers willing to risk technological obsolescence by working in an outdated environment may force an upgrade to state-of-the-art equipment.

- Exclusion of the EDP function from normal organizational discipline, where it still occurs, is a temporary phenomena. Sooner or later data-processing performance must measure up to expenditures and expectations. EDP managers should never delude themselves into believing that their arcane craft is forever beyond the comprehension and control of corporate management.

- Major changes in computer use and in the organization of the computer function will continue to be influenced primarily by technology. Most of the significant trends over the past 30 years were triggered by advances in technology. For example, the use of powerful operating systems and high-level user-oriented languages was made possible by the tremendous drop in the cost of memory, distributed processing was made possible by the development of mini- and microcomputers, and the proliferation of on-line and real-time applications was influenced, in large measure, by advances in telecommunications and display terminal technology.

- Computer technology does not exist in a vacuum. It is most influential when it can be translated into systems that support real user needs and when it does not clash with deeply ingrained attitudes. Thus, high-level languages, minicomputers, and teleprocessing systems have enjoyed great popularity. Computer modeling and MIS applications, on the other hand, have met with mixed results, despite the availability and reasonable cost of the requisite technology. The reason is that high-level languages, minicomputers, and TP applications have produced tangible results for end users. But, in many cases, modeling and MIS applications, for reasons discussed elsewhere in this book, have not. The key fact is that without the support of the ultimate consumer, the end user, technological advances will not be translated into usable forms.

Discussion Questions

1. Describe the evolution of hardware and software through the 1950s, 1960s, and 1970s.
2. Describe the changing nature of applications systems.
3. What impact have computers had on clerical personnel, middle management, and top management?
4. What role has the computer played in reducing costs and performing functions that were never done before?
5. Describe the evolution of management control over the EDP function.
6. What lessons can we learn by studying EDP history?

2 PLANNING

IMPORTANCE OF PLANNING

Planning is the process of making risk-taking decisions systematically and with forethought and then organizing efforts to carry out those decisions. Risk is a necessary ingredient. If there is no risk of making a wrong decision or mismanaging the execution of a decision, planning becomes trivial. And planning must be done systematically and with forethought or it becomes spontaneous action, the direct opposite of planning.

Planning is *necessary* because the work to be done generally exceeds available resources. This forces the establishment of priorities, a task that cannot be performed in a rational manner without planning. Planning is *important* because it enhances our ability to design and implement effective computer systems that support corporate goals and objectives. In addition, planning has the following virtues:

- A plan provides a framework for orderly change by enhancing our ability to make changes compatible with the general direction and scope of a project.
- Planning is consistent with the strong human need for order, predictability, and routine. People become frustrated and disoriented if called upon to constantly improvise.
- Planning forces careful evaluation of priorities and systematic consideration of factors that may not have surfaced without special attention.
- The existence of a written EDP plan indicates deliberation and forethought on the part of the EDP manager. This places her or him in a stronger position when lobbying for and justifying the EDP budget. The plan is a tangible record of how the department supports company goals and how the money will be spent.

In recent years, the importance of EDP planning has increased dramatically. This is due to several important trends:

- Computers are now at the heart of many corporate functions. Twenty years ago, EDP was used mainly to support and streamline administrative functions. These functions were important but not necessarily critical to the main business of the company. Late bills, even late payrolls, though not easily tolerated, would not critically affect the competitive position of a company unless the problems persisted. Today, however, the collapse of an airline reservation system or an inefficient order entry system could cripple an entire company. The price we pay for poor or inadequate EDP planning is much higher today than it was 20 years ago.

- The amount of money spent on EDP as a percentage of the Gross National Product or corporate expenditures has increased dramatically. In the 1950s, expenditures on EDP typically represented 1 to 1½ percent of gross sales. This figure for many companies now stands at 2 to 3 percent and is sometimes as high as 15 percent in certain industries, such as insurance, that are inundated by paperwork. Therefore, the sheer size of EDP expenditures warrants greater attention by management. This, in turn, increases the importance of planning.

- More computer systems now cross departmental boundaries. The increasing complexity of computer systems, including the development of data-base technology, has increased the sharing of files and data banks. This requires greater coordination between EDP and various system users and forces everyone to plan more effectively. For example, as long as an order-entry system simply produced bills and shop orders, little interdepartmental coordination was necessary. But once that system begins to automatically trigger production schedule changes and finished goods inventory reductions, a great deal of planning becomes necessary to synchronize and control these activities.

- Increasing government regulations necessitate more careful coordination and planning between system designers and other company personnel. Accountants, lawyers, and planners may need to be consulted in order to incorporate needed system features. Privacy legislation, equal opportunity initiatives, tax and accounting regulations, ecological considerations, and safety rules may all require system control and reporting features that were unnecessary 10 years ago. In addition, if a company is a defense contractor or receives grants and subsidies, special accounting features are required. The EDP plan is particularly important for governmental and quasi-governmental organizations. Since funding agencies are frequently not familiar with the day-to-day functioning of the funded organization, the EDP plan may be the most important single source of information about that organization's EDP activities.

EDP planning is important on both the corporate and project levels. Corporate EDP planning is generally long range (i.e., 3 to 5 years) and is concerned with supporting overall corporate goals and objectives. This type of planning is described in this chapter. Project planning corresponds with the length of a project (rarely more than three years) and is mainly concerned with the effective scheduling, organization, and execution of individual projects. Project planning is exhaustively covered in many excellent project management texts and is explored from a management perspective in Chapter 4. The remainder of this chapter describes the information an EDP plan should contain, suggests a methodology for plan development, and proposes a strategy for defining application priorities.

CONTENTS OF THE EDP PLAN

The EDP plan should contain sufficient information to answer the following questions:

- How is the EDP department organized, what is its philosophy, how has it evolved, and what kind of hardware and software does it use?
- What applicaton systems are currently operational or under development?
- How is EDP supporting major corporate activities and goals?
- What systems should be developed over the next 3 to 5 years, what should their development priorities be, and what resources will be needed to support systems development?
- What internal improvements and projects is the EDP department engaged in?

The audience for the EDP plan is corporate and user management, as well as EDP personnel. The plan is, in fact, at least as much an external document as it is an internal document. It is a vehicle for presenting the EDP story to people outside the EDP department and should be understandable to nontechnical people. Thus, conflicts over terminology and level of detail should generally be settled in favor of the lay audience, the non-EDP personnel. Data processors who need extra detail can examine working papers, detailed system write-ups and other background documentation used to prepare the plan.

The following is a description of each part of the plan. A detailed contents checklist is included.

Philosophy, Organization, and History of the EDP Department

This section of the plan is important because it defines the theoretical, historical, and organizational framework within which the actions of the EDP department take place. By reading the philosophy portion of the plan, the reader should gain an understanding of how systems are selected for development; how time and resources needed for their development are estimated, including a description of capacity planning; and how projects are controlled. It also imparts an understanding of how EDP interacts with the user community, particularly with respect to how it bills for its services, how it protects its resources (e.g., data files and equipment) and what it is doing to improve the efficiency and effectiveness of its internal operations. In addition, disaster recovery provisions, such as off-site storage of master files, should be described.

The organization section defines the reporting structure and describes the activities and responsibilities of each organizational unit within EDP.

The history section describes the evolution of the EDP department in terms of hardware, software, physical facilities, and applications systems. It establishes the context within which EDP in this organization should be viewed. It provides a picture of the sequence in which applications were developed and the relative emphasis given to various functional areas in the organization by EDP. Also of interest is a description of progress that has been made since the issuance of the last EDP plan. If a new plan is issued every two or more years, a separate section should probably be devoted to progress since the last plan.

Relationship between Company Activities, Goals, and Potential EDP Systems

This is potentially the most difficult and most important section of the plan. The reason is that the selection of and setting priorities for application systems for development hinge in large part on the accuracy with which these systems are identified with important company activities and goals. A graphic representation accompanied by a narrative is generally the most effective method of describing these relationships (see the sample management systems requirements chart at the end of this chapter). Corporate activities and goals that form the basis of development recommendations should also be stated. The process of identifying EDP systems with organizational goals and activities is described in the plan development section.

Hardware/Software Inventory

This part of the plan provides the reader with an inventory and summary description of the hardware and software components that support the firm's EDP activities. Of particular interest are components with which the user interacts directly, such as terminals and high-level query languages. Other important components include job accounting and capacity planning software. Applications should be described in the next section.

Current EDP Activities

This part of the plan describes currently operational application systems and their benefits. It also identifies projects under development and may include a description of enhancements to current systems. The level of detail should be commensurate with the size and importance of the systems being described. In addition to application systems, internal projects such as the installation of new software and hardware, the development of standards, and the tuning of applications and operating systems should be described.

Proposed Systems

This section describes the features, characteristics, and benefits of application systems proposed for development within the next 3 to 5 years. Systems proposed for development within the next year or two should be described in greater detail than systems proposed for development toward the end of the plan period.

Priorities and Schedules

This is generally in the form of a Gantt chart[1] representing the sequence and elapsed times for implementing the systems proposed for development. Since some of the proposed systems may not yet have been subjected to a feasibility study, the elapsed times are very rough estimates. Nevertheless, a "guesstimate" of development times must be attempted in order to define system dependencies and to project employee availability.

---

[1]See Glossary.

Resource Requirements

This section of the plan describes the hardware, software, people, facilities, and budget needed to implement the systems proposed in the plan. If carefully researched, it serves the important function of bringing the "wish list" of desirable systems into conformity with the real world of limited resources. Estimating resource requirements is described in Chapter 4.

Constraints and Assumptions

This section also helps inject a sense of reality into the plan. Some very important constraints and assumptions, such as the following, can spell the difference between success and failure:

- Availability of key people.
- Support of top management, particularly with reference to an adequate budget allocation.
- Support of user management, especially the availability of user personnel to help with systems definition.
- On-time delivery of hardware and software.

DEVELOPING THE EDP PLAN

Six steps must be performed to develop an effective EDP plan:

- Organize plan development.
- Prepare the plan context.
- Identify major corporate activities and goals.
- Relate data processing and manual systems to these activities and goals.
- Select development priorities.
- Define resource requirements.

These steps are initiated in the sequence listed. However, overlap will occur because some information needed to complete one step may not be available until the next step. For example, resource requirements necessarily affect the selection of development priorities, and development priorities may, in turn, influence the technological orientation described in preparing the plan context.

The following sections describe each plan development step.

Organizing Plan Development

Who should be responsible for developing the EDP plan? Some organizations support a full-time planning staff. If this is the case, the planning section is the natural choice. However, just as war is too important to be left to the generals, planning is too important to be left exclusively to planners.

The most common problems of EDP plans developed by professional planners are unreality and bureaucratese. Since planning is usually a staff function removed from life in the trenches and since planners use jargon unfamiliar to computer users, plans produced under the aegis of the "planning department" frequently suffer from these twin ailments. It is, therefore, wise for line EDP management to carefully monitor plan development.

If no planning group exists, the person responsible for developing the plan should be a senior project leader or manager with the following abilities:

- Writes well.
- Can organize effectively.
- Is familar with the day-to-day activities and problems of EDP.
- Has a good knowledge of existing and planned application systems.
- Has good contacts within the user community.

Admittedly, this is a tall order. However, long-range planning, at least in medium-sized installations, need not be a full-time job. An individual meeting these qualifications can be "borrowed" for several months to develop the plan. (Since the process of developing the EDP plan provides excellent exposure to user management and to the workings of the entire EDP department, plan development may be a very good transitional assignment for a capable project leader slated for promotion.)

Regardless of whether the planning section or a line manager is responsible for plan development, major activities will include the following:

- Collection of information from users of EDP services and from internal EDP sources.
- Collation and editing of this material.
- A substantial amount of original writing.
- A significant amount of analysis and interviewing.

Project leaders, managers, and, perhaps, senior systems analysts, representing all major functions in the EDP department, should attend a meeting at which the intention to develop the EDP plan is announced by the director of EDP. The importance, general contents, and development schedule for the plan should also be discussed.

This "kickoff meeting" is important because it puts the entire EDP department on notice that cooperation with the plan developer is expected, that assignments given to individuals by the plan developer must be completed on time and in a workmanlike fashion, and that plan development is a serious project that will be controlled and managed with the same vigor as an application development project. The reason for this emphasis is that planning has traditionally taken a back seat to the ongoing, day-to-day activities of the EDP department. Therefore, people tend not to take plan development seriously unless EDP management is visibly and emphatically supportive. The plan developer cannot be expected to produce the entire plan "from scratch." In addition to extensive discussions with users and potential users of EDP services, many pieces of the plan must come from people who represent the EDP areas that the plan covers. The plan developer is particularly dependent on applications development, operations, program maintenance, and systems programming people. The kickoff meeting is a convenient place to request information from people in these areas. This information should include the following:

- Status of current activities
- Summary descriptions of current systems
- Current short- and long-term commitments
- Inventory of hardware and software

Preparing the Plan Context

This step of plan development consists of preparing and incorporating into the plan the following items:

- Philosophy, organization, and history of the EDP department
- Current EDP activities and commitments
- Constraints and assumptions

Typically, this information is received from project leaders, systems analysts, and managers in the EDP department through assignments made at the kickoff meeting. However, since the quality and writing style of material submitted to the plan developer will vary widely, a substantial amount of rewriting generally takes place. In addition, original research and writing is required, particularly when formal documentation describing the EDP charter and philosophy does not exist. Plan development may, in fact, be an excellent opportunity to define the role, philosophy, and constraints of the EDP function. However, unless the stated philosophy is reasonably congruent with actual practice, the credibility of the entire plan will suffer.

Identifying Major Company Activities and Goals

The EDP function must be in tune with the major activities, goals, and objectives of the host organization. Data processing has no life of its own outside that of the customers it serves, and its only reason for existing is to satisfy their needs. American business is littered with the bones of EDP managers who lost sight of this critical fact.

The identification of major activities and functions performed by a company requires an organizational analysis that answers two questions: (1) What is the major business of the company? and (2) What functions and activities must be performed to support this business? The answer to the first question is apparent in a single-business company such as a manufacturing firm, a public transportation company, or a retail store. The major business may be manufacturing shoelaces, operating busses or selling consumer goods. Frequently, however, companies consist of divisions engaged in different lines of business. In this case, divisional EDP plans can be combined into a single corporate plan.

The identification of functions and activities needed to support the company's major business is triggered by examining the company organization chart. Each major organizational component is analyzed to identify the following:

- The functions that it performs.
- The information it needs to perform these functions.
- The bottlenecks and inadequacies that prevent more successful performance.

Unless a company is a first-time computer user, this type of analysis is performed over a period of years. As individual systems are evaluated and developed, more information on how the company works and what its problems are is accumulated. When developing the plan, this information is interpreted and organized into a form suitable for inclusion. Despite the fact that much of this information may be available in old feasibility studies, memos, and system development requests, a substantial amount of original research and systems analysis must still be done. User interviews, information flow and forms analyses, job and function definitions, and an examination of volumes and processing schedules are employed.

Major company activities and functions can be recognized by attention to the following guidelines:

- Important activities are controlled by powerful, influential executives.
- Important activities have large budgets.
- Important activities report to a high organizational level.
- The organization structure of most companies reflects the company's critical functions.
- The budgets of important activities are resistant to cutbacks and economies during periods of slow business activity.
- The problems of important functions are widely discussed, gossiped about, and generally considered to be critical to the welfare of the organization.

The identification and interpretation of corporate goals may be a more difficult task than defining major activities. Company goals may be contained in a formal corporate long-range plan or they may exist only in the everyday actions, comments, and memoranda of management. If available, both formal and informal sources of information should be used.

A formal corporate plan is probably the most accurate written indication of corporate goals. Annual reports, sales brochures, and other public documents are self-serving and, therefore, less accurate and candid. But formal documentation rarely tells the full story. For an EDP manager to be aware of real as opposed to stated corporate goals and objectives, he or she must be tuned in to the thinking and actions of top management. This requires a dedicated interest in non-EDP business matters and a highly developed political sense, qualities that, unfortunately, are often not found in EDP managers. Although much has been written in the trade press about the evils of insularity and narrow technical orientation, the continuing high turnover among EDP managers clearly indicates that they are less at home in the management community than, say, marketing or production executives.

The recognition of corporate goals must be followed by their translation into objectives that are meaningful to EDP. For example, to be useful, the following goals require further explanation:

- Increase profit margins.
- Increase market share.

- Reduce production costs.
- Decrease clerical costs.

Until we understand the *magnitude* of change that is expected and the projected *means* of achieving it, we cannot develop an accurate tie in to EDP. Therefore, the identification of goals must go beyond generalities and platitudes. It requires the agreement of senior management on numbers and strategies.

Numbers are important because, if examined in context, they indicate the seriousness with which goals are to be pursued. For example, a 10 percent increase in sales in a moribund or declining market will require enormous sales effort and, probably, a large commitment of resources (more salesmen, better market intelligence, and the like). On the other hand, a 10 percent increase in a rapidly growing market may not require any additional resources. The greater the degree of sacrifice needed to achieve a specific goal, the greater the esteem in which that goal is held by top management—and the greater the potential EDP budget for its support. This is an important consideration when development priorities are established.

The explication of how corporate goals are to be achieved is also important because it helps to define the role EDP must play in meeting those goals. For example, if increased market share is to be accomplished through acquisitions, EDP support may be limited to tailoring current corporate financial systems to accept accounting data from new subsidiaries. However, if market share is to be increased through more accurate sales forecasting and faster product deliveries, EDP may play a major role by developing market models, production scheduling systems, and material requirements generation systems.

Table 2–1 illustrates how general goals may be translated into objectives meaningful to EDP. Once that is done, we can begin to define the specific computer systems needed to support those goals.

Relating Computer Systems to Major Company Activities and Goals

This step of plan development consists of matching the needs of the organization with potential data-processing applications. Organizational needs were defined in the previous step of plan development by an organizational analysis. This analysis identified the functions of each organizational unit, the information required to perform these functions, the products that each organizational unit produces, and the problems that reduce efficiency.

The matching process requires developing general specifications

TABLE 2–1. Translation of Corporate Goals

General Goal	Magnitude	Means of Achievement	Possible Computer Support
Increase profit margins	+10%	Increased volume of sales	Market analysis; profitability analysis
Increase market share	+20%	Acquisition of other companies in the same business	Integration of corporate-wide computer resources and systems
Reduce production costs	−5%	Improve production scheduling and reduce waste	Production scheduling; production "rnix" analysis
Decrease clerical costs	−10%	Improve efficiency of order processing	Order entry

for systems, both automated and manual, that will support organizational needs. Normally, these have evolved over a period of years as a by-product of feasibility studies. However, appropriate formating and description are required before inclusion into the plan.

A systems analyst experienced in a broad range of applications can frequently match organizational needs with EDP systems through knowledge of commonly used applications such as payroll, personnel, inventory, and accounts payable. More arcane applications are more difficult to match. Table 2–2 illustrates the relationships between departments and functions, products, and type of EDP system. A convenient analysis technique is to categorize EDP information needed by various organizational units into *decision support* data and *transaction* data that directly affect the products produced by a department. Decision support data, such as the following, provide information for people to use in making business decisions:

- Sales statistics
- Cost accounting data
- Budget projections
- Inventory use statistics

Transaction data trigger concrete activities and events. These activities may result in the production of the following:

- Customer bills
- Payroll checks
- Inventory reorder notices
- Mailing lists

TABLE 2–2. Relationship of Department to Function, Product, and System Type

Department	Major Functions	Products	System Type
Marketing	Make sales and enter orders	Customer orders	Transaction
	Pay commissions	Commission checks	Transaction
	Perform market analysis	Statistical reports	Decision support
	Develop product pricing models	Pricing models	Decision support
Budget/Finance	Monitor expenses and income	Accounting entries	Both
	Prepare and process annual budgets	Budget documents	Both
	Perform financial modeling to support budget preparation	Budgeting alternatives	Decision support
Payroll	Pay employees	Payroll checks	Transaction
Inventory	Plan requirements	Component estimates	Decision support
	Record issues and receipts	Records of issues and receipts	Transaction
	Monitor inventory and reorder when needed	Reorder notices	Both
Purchasing/accounts payable	Match materials receipts with payments	Payment authorization	Transaction
	Track and analyze vendor performance	Performance reports	Decision support
	Print checks to vendors	Checks	Transaction
	Select vendors	Selected suppliers	Decision support
Personnel	Monitor job and skill histories	Support promotion and transfer policies	Decision support
	Monitor and schedule annual physical examinations	Physical examination schedules	Transaction
	Monitor minority hiring and promotion programs	Reports to government agencies and hiring decisions	Both

Decision support systems are commonly used in modeling, statistical analysis, performance reporting, and historical studies. Transaction-oriented systems are used for data collection, payroll, accounts payable, inventory, accounts receivable, and other systems that result in a tangible product. Most modern systems have both decision support and transaction processing characteristics. However, usually one or the other set of characteristics predominates.

Accounting is an example of an application that is used for both decision support and transaction processing. Accounting systems are the lifeblood of a commercial organization because they inform management of expenditures and income. This information is used as a decision support tool to determine pricing strategies, production decisions, inventory levels, staffing requirements, and the like. But, in addition, accounting systems are transaction systems because they produce information used in annual reports and tax returns. These are tangible products.

Selecting Development Priorities

Choosing application priorities is, in the final analysis, a political decision. By "political," I mean a decision based on the web of personal and professional relationships that exist among people in every organization. It must be emphasized that "political" is not necessarily synonymous with "nonrational." Quite the contrary. If the system of rewards in an organization is predicated, however imperfectly, on the quality of an individual manager's performance, the "political" nature of the relationship will coincide to a large extent with what is perceived to be good for specific departments. These departmental needs must, of course, be balanced in such a way as to provide maximum benefits to the organization as a whole.

Since few, if any, EDP alternatives are overwhelmingly persuasive strictly on their merits, the costs and benefits of a computer system are largely a function of the perception of individual managers. An "objective" decision based "on the facts" (graphs, charts, impressive figures) may, in reality, consist of a gut feel judgment. This is particularly apparent when management information systems (MIS) or decision-support systems are being evaluated. Their success or failure frequently lies in the realm of self-fulfilling prophecy: a strongly supported, enthusiastically accepted system may improve the management of a particular function even if the technology is weak and the justification for the system is questionable. On the other hand, EDP history is replete with technologically elegant systems that failed through lack of user acceptance.

The 12 questions outlined next cover the most critical issues that must be faced when committing resources to sizable projects.

1. Does the application affect a major corporate activity or is the activity trivial?

2. Does the application support major corporate goals? For example, market research and sales analyses are appropriate for companies trying to increase market share; on the other hand, systems that can reduce costs or quicken cash collections are important for companies trying to increase profit margins and improve cash flow.

3. Does the system contribute to cost savings or cost avoidance?

4. Is user management enthusiastic and supportive? Does this support extend to the organizational level that will actually operate and use the system?

5. Is the complexity and character of the system consonant with the character of the company and the level of EDP experience of the user? A boldly innovative system in a conservative, tradition-bound company is implanted at great risk because it is a departure from "the way things are done." Similarly, a system requiring great sophistication on the part of the user is inappropriate as a first computer application for a department.

6. Are company politics "right?" Is the user in a relatively strong position within the company or is she or he vulnerable to budget cuts that will reduce the ability to support the new system?

7. Is the user's level of competence reasonably high and is the department adequately managed? Computer systems are difficult enough to implement in well-run, highly competent departments; they are extremely difficult to implement if the user is not very good at his or her own job. Unfortunately, users with chronic personnel or operating problems sometimes delude themselves into thinking that a computer system will be a magic substitute for competence and hard work. This is never the case.

8. Does the development of the system enjoy top management support or is it supported only by the immediate user? Without top management support, development efforts may be vulnerable to budget cuts and even cancellation, particularly when deadlines are missed or cost estimates are inaccurate.

9. Does the proposed system enhance or support a "balanced portfolio" of high-risk versus low-risk projects? The repertoire of projects for an EDP installation is analogous to an investment portfolio: it should attempt to maintain a balance between risky, high-payoff systems and safe, low-return systems. The concept of risk as it applies to EDP projects is discussed in the Risk Analysis section of this chapter.

10. What degree of adjustment is required before the user can effectively work with the system? Systems requiring drastic reorientation will be more difficult to implement successfully than sys-

tems that closely follow the habitual rhythm of the user department.

11. Can the system be implemented in small modules or stages without substantially lowering its payoff? There are three advantages to modularity: "results" are achieved faster, thus allaying management doubts about a system's effectiveness; experience gained in developing and operating one stage can be transmitted to the development of the next stage; and, in case of difficulties such as overruns, schedule delays, and design oversights, a scaled-down version of the system can be adopted without sacrificing system usefulness.

12. Does the system provide EDP with visibility and a positive image? This may seem like a more fitting concern for public relations people than for EDP professionals. However, the reality is that data processing, like every other function in an organization, must compete for a chunk of a finite budget that will be allocated according to *perceived* achievements and needs. Therefore, EDP must lobby on its own behalf by developing systems that lend themselves to favorable publicity.

Defining Resource Requirements and Commitments

The development of the systems defined in the plan requires the commitment of personnel and computing resources, without which the projects cannot be undertaken. Therefore, the plan should always include a best-guess estimate of the following:

- EDP and user personnel required to develop, maintain, and operate each proposed system.
- The hardware and software needed to develop and operate each proposed system (CPU capacity, terminals, disk space, software packages, and so on).
- Total EDP and user resource requirements for all systems included in the plan, based on estimates for individual systems.

The development of detailed estimates is described under feasibility studies in Chapters 5 and 6. However, in the plan it is frequently not possible to achieve a great level of detail, because not all systems proposed for inclusion will have been thoroughly researched. Indeed, it is almost impossible to develop a long-range EDP plan without a good deal of speculation and guesswork, particularly on systems scheduled for development 3 to 5 years in the future.

However, some resource requirements, such as the following, may be predicted at the time the plan is developed.

- Terminals and networks needed for some new TP applications.
- Application software packages for systems that will not be developed in-house.
- The addition of third-shift operations personnel for high-volume batch systems that may overwhelm current operations schedules.
- User data entry personnel for systems with distributed data entry.
- Sufficient personnel coverage for systems requiring 24-hour attention.
- The installation of a data-base management system or other software that requires upgrading to a different version of the operating system.
- The implementation of a system whose master files will consume mass storage space not currently available.

Personnel estimates for systems that have not yet been exposed to a feasibility study may be off by as much as 100%. However, an estimate must still be made, because inclusion and scheduling of each system into the plan will depend on the resources used by every other system. Approximations based on past experience may be used to calculate the number of programs, predicted system complexity, and other variables described in the resource estimating section of Chapter 4.

A very important resource estimate that is frequently neglected is user commitment of personnel during system development. Since the development process is a partnership between the client and EDP personnel, the plan should always contain explicit descriptions and estimates of user involvement.

UPDATING THE PLAN

To reflect changes and current conditions, the plan should be periodically updated. Every 2 years is probably appropriate. Each new version of the plan will, therefore, stretch about 2 years farther into the future than the preceding version.

The following portions of the plan are particularly susceptible to becoming dated:

- Current EDP commitments and activities
- Proposed systems
- Priorities and schedules
- Resource requirements
- Hardware and software configuration

A suggested approach to updating the plan is to carry out an abbreviated version of the first step described in the preceding section, Organizing Plan Development. EDP personnel should be asked to review the current plan for completeness, accuracy, and currency. Non-EDP personnel involved with system planning should be asked to reevaluate their needs and commitments. Comments and suggestions offered through this process will be incorporated into the new version of the plan. The plan should then be reviewed and modified according to the remaining development steps.

RISK ANALYSIS[1]

The risk analysis concept postulates that, all other things being equal (e.g., a competent staff, sufficient resources, a meaningful application), project risk will depend on the following factors:

- Degree of predetermined structure in the system
- Use of new computer technology
- Project size

Predetermined Structure

Predetermined structure is the extent to which a computer system emulates tasks or activities being currently performed. A high degree of predetermined structure is present if many of the new system's major functions are already defined and are being performed manually or by an existing computer system. For example, a payroll or accounts receivable system generally results in the automation of a series of known steps. A logical, predefined methodology exists for calculating hours worked, deductions, and other information required to produce payroll checks. Likewise, the printing of invoices and the calculation of charges is a well-practiced activity. Because the nature of the information, its method of production and its uses are well known, the risk of problems is minimized.

By the same token, computer applications are subject to greater risk when they produce information that has never been used before or produce information in a totally unique fashion (e.g., through the

---

[1]This section is based, in large measure, on ideas of project risk presented by David Norton of Noland, Norton, & Company, Lexington, Massachusetts, and F. Warren McFarlan of Harvard University. It is taken from the *Information Systems Handbook*, F. Warren McFarlan and Richard L. Nolan, eds., Dow Jones-Irwin, Inc., Homewood, Ill., 1975.

use of data-entry terminals at the source of the information). The degree of predetermined structure of such systems is low.

New Technology

New technology refers to the degree to which technology that has not been used before by an organization will be used by this system. The technology could be state-of-the-art or merely hardware and software that company personnel are unfamiliar with. The development of systems utilizing new or unfamiliar technology is more prone to unanticipated problems than systems using familiar, tried and true hardware and software. These problems include the following:

- Incomplete or inaccurate documentation of the products being used.
- The presence of software "bugs".
- Untested hardware.
- Lack of experience in the use of system features and options.
- Unavailability of high-quality support from the vendor.
- Inaccurate project scheduling due to inexperience with the new components.

Project Size

Project size is also an important risk factor. The sheer size of a project in terms of resources applied, number of computer programs and manual procedures required, and volume of data the system must eventually process severely affects project risk. The reasons large projects are more prone to serious problems than small projects are as follows:

- Coordination and communication problems are magnified out of proportion to project size. Interactions among 20 project team members are more than twice as complex as interactions among members of a 10-person team. This phenomena is explained in Chapter 4.
- System testing is more complex in systems that contain many programs, and system problems are more difficult to trace.
- User training must be carried out on a larger scale and must be better coordinated and more formalized.
- Reruns, backups, conversions, and other data-manipulation procedures are more difficult and time consuming.

Risk Analysis Summary

- *The degree of risk is inversely proportional to the degree of predetermined structure of the system being automated; that is, less structure equals greater risk.*
- *The degree of risk is directly proportional to the degree to which new technology is used. That is, the greater the use of new technology, the greater the risk of project failure.*
- *The degree of risk is directly proportional to the size of a project. Large projects are riskier than small projects.*

As stated earlier, a data-processing manager is well advised to keep a balanced portfolio of high- and low-risk projects. High risk projects are large, utilize unfamiliar technology, and result in systems that produce new information and require drastically different manual procedures. Medium-risk projects may have one or two high-risk factors:

- A large project using familiar technology but producing unique information.
- A small project using new technology but having a low degree of predetermined structure.
- A state-of-the-art system that automates a familiar process and does not require great resource expenditures.

Low-risk projects are usually small in scale, utilize familiar components and automate a well-established process.

PLAN CONTENTS CHECKLIST

The following is a listing of information the long-range plan should contain.

Philosophy, Organization, and History of the Data-Processing Department
- EDP charter, mission, and statement of responsibilities.
- Scope of EDP activities.
- Systems development philosophy.
- Hardware and software acquisition (e.g., financing) philosophy.
- Project control philosophy.
- Compliance with privacy legislation and computer support of government-mandated regulations.

- Criteria used to establish development priorities.
- System backup, security, and disaster recovery provisions.
- Project estimating techniques.
- Capacity planning methodology.
- Types of formal standards that exist in the department.
- User request procedures.
- User billing (charge-out) philosophy.
- Technological orientation of the department.
- Departmental organization chart and a description of major organizational units.
- Hardware, software, physical facilities, and applications systems evolution.

Relationship Between Company Goals and EDP Systems

- Pictoral representation and narrative description of major company activities cross-referenced with systems that support those activities. Also see sample Management Systems Requirements (Figure 2–1) at the end of the chapter.
- Description of how EDP supports corporate goals.

Hardware and Software Inventory

- Current hardware (including schematics).
- Current software (operating systems, utilities, language processors, and the like).
- TP network.

Current EDP Activities

- Application systems: operational.
- Application systems: under development.
- Internal projects (standards development, operating system tuning, installation of new hardware, and so on).
- Benefits of current systems and projects.

Proposed Systems

- Features and characteristics
- Benefits

Priorities and Schedules

- System dependencies
- Proposed development schedules

Resource Requirements

- Budgets
- Hardware
- Software
- People
- Facilities

Constraints and Assumptions

- Top management and user support, including the availability of key people.
- Budget availability.
- Vendor considerations (delivery schedules, new product developments, availability of financing arrangements, and the like).

CHARACTERISTICS OF AN EFFECTIVE LONG-RANGE EDP PLAN

- It covers a specific time period, usually 3 to 5 years.
- It contains sufficient detail to be meaningful but not so much detail as to become easily dated when changes occur. Specifically, the plan should contain more detail for the first year than for the last.
- It contains clearly defined objectives (what do we want to accomplish?), goals (what will be our milestones and checkpoints?), and strategy (how will we accomplish our objectives?).
- It indicates the constraints and assumptions on which the plan was based, including the following:
  —EDP resources needed to support the plan (budget, hardware, software, personnel).
  —Timeliness of management decisions needed to implement various portions of the plan.
  —Required user commitments.
- It clearly relates EDP goals and objectives to corporate goals and objectives.
- It is supported by top management, represents a consensus of corporate thinking, and reflects substantial input from the functional areas affected by the plan.
- It indicates the specific responsibilities of EDP and each user department affected by the plan.
- It is practical and feasible in terms of technology, corporate resources, the political and economic environment, and the capabilities of the EDP staff. Realization of the plan cannot be contingent

on unlikely events (e.g., a 30 percent sales increase in a dormant industry), fundamental changes in company thinking (e.g., conservative management rapidly becoming innovative), technological breakthroughs (e.g., quantum increases in teleprocessing capabilities), or dramatic productivity increases in the EDP staff (e.g., wholesale elimination of "deadwood," the successful implementation of productivity techniques, the use of "programming machines").

- It is reviewed and updated on a periodic basis (usually every 2 years).
- It is written in language that is easily understood by non-EDP people. The plan is, after all, a declaration to the rest of the company of what EDP has accomplished, and hopes to accomplish in the future, and why the firm should continue to support its activities.

SAMPLE MANAGEMENT SYSTEMS REQUIREMENTS CHART

Figure 2–1 identifies the array of systems a fictitious company, Gotham City Bus Lines, needs to operate successfully. It is derived from an actual 5-year EDP plan developed by the author for the Chicago Transit Authority. The degree of automation in each system identified in the chart will depend on the importance of the business function the system affects, the costs and benefits of automation in each area, and the availability of EDP and user resources. Note that not all the functions listed will or should be automated. Some of the indicated systems may have already been automated; others will be automated in the future; some may never be automated owing to cost and technology considerations.

The vertical axis of the chart presents the following groupings of major types of systems:

- *Strategic planning.* These systems provide top management with summary information necessary to make major policy and strategy decisions. They include labor negotiation strategies, the construction of new bus facilities, major route changes, investment and borrowing decisions, and high-level personnel and budget planning.
- *Management information and control.* These systems provide supervisory and middle management with detail and summary revenue, expenditure, and performance information needed to effectively manage major activities on a day-to-day basis. These systems produce maintenance scheduling information, personnel attendance data, Equal Employment Opportunities Commission compliance information, various accounting reports, materials management control information, and other operating data.

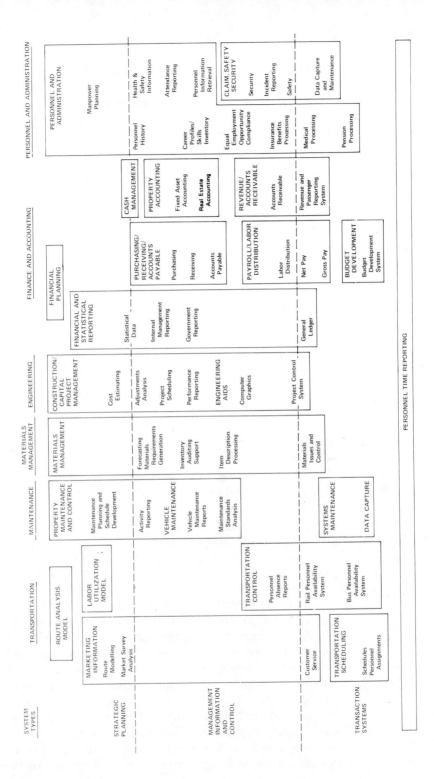

FIGURE 2–1. Gotham City Bus Company Management Systems Requirements

- *Transaction systems.* These systems perform three major functions: they capture and edit data at its source for later use by management information and strategic-planning-systems; they produce tangible products such as payroll checks; and they replace well-defined clerical procedures in the interest of efficiency. Examples of the data-collection and editing functions are input from badge readers in bus repair garages, revenue data entry through display terminals, and the collection, keypunching, and editing of payroll information. Examples of clerical mechanization include calculation of payroll data and the production of reports that list all employees due for physical examinations.

The following major business functions of Gotham City Bus Lines are identified on the horizontal axis.

- *Transportation.* The major business activity performed by Gotham consists of the actual operation of busses and directly related support functions such as the development of bus routes and schedules.
- *Maintenance.* Busses must be maintained at regular intervals and repaired when breakdowns occur.
- *Materials management.* This function provides spare parts for the repair of busses.
- *Engineering.* This function supports transportation and maintenance by enabling the contruction of bus shelters, repair facilities, and garages.
- *Finance and accounting.* Gotham requires effective systems for recording and monitoring revenues and costs in order to qualify for government subsidies, as well as for internal control purposes.
- *Personnel and administration.* Logical procedures for hiring, firing, and transferring people must exist to support transportation and maintenance activities. In addition, payroll systems must exist to pay employees.

Each major function is related to the others and can be subdivided into supporting activities. For example, the transportation function must include the preparation of bus schedules and must allocate people to drive the busses. Maintenance must be supported by materials management activities that ensure a timely and adequate supply of spare parts. And financial reporting relies on the ability to accumulate costs and revenues by various expense and organizational categories. This requires clerical and automated procedures for the collection and storage of accounting data.

Each activity can be further reduced to a level on which a meaningful definition of computer or manual systems can take place. For example, the maintenance function requires scheduling systems to ensure an adequate supply of mechanics for the performance of timely oil changes, tune-ups, and other maintenance activities.

Discussion Questions

1. Why is long-range EDP planning important?
2. Identify and describe the eight components of an EDP plan.
3. Describe the process of identifying company activities and goals meaningful to plan development.
4. What is the difference between "decision support" and "transaction processing" systems? Give examples of each.
5. What are some of the questions an EDP manager should ask when prioritizing the commitment of resources to projects?
6. Define the three factors that play a key role in determining project risk. How does each factor affect project risk?
7. Describe low, medium, and high risk projects in terms of the three risk factors.
8. Identify three characteristics of an effective long-range EDP plan.

3

EDP ORGANIZATION

This chapter covers the following organizational issues:

- *Distribution.* The degree to which computing power, staff, and control should be dispersed throughout the firm and the advantages and disadvantages of each degree of dispersal.
- *Organizational placement.* The placement of the EDP function in the organization.
- *EDP organization structure.* The formal organization of the EDP department.
- *Relationships within EDP.* The informal relationships within the EDP department.
- *Relationships with users.* Interactions between EDP and the user community.
- *Systems and procedures function.* Its definition, importance, organization, placement, and major activities.

DISTRIBUTION OF THE EDP FUNCTION

Over the past 25 years, the data-processing function has been subject to a major trend toward decentralization, followed by a retrenchment resulting in centralization. Currently, there is some momentum toward a version of decentralization called distributed processing. The decentralization phase was characterized by the relatively uncontrolled expansion of EDP resources into various geographic locations, departments, functional areas, and organizational units.

Typically, the corporate headquarters of a company acquired a computer in the 1950s or 1960s and automated its payroll, billing, and, perhaps, some inventory functions. As the cost of computer power decreased and awareness of the computer's capabilities increased, each division of the company demanded access to the computer. However, since telecommunications was still in its infancy and since the physical transmission of data posed formidable logistical problems, the tendency was to acquire on-site hardware, software, and staff, thereby ignoring the "central" computer.

Another common scenario was decentralization after futile attempts were made to reconcile the perceived needs of remote locations with the discipline and standardization required for centralized processing. The frequent result of a central computer site serving multiple remote users was insensitivity to user needs in the development of application systems and poor responsiveness in the subsequent operation of the systems.

Additional factors leading to the decentralization of EDP resources were the emergence of the conglomerate and the increasing autonomy of organizational units. Conglomeration resulted in diverse, sometimes unrelated, business enterprises coexisting under one corporate umbrella. Each company had its own unique processing needs that could not be successfully translated into common application systems. Each new company added to the corporate family came equipped with its own data-processing hardware, software, and staff, which it was loathe to surrender. The trend toward greater organizational autonomy enabled smaller and smaller units to acquire EDP resources without home office approval.

As data processing gained more corporate visibility and gobbled up an increasingly large share of company resources, top management began to question the wisdom of so many computers and staffs doing so many things that, on the surface at least, were amenable to economies of scale. Why, for instance, did each division need its own payroll system, accounts receivable system, billing system, and so on? Not only were seemingly redundant applications sometimes developed for different company divisions, but there was frequently a proliferation of management and equipment overhead: multiple data-processing managers, multiple operations managers, multiple computer rooms, multiple keypunch staffs, a myriad of small (or not so small) computers, and so on.

Common sense dictated greater control of staff and hardware acquisitions at remote sites and the gradual reprogramming and transfer of systems to the central computer. Meanwhile, large computers were becoming increasingly affordable. They came equipped with sophisticated operating systems capable of multiprocessing and could support teleprocessing applications at a reasonable price.

The trend toward centralization was also helped by greater personnel specialization and the increased software overhead required to operate and maintain modern computers. Thus, even if top management sentiment had favored retention of disbursed computing power, which it emphatically did not, it became less and less justifiable from a staffing viewpoint. Complex operating systems, for example, spawned the systems programmer, the person who generates and maintains the operating and utility systems. This individual was frequently needed in medium-sized as well as large installations. Therefore, the reasoning went, why have two or more of these highly paid specialists when one is sufficient?

The rapid development of minicomputer technology in the 1970s has resulted in a trend back toward decentralization, but with a difference. The current version is called *distributed processing*. Although there is no commonly accepted definition of distributed processing, it is generally characterized by the dispersal of minicomputers and/or terminals with some data editing and manipulation capabilities to small organizational units such as an accounting department or a production control section. If the hardware component is a minicomputer, the user department provides an operator and, perhaps, a programmer-analyst. More sophisticated technical expertise is borrowed from the central site, which usually continues to exist in some form even in a fully distributed network. Systems analysis and application programming may also be done by the central site.

If the network includes intelligent terminals, and it usually does, the user organization performs data entry. Since intelligent terminals are, by definition, capable of performing simple editing previously done on the central computer, the user now becomes responsible for input editing and error detection. Another common characteristic of distributed networks is the provision of summary files to individual users with access to the main files only on a need-to-know basis.

Intelligent terminals and minicomputers generally require a narrower range of technical expertise than large, general-purpose computers. This is because programming languages for these machines are frequently oriented toward the lay person, and because the physical operation of the system is relatively simple. Of course, the scope and complexity of applications that can be programmed may be more limited. However, judging from the popularity of minicomputers, their capability is sufficient for the needs of most users.

It is premature to draw conclusions from the current trend toward distributed processing. Each organizational swing since the 1950s—decentralization, centralization, and distributed processing—has had advantages and disadvantages, has helped correct some undesirable condition or abuse, and has, in its turn, resulted in a new set of problems. Any degree of dispersal can lose its effectiveness if followed slavishly, and each method can have distinct advantages if used under appropriate circumstances.

The following three factors help define the optimal dispersal of computing power, staff, and control:

- *Degree of commonality between functions and systems.* Related businesses (banks, for example) frequently have very similar systems needs and information processing characteristics. When this happy circumstance occurs, one computer system can be used to process the major systems of the entire corporation. On the other hand, diverse members of a conglomerate are often in widely differing businesses; therefore, very little commonality exists. Only some corporate-wide accounting applications may be processed centrally. Different geographical locations of the same company may also have widely differing needs: one location may house the manufacturing plant while another is the warehousing and distribution center. Each location may need its own unique systems, and these systems are not always practical to develop and operate at a central site.
- *Size of the EDP function.* A very large company the size of General Motors or Exxon cannot meet its total EDP needs with one centralized computer installation. This is technologically infeasible. Even if it could be done, the problem of management control would be overwhelming. Therefore, the sheer size of the company and the extent of its EDP function sometimes dictates a substantial degree of decentralization. Conversely, once a "critical mass" is reached, centralization may be justified. For example, there may be little benefit in replacing two very small computer systems using rudimentary operating systems with one medium-sized computer; however, once these small computers are upgraded to the point where they are multiprogrammed and are performing other tasks that require sophisticated operating systems, it may be cost effective to transfer all processing to a large, centrally located computer.
- *Personality of the company.* The degree of dispersal of the EDP function will tend to reflect the autonomy of the other organizational units in the company. If individual divisions, plants, or departments are highly independent or are profit centers, each will tend to demand, and get, its own computing facilities. On the other hand, a highly centralized company with a steep "pyramid" management hierarchy will tend to centralize EDP activities and will frown on efforts of individual units to acquire computers.

ADVANTAGES OF DECENTRALIZATION

Decentralization of the EDP function gives users a high degree of control over the development and operation of their systems. This results in the following advantages.

Sensitivity to User Needs

A management truism is to "make decisions as close to the source of the action as possible." A system designed by people who are geographically and organizationally close to the user will generally be more in tune with the user's needs than a system designed by "outsiders." Physical proximity of EDP to the user can also result in a greater degree of confidence, trust, and cooperation between the designer and her or his client, even if, objectively, the people from "home office" are just as competent and are equally familiar with the user's needs and problems.

Operational Responsiveness

Except where effective telecommunications between the central computer and the user exist, the time between job submission from remote sites and the receipt of output at those sites is generally less under decentralization than under a centralized system. When cards, tapes, records, and the like must be physically moved from one location to another, system responsiveness is affected. However, the introduction of remote printers, data-entry terminals, and microform output has substantially reduced the logistics problem. System performance can also suffer in a centralized environment. Excessive competition for scarce resources with other systems can be a persuasive argument for dedicating a remote site to a critical application.

Physical proximity may also be important when hardware, software, or application system problems are encountered. Reruns are usually more difficult to arrange at remote locations with multiple users than at single-user sites.

System Flexibility

The time required to make system modifications that respond to changing user needs is usually shorter under decentralization. The chain of approvals necessary to make system changes is not as long, and systems and programming assistance is often available sooner. In a centralized organization the larger number of users frequently guarantees a long wait. This is not necessarily a disadvantage: modifications that have not been carefully thought out frequently result in a system that does not perform either the original or the new functions well.

ADVANTAGES OF CENTRALIZATION

The advantages of centralization are enhanced personnel utilization, hardware and software economies, and increased management control. Following are descriptions of how these benefits can be achieved in a centralized EDP organization.

Personnel Utilization

Personnel utilization is enhanced by the avoidance of personnel duplication and by the superior ability of larger installations to attract and keep talented individuals. The duplication of personnel, mainly in the areas of management, computer operations, and technical support, is avoided in a centralized environment because only one EDP installation is maintained.

* Every installation, whether one large installation or multiple smaller ones, requires an EDP manager, an applications development manager, and an operations manager. Therefore, one computer center requires less management overhead.
* The need for computer operators is dependent on the number of shifts and the number of installations. Therefore, more operators are needed to run several small computer centers than one large one.
* Modern computer installations, with their complex operating systems, data base management systems, telecommunications networks, and powerful hardware, require the talents of many technical specialists to support the activities of the applications development and operations staffs. Systems software programmers generate and "tune" the operating system; a data-base administrator coordinates the design and implementation of data bases; telecommunications experts design and monitor telecommunication networks; and instructors develop training programs and teach classes. There is, however, no linear relationship between the size of an installation and the number of "overhead" technical specialists that are needed. Once the appropriate people are hired, net additions to staff are not necessary until significant growth occurs.

The ability to attract and keep competent personnel is another aspect of personnel utilization. A large organization usually has more career opportunities, educational benefits, and work assignment variety than a small organization. Therefore, large installations, if properly managed, are frequently more effective in retaining competent people than small installations. Of course, a data-processing organization is not primarily organized for the gratification of its staff. Nevertheless, in a market where demand traditionally exceeds supply, the creation of an environment that attracts qualified people deserves attention.

Hardware and Software Economies

Economies in the acquisition and operation of hardware and software may be achieved through the following:

- More advantageous financing arrangements
- Better vendor service
- Improved price-performance ratio
- Higher computer utilization rates
- Avoidance of duplication

Reduced costs and more advantageous financing arrangements are achieved through increased concentration of buying power. One large installation can usually command a greater degree of flexibility in rental and purchase arrangements with its vendors than multiple smaller sites. In addition, a larger site is more amenable to quantity discounts as well as "mix and match" hardware selection (i.e., a variety of vendors supplying different components to the system).

Better service can sometimes be achieved through larger-scale purchases and rentals. A salesperson who services an account worth $100,000 in monthly rentals will tend to be more responsive than five salespeople each with a $20,000 account. Even when an account manager is charged with servicing multiple sites, the split responsibilities resulting from geographical factors and vendor reporting structures (e.g., different systems engineering organizations servicing different sites) do not constitute the most effective service arrangements.

The price-performance structure of most hardware systems encourages the use of large machines. Each succeeding cost increment in a hardware upgrade generally produces a disproportionate increase in performance. Therefore, a proliferation of small computers may not be as cost effective as one or two very large computers. However, the spectacular advances being made in hardware technology may significantly reduce or even eliminate the price-performance differences between small and large machines.

Higher utilization is achieved through more intensive use of software and computer peripheral equipment and through the elimination of the idle time that occurs when there is less than a three-shift operation. For example, it is generally less expensive to operate one high-speed printer three shifts per day than several slower printers at different sites for only a few hours per day.

Avoidance of duplication results from the ability to use fewer, more powerful hardware and software components. The total hardware and software cost in one large, centralized computer installation is frequently less than the cost of processing the same volume of work through multiple smaller sites. Each small installation has fixed hardware and software requirements such as a card reader, printer, disk and tape drives, central processing unit (CPU), operating system, and various utility programs. A large installation has the same requirements, but only one CPU, card reader, and so on, is required. In addition, duplicate-site preparation costs for air conditioning, flooring, power supply backup, and fire protection are avoided.

MANAGEMENT CONTROL

Management control over EDP expenditures, standards, and activities is enhanced when the EDP function is centralized. Multiple data centers, with their own networks of loyalties and interests, are much more difficult to control than a single large installation.

The superiority of centralization stems from a time-honored organizational fact of life: "solid-line" control is invariably more effective than "dotted-line" relationships. It is very difficult to enforce meaningful compliance with uniform systems development practices, the use of common programming languages, hardware compatibility standards, and consistent security procedures without direct-line authority. The "corporate MIS director" whose fiefdom crosses divisional lines is powerless unless he or she has direct budgetary control over the EDP establishment and can, therefore, command the loyalty and obedience of local EDP managers. The most powerful management tool is still control of the purse strings.

ORGANIZATIONAL PLACEMENT OF EDP

Who should control the EDP function depends on who the major EDP user is, the degree to which EDP systems cross organizational lines, and the degree to which computer activities influence the main business of the company. In addition, the size, type, and personality of the company, as well as the weight of tradition, influence EDP placement.

The Major User

The major user of EDP services within a company is the single most important factor influencing the organizational placement of data processing. Traditionally, the accounting department was the major user. Payroll, accounts receivable, general ledger, and other accounting applications were computerized first. Therefore, the chief financial officer was the logical reporting point for EDP. In colleges and universities the EDP function frequently reports to an administrative dean because of the importance of admissions, registration, and student billing systems. In high-technology companies with extensive research and development, the EDP function often reports to the engineering or operations research group, or that group has its own computer center specializing in scientific work. If computer usage is evenly divided between several company areas, it is advisable to place EDP on the same organizational level with the departments it serves. This enables EDP to exercise a needed influence on resource allocation, systems development, and maintenance priority decisions. One reason the development of nonaccounting applications often took a back seat to the development of accounting systems is that EDP has traditionally reported to the controller, thus causing the development of important nonaccounting applications to be postponed.

Crossing Organizational Lines

The degree to which EDP systems cross organizational lines is also a powerful contributing factor to EDP placement. It is difficult to effectively resolve the conflicting demands engendered by systems that affect multiple departments if the computer function reports to the executive in charge of one of those departments. For example, if the inventory system of a manufacturing company affects the production department, which it invariably does, the data-processing manager should report to the executive in charge of both of these functions. He or she should not report to either the materials management (inventory) or manufacturing department.

Impact on the Company's Main Business

In a company whose central business activity is directly and critically influenced by the computer function, the EDP manager should report to the chief executive officer or a senior vice-president. Airline companies are a case in point: if the airline reservation system of a large airline malfunctions, a serious loss of business would occur through excessive overbooking, delays in check in, and other problems associated with the system failure. Similarly, in the banking and insurance industries, EDP often reports to the vice-president of operations because data processing constitutes a disproportionate part of company activities. In the case of banks, the speed with which checks are processed determines the amount of money in "float" (i.e., checks in transit). This affects the interest a bank can earn on that money. In companies where the computer performs support activities that affect, but not critically, the business of the company, the EDP function tends to report to lower organizational levels and less influential managers.

Future Trends

Trends in the organizational placement of EDP are conflicting. On one hand, the development of large, sophisticated hardware-software systems linked by powerful communications networks calls for control of EDP at a high organizational level. On the other hand, distributed data processing (DDP) is enabling the development of independent systems at increasingly lower levels. Evidence suggests that distributed processing, pervasive as it is becoming, will probably not reduce the need for a high degree of centralized control over expenditures and technology; it merely provides the wherewithal for increasingly smaller organizational units to develop their own systems.

In addition, distributed processing does not reduce the need for uniform, accurate data collection, storage, and manipulation on a corporate level. This cannot be accomplished without substantial standardization of hardware-software components. Perhaps even more important, the high level of skill required to develop sophisticated systems will probably not be available at the organizational level that controls the hardware. A central EDP organization may still be needed to provide support to users. Otherwise, distributed processing may become "distributed incompetence."

EDP INTERNAL ORGANIZATION

The internal structure of an EDP installation is governed mainly by its size and hardware-software complexity. A number of basic functions such as programming, systems design, computer operations, and data entry must always be performed. However, some or all of these functions may be shared between EDP and its users in a distributed or decentralized environment. In larger installations, systems programming, telecommunications, formal classroom training,

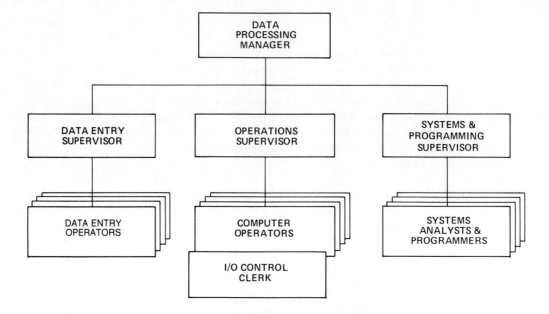

FIGURE 3–1. Typical Small EDP Installation

and a variety of other support functions must also be performed. Figures 3–1, 3–2, and 3–3 illustrate typical reporting structures for EDP installations of various size.

It must be noted, however, that real-life EDP organization structures—particularly in large companies—do not always follow a consistent pattern. Their evolution over time is influenced by organizational politics, the strengths and weaknesses of individual managers, and the needs of various end users.

RELATIONSHIPS WITHIN EDP

The data-processing department, like any other organization, has competing factions and is subject to conflicting interests. Although commonalities outweigh differences, the dynamics of the relationships within EDP can be understood best by examining the differences.

Operations and Systems Development

The most significant area of conflict within any EDP installation is between the developers of a system, the programmers and systems

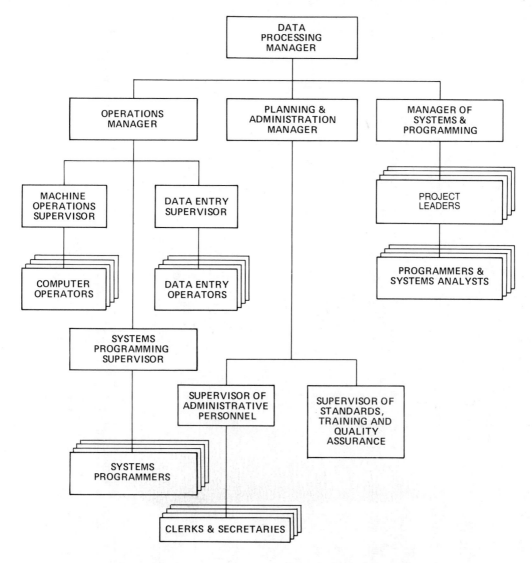

FIGURE 3–2. Typical Medium-sized EDP Installation

analysts, and the people responsible for the daily operation of that system, the operations staff. This conflict always exists when one group of people is responsible for the design and development of a product and another group is responsible for its operation. The reason for the conflict is the inevitable existence of trade-offs between the effectiveness of a product's design and the practicalities associated

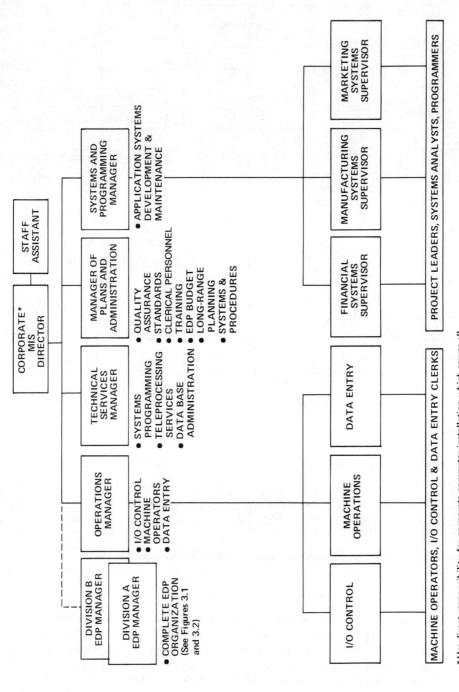

FIGURE 3-3. Typical Large EDP Organization

CORPORATE* MIS DIRECTOR

STAFF ASSISTANT

DIVISION B EDP MANAGER

DIVISION A EDP MANAGER
- COMPLETE EDP ORGANIZATION (See Figures 3.1 and 3.2)

OPERATIONS MANAGER
- I/O CONTROL
- MACHINE OPERATORS
- DATA ENTRY

TECHNICAL SERVICES MANAGER
- SYSTEMS PROGRAMMING
- TELEPROCESSING SERVICES
- DATA BASE ADMINISTRATION

MANAGER OF PLANS AND ADMINISTRATION
- QUALITY ASSURANCE
- STANDARDS
- CLERICAL PERSONNEL
- TRAINING
- EDP BUDGET
- LONG-RANGE PLANNING
- SYSTEMS & PROCEDURES

SYSTEMS AND PROGRAMMING MANAGER
- APPLICATION SYSTEMS DEVELOPMENT & MAINTENANCE

I/O CONTROL

MACHINE OPERATIONS

DATA ENTRY

FINANCIAL SYSTEMS SUPERVISOR

MANUFACTURING SYSTEMS SUPERVISOR

MARKETING SYSTEMS SUPERVISOR

MACHINE OPERATORS, I/O CONTROL & DATA ENTRY CLERKS

PROJECT LEADERS, SYSTEMS ANALYSTS, PROGRAMMERS

*Has direct responsibility for corporate computer installation which serves all divisions except A and B which are autonomous. EDP managers for A and B report to their own division management but are responsible to the corporate MIS director for adherence to corporate EDP standards and plans.

with its use. The specifics of this conflict as it relates to EDP can be described in terms of competing interests. The major goals of systems development personnel are as follows:

- Get the job done as quickly as possible.
- Use programming techniques that result in easy-to-maintain code.
- Develop a product that satisfies the user.

Operations, on the other hand, is interested in the following:

- Simple, easy-to-run job steps.
- Short running time.
- Minimum operational interference, such as mounting and dismounting disk packs and loading special forms into the printer.
- Minimal report balancing, bursting, and decollating.

Some of these goals are in conflict:

- Efficient programming techniques and high-level, easy-to-use languages do not necessarily produce the most efficient code. In fact, there is frequently an inverse relationship between ease of programming and operationally efficient code.
- Hasty programming necessitated by emergency requests and program problems frequently results in unreliable code, poor documentation, and awkward operating procedures. Unfortunately, rush work is a fact of life in most data-processing installations.
- User requirements sometimes result in unavoidable complexities, awkward operating procedures, and complicated input-output handling.

The basic conflict can be summarized as a trade-off between *system effectiveness* and *operational efficiency*.

Effectiveness is the degree to which a system produces maximum results for the user in a minimum time period. Efficiency is the degree to which the system makes good use of computer resources. In a cost-benefit analysis, effectiveness exerts an upward pressure on the benefit side of the equation and efficiency exerts a downward pressure on the cost side.

In addition to the effectiveness and efficiency issues, the relations between operations and development personnel are aggravated by the fact that system failures often cannot be readily traced to either an operations problem (i.e., hardware or software or operator error) or to a program "bug" (i.e., an applications error). Both sides instinctively plead innocence.

Systems Analysts and Programmers

The conflict between systems analysts and programmers has two dimensions: functionality versus aesthetics; and time-cost constraints versus program quality. Systems analysts are generally interested in developing a useful product for the user in a minimum time frame. Programmers and other technical specialists, because of their distance from the user and from the business problem, are sometimes overly concerned with technical elegance and clever solutions. Unfortunately, elegant solutions are frequently difficult to implement and laborious to maintain, and do not necessarily produce timely results for the user. Furthermore, programmers, like engineers, sometimes spend inordinate amounts of time achieving inconsequential increments of perfection. Thus, there is a conflict between cost effectiveness and "good engineering."

Managers and Everyone Else

One of management's major tasks is to assign priorities and allocate resources. Occasionally, past mistakes, the constraints imposed by resource scarcity, constantly changing user demands, and the politics of organizational life require shifts in resources and the termination of seemingly promising development projects. These actions are very difficult for technical people to accept and are invariably construed as positive proof of management incompetence. After all, it is frustrating to work diligently for 6 months on a project only to be told that your efforts were in vain and that the system will never see the light of day. Such frustrations are a necessary fact of organizational life. The accommodation of changing needs requires actions that may seem irrational from a technician's perspective but may, in fact, be eminently logical from the standpoint of overall organization needs.

RELATIONSHIPS WITH USERS

Three basic levels of interaction between EDP and its users exist within a company: the working level, the supervisory level, and the policy level.

Working Level

The working level represents the day-to-day interaction of systems analysts and programmers with the user personnel who are most directly affected by the computer system and who are primarily responsible for its successful operation. In addition, the working level includes operations personnel such as input-output control clerks, computer operators, and keypunch supervisors.

In some instances, a systems coordinator or liaison is appointed by the user department to act as the major contact with EDP. This individual may assume this coordination function in addition to other duties or may participate in EDP projects on a full-time basis. His or her main function is to bridge the gap between the world of the computer-oriented technical experts and the business orientation of user department personnel. In addition to participating in the working-level relationship, the coordinator may participate in the supervisory level.

The systems coordinator should be familiar enough with computers to know what to reasonably expect from computer systems. She or he should also be familiar enough with the business problems of the department to help the systems analyst define the functional requirements of new systems and assign priorities to improvements of current systems. However, the systems coordinator should refrain from interfering in the strictly technical aspects of systems development. This is the province of EDP people.

Working level relationships should be based on the following guidelines:

- *Do not make commitments.* Schedule and personnel commitments, as well as major system features, should be negotiated at the supervisory and policy levels, not between analysts and first-line system users.
- *Coordinate activities through the supervisory level.* All user components for assistance or system modifications should be communicated to the supervisory level. Work should not be commenced until approvals are received.
- *Inform management of all unusual events.* System failures, extraordinary requests, personnel problems, and other unusual events and conditions should be communicated to the project leader.
- *Do not "marry" the user.* Sometimes, a systems analyst or programmer develops a strong interest in protecting the user and, in effect, becomes a lobbyist. In addition to functioning as a day-to-day problem solver, the analyst cajoles the EDP department into providing better service to the user and sometimes even performs surreptitious programming favors not sanctioned by management. Although this represents an admirable dedication to providing quality service to EDP users, it is ultimately detrimental to the interest of the EDP department. A certain emotional distance must be maintained in order to make objective decisions.

Supervisory Level

The purpose of EDP and user interaction at the supervisory level is the following:

- Achieve a clear understanding of mutual commitments.
- Maintain agreement on project schedules.
- Monitor the progress of current projects.
- Resolve personnel problems.
- Address major technical issues.

The relationship is usually between the EDP project leader and the section or department supervisor in the user area. The major elements of the relationship are frequent (usually weekly) progress reviews, the resolution of problems requiring decisions by first-line management, and the guidance of projects toward completion.

Typically, the project leader spends 25 to 50 percent of his or her time managing the project. The user generally spends less time, about 25 percent. Weekly status meetings include EDP and user personnel. They are held to monitor project progress, resolve problems, allocate project resources, and consider minor changes in specifications. These meetings may be fairly informal and may even be held on an as-needed basis. Sometimes, the time interval between meetings is punctuated by actions to resolve problems that cannot be allowed to continue until the next meeting. Confidential discussions between the EDP project leader and the user supervisor can be held at lunch or over drinks (or both) to discuss sensitive issues, such as the performance of various team members.

Policy Level

At the policy level, the interaction between EDP and the user revolves around the allocation of resources, the development of broad EDP priorities, and the definition of project and functional responsibilities. This interaction is usually carried out at the vice-presidential and EDP manager level.

Resource allocation and the development of EDP priorities deal with the following questions:

- Which systems will be developed?
- In what sequence?
- With what degree of resource concentration (e.g., in 6 months by six people or in 1 year by four people)?

- Who pays for what and out of which budget? (e.g., does the user pay for outside consulting services or does EDP? Who pays for the communications terminals located in the user area?).

The definition of project and functional responsibilities has a direct impact on the control of systems development and operations. It also has an important bearing on how successfully the user will interact with the computer system. The most important issues are as follows:

- Who controls large projects, the user or EDP?
- Who makes the final decisions regarding project scope?
- How is the power to direct, hire, and fire project personnel distributed between the user and EDP?

EDP steering committees and project review boards frequently provide the formal structure within which resource allocation and project responsibility questions are discussed.

The job of steering committees is to set priorities, monitor system progress on a very general level, approve major expenditures, and represent interdepartmental interests on the policy level. Steering committees should not (but sometimes do) get embroiled in the minutiae of systems development. Their function is to provide high-level direction and arbitrate high-level disputes, not to track progress on individual systems.

Project review boards are similar to steering committees except that they operate on a project level. Their function is to monitor the progress of large projects, particularly those that have great interdepartmental impact. The members of project review boards are frequently on a lower organizational level than members of steering committees. For example, the EDP steering committee in a manufacturing company may include the senior vice-president and the vice-presidents of manufacturing, finance, and marketing. A project review board, on the other hand, would be composed of area or departmental heads.

The critical factor at all levels of interaction between EDP and its users is the ambition, drive, intelligence, and political sagacity of each party. As with any other organizational endeavor, individual people, not formal structures or job descriptions, ultimately determine organizational relationships. The degree of leadership exercised by EDP personnel and, more importantly, their success at implementing successful systems will determine EDP success at capturing resources, controlling projects, and winning organizational battles.

SYSTEMS AND PROCEDURES

The systems and procedures department, if it exists at all, is a neglected stepchild in most companies. This is unfortunate, because its activities can have a great impact on the design and operation of computer systems. The manual, organizational, and forms dimension of automated systems is frequently the weakest part of EDP. Seemingly innocuous processes can make or break a system: if data are incorrectly transcribed owing to poor forms design, if reports are not properly audited, if file maintenance is not faithfully performed, a system becomes unreliable and falls into disuse.

The responsibilities of the systems and procedures department are normally the following:

- *Develop and maintain organization charts and statements of functional responsibility.*
- *Perform general system studies.* This includes the study of functional activities and administrative problems and is the department's most multidimensional function. General system studies tie together the personnel, procedural and computer aspects of information systems.
- *Develop and publish corporate policy statements, procedures, and bulletins.*
- *Design and control forms.* This is a much-neglected corporate activity which may be the single most important function of Systems and Procedures. Poorly designed forms and the uncontrolled proliferation of forms can have a depressing effect on the efficiency of many departments. In addition, poorly designed forms that are used out-of-house can produce very negative public reaction.
- *Perform report analyses.* This consists of the review of manual and computer reports for accuracy, usefulness, timeliness, and minimum of redundancy. Report analysis by people outside the user department is important because information recipients will rarely take the initiative to eliminate reports, even when they do not use them.
- *Perform time and motion studies.* These are the traditional work-measurement techniques that are used as the basis for developing work standards.
- *Participate in records management.* This involves the development of retention schedules and purge policies for both computer and noncomputer records. It also involves the removal and destruction of inaccurate or out-of-date records.

- *Select office equipment and participate in office layout design.* This function is particularly important in "paper factories" such as banks and insurance companies, where voluminous clerical and paper-work procedures necessitate efficient office layouts and careful equipment selection.
- *Assume a leading role in the selection and implementation of word processing and other office automation systems.* Responsibility for this activity, which is fragmented and disorganized in most companies, may be the most important function that systems and procedures perform in the 1980s and 1990s.

The systems and procedures function can be placed either within the jurisdiction of EDP or parallel to it. The advantage of placing it within the EDP department is that the systems skills necessary to perform high-quality systems and procedures work are most readily available in the computer department. In addition, since forms design, report analysis, general systems studies, and records management directly affect computer systems, better coordination can be expected if systems and procedures is under the same organizational umbrella. The close relationship of office automation systems and main-frame computers further argues for this placement.

The disadvantage of placing systems and procedures within EDP is that computer people normally show lukewarm interest, at best, in manual procedures and other "nontechnical" tasks. These are considered demeaning and less interesting than computer exotica.

Regardless of where systems and procedures is placed organizationally the functions it can perform are important. Unfortunately, they are neglected in most companies.

Discussion Questions

1. What were the major reasons why many organizations decentralized their EDP activities? What caused the trend back toward centralization?
2. Describe the benefits traditionally associated with a centralized environment. What are its disadvantages?
3. What is Distributed Data Processing (DDP)?
4. Discuss the impact of centralization, decentralization, and DDP on management control of the EDP function.

5. What are the major factors that influence the organizational placement of EDP? To which company function has EDP traditionally reported?

6. Describe several alternative organization structures for EDP.

7. What are the major "interest groups" within EDP, and how do they interact to protect their own turf?

8. Describe the appropriate relationships between various levels in the user organization and EDP.

9. What is the purpose of project review boards and steering committees? How do they differ?

10. What are the major functions of a typical systems and procedures group? Why are these functions important?

4

PROJECT MANAGEMENT

The aim of this chapter is to summarize basic project management concepts and to offer guidance on how to exercise effective management control over project leaders. Detailed how-to information is not presented since it can be found in a number of textbooks that deal exclusively with project management. A seemingly mundane topic is also included, how to hold effective meetings, because meetings represent a very large and critical expenditure of management time. They can, therefore, have a substantial impact on the successful completion of EDP projects.

SUMMARY OF PROJECT MANAGEMENT CONCEPTS

A project is a finite, time-oriented activity with specific objectives and constraints. A project, by definition, should have the following:

- Objectives.
- A starting and ending point.
- A specific budget in terms of money, people, and time.
- A schedule and milestones.
- A task plan, that is, a listing of activities that must be completed to fulfill the objectives and satisfy the schedule.

In an EDP context, ongoing activities such as systems maintenance, keypunching, and computer operations are not considered "projects." These activities have no finite start and stop points and no total budget, only an annual one. However, any ongoing activity may be organized into separate projects if this proves necessary or desirable.

Project management may be categorized into three overlapping activities: planning, scheduling, and control.

Planning and Scheduling

EDP project planning requires a work plan, an estimate of resource requirements, and the development of schedules and milestones. A *workplan* identifies each task that must be performed in order to successfully complete the project. *Resource requirements* for each task are then estimated and are stated in person hours, days, weeks, or months depending on the size of the project. Total requirements are calculated by adding these items together. This represents the total person days (or hours, or weeks, or months) needed to successfully complete the project.

Schedules are developed by estimating the available resources that can be effectively used on the project and dividing this into the total time required to complete the project. Or, more likely, it is done by starting at what seems to be a reasonable completion date and working back. This enables an estimate to be made of the resources required to meet a desired completion date. An iterative process usually ensues, which should result in the commitment of a reasonable level of resources and the establishment of a reasonable completion date. It involves the assignment of specific time frames, dates, and people to tasks and subtasks. The development of a project schedule must also include identification of task dependencies. This is necessary in order to schedule tasks in the appropriate sequence. Critical path analysis is an effective technique to use for this purpose, especially for large projects.

Milestones are "100 percent events" or "deliverables" that signify the completion of important parts of the project. They are generally used as control points in monitoring schedules and work plans.

Control

Project control is a monitoring and correcting function. It consists of a feedback mechanism and correction procedures. The feedback mechanism is used to report project progress and resource expenditures on a periodic basis. A comparison of actual to planned progress and resource expenditures takes place, and correction procedures begin. Corrective action may consist of increasing the efficiency with which project tasks are being performed, changing the schedule to conform to actual progress, renegotiating user expectations in order to permit elimination of nonessential system features or—the least palatable alternative—lowering the overall quality of the end product by short-cutting.

Project control is greatly enhanced by following these rules:

- Keep the feedback mechanism simple and understandable. Gantt charts accompanied by periodic status reports are best. A typical project Gantt chart is illustrated in Figure 4–1.
- Be consistent. Gantt charts and status reports should always follow a standard format and should be due at the same time each period—usually at the end of the week, at month's end, or on the fifteenth of each month. Status meetings should be held on the same day at the same time and place whenever possible.
- Concentrate on the quality of the feedback rather than the particular technique used. The technique is of secondary importance. Beware of sloppy or inaccurate computerized project reporting; it is worse than good manual reporting.
- Don't overdo it. Remember, project reporting and control are not an end in themselves; the purpose is to help produce a better system in a shorter time frame. If the cost of the project control mechanism outweighs the benefits derived, a less elaborate mechanism should be found. A good rule of thumb is that, with the exception of project leaders, project team members should not spend more than about 10 percent of their time on project status and time reporting.
- Encourage solutions. The Project Problems section of the status report should always be named Problems and Solutions. Each problem entry should be accompanied by a solution entry, even if the suggested solution is "none."
- Status meetings should be separate from "action" meetings or brainstorming sessions. Instant phone calls and hurried orders by the project leader to resolve a problem brought out during a status meeting can embarrass project team members and discourage future candor. Therefore, resist the temptation to solve problems as soon as you become aware of them. Save the action for later.

MANAGEMENT CONSIDERATIONS

Following are suggestions for strengthening the management of EDP projects. To have a positive impact, they must be strongly endorsed and supported by middle- and upper-level management, as well as by project leaders.

Develop a Strong Commitment to Good Management

Every manager pays lip service to managing. Unfortunately, many project (and EDP) managers are ambitious ex-technicians who have

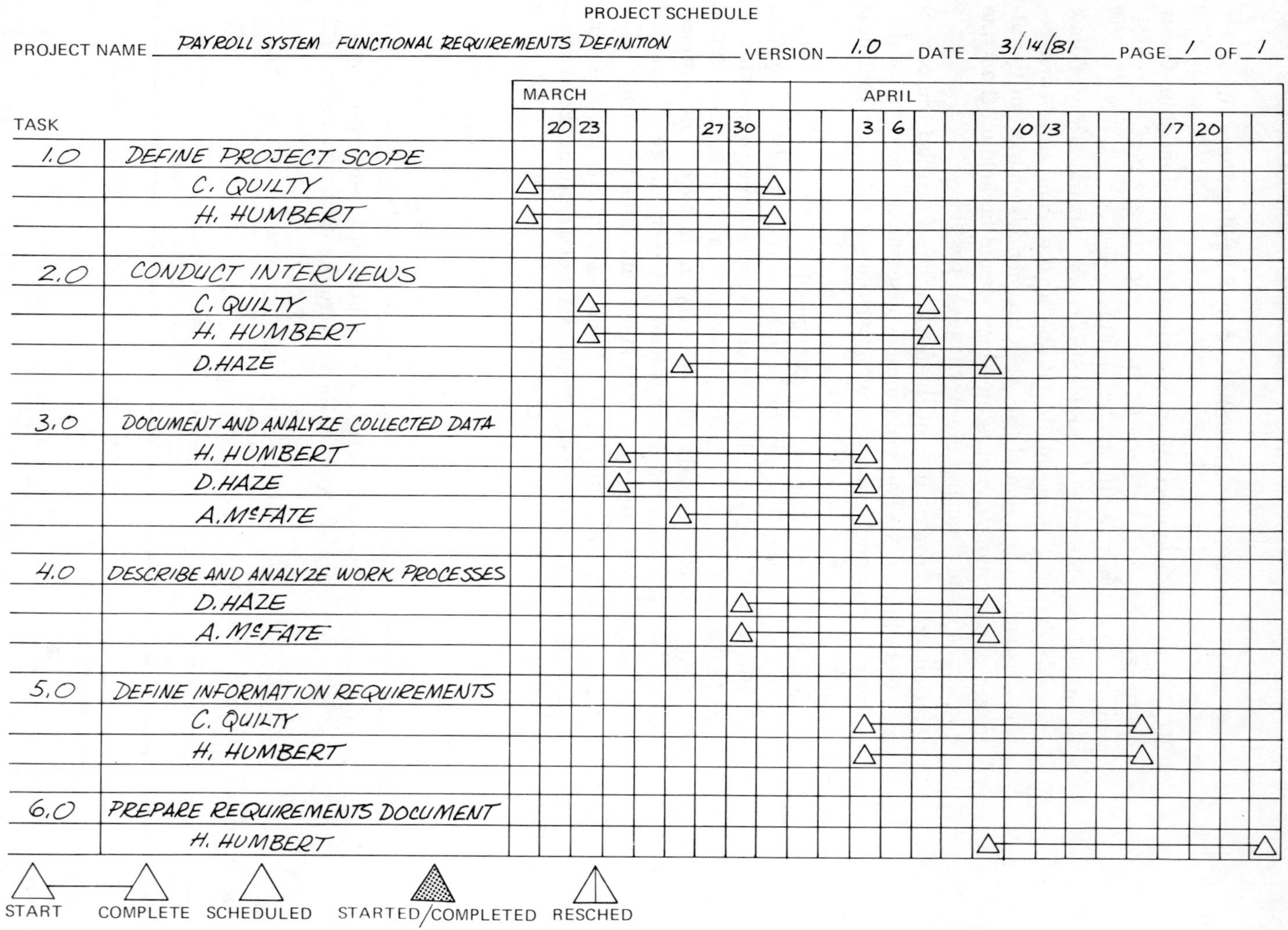

PROJECT NAME ___PAYROLL SYSTEM FUNCTIONAL REQUIREMENTS DEFINITION___ VERSION ___1.0___ DATE ___3/4/81___ PAGE __1__ OF __1__

TASK		MARCH				APRIL				
		20	23	27	30	3	6	10	13	17	20
1.0	DEFINE PROJECT SCOPE										
	C. QUILTY	△		△							
	H. HUMBERT	△		△							
2.0	CONDUCT INTERVIEWS										
	C. QUILTY		△			△					
	H. HUMBERT		△			△					
	D. HAZE			△			△				
3.0	DOCUMENT AND ANALYZE COLLECTED DATA										
	H. HUMBERT		△			△					
	D. HAZE		△			△					
	A. McFATE			△			△				
4.0	DESCRIBE AND ANALYZE WORK PROCESSES										
	D. HAZE			△			△	△			
	A. McFATE			△			△	△			
5.0	DEFINE INFORMATION REQUIREMENTS										
	C. QUILTY					△	△		△		
	H. HUMBERT					△	△		△		
6.0	PREPARE REQUIREMENTS DOCUMENT										
	H. HUMBERT						△				△

△ START △ COMPLETE △ SCHEDULED △ STARTED/COMPLETED △ RESCHED

FIGURE 4–1.

62

little real commitment to being good managers. They are fulfilling a management role because it represents a promotion and generally pays better than technical work. A lack of sincere commitment to planning, scheduling, project reviews, and the like, is quickly recognized by lower-level people and ultimately results in a casual attitude toward meeting project schedules. The absence of commitment by management is difficult to hide. Telltale signs are the following:

- Lack of incisive, intelligent questioning of project tasks, schedules, and work assignments.
- Sporadic, disorganized project review meetings.
- Tolerance of sloppy, inaccurate status reporting.
- Ready acceptance of excuses.
- Generous stretching of deadlines (or, conversely, irrational insistence on clearly unreasonable deadlines).
- Tolerance of poor project documentation.

The result is ineffective project management that may fulfill the letter but not the spirit of good management.

The solution is to impart a sincere respect for the importance of good project management. This is done by convincing people that there is a very strong causal relationship between good project management and successful projects. It is sometimes a difficult task. Many people are secretly convinced that "whatever I do, the project will not be implemented on schedule." Surprisingly, many people in EDP have never met a schedule and therefore believe it is impossible. However, 30 years of experience has shown that EDP is no different from any other team endeavor: it *is* possible to complete projects on time by careful attention to project planning, scheduling, and control.

Keep Your Communications Channels Open

Social and organizational protocol in Western society has been strongly influenced by the hierarchical nature of our institutions. Despite our egalitarianism and distaste for blindly following orders we essentially cling to chain-of-command thinking. For example, organizations rarely approve of employees jumping levels to present complaints or ideas to management. Although the highly organized, industrialized nature of our society demands substantial adherence to these hierarchical principles, chain-of-command thinking sometimes gets us into trouble. This is true in EDP if the information pipeline does not allow accurate, candid information on the progress and quality of projects from reaching appropriate management levels.

How can the integrity of information be protected without undermining the authority of the project leader and without destroying organizational protocol? Three steps can be taken by the EDP manager to help alleviate this problem:

- Encourage the attitude that every person, regardless of rank or position, must "pay his way"; that everyone's performance is subject to scrutiny and that there is no organizational protection from legitimate criticism.
- Conduct regularly scheduled project review meetings with *all* members of the project team, regardless of rank. Ask tough questions and direct those questions at everyone, not just the project leader.
- Conduct walkthroughs and other peer reviews that encourage a free exchange of ideas.

An important cause of mediocrity at management levels is the you-scratch-my-back-and-I'll-scratch-your-back attitude that develops when appropriate checks and balances do not exist. This self-protective attitude can be kept in check only when communication channels are left open.

Don't Accept Excuses

Excuses are for people who don't anticipate problems. Although the prevention or effective resolution of problems in EDP is frequently beyond our control, the *anticipation* of most problems is not. Careful project planning and timely awareness of potential difficulties causes two good things to happen:

- Some problems become nonproblems because we factor them into our development schedules.
- Some problems are resolved because their anticipation buys time to find solutions or alternative courses of action.

For example, insufficient computer test time is only a "problem" if it is not factored into project schedules. It ceases to be a problem when schedules are developed to accommodate it. Problems with new software can sometimes be resolved when the systems programming staff is given sufficient lead time to conduct appropriate tests. Conversion problems can frequently be solved by developing conversion programs and temporary processing alternatives.

Following are examples of problems that are avoidable when careful planning takes place.

- "The key user person went on vacation" (Was he ever asked for his vacation schedule?).
- "The user keeps changing the specifications" (Was an allowance for changes built into system development schedules?).
- "A key programmer was taken off the project for 3 weeks to modify our year-end accounting programs" (Don't such modifications occur every year and isn't the key programmer the person who is always responsible for them?).

Choose the Right Project Managers

The best technicians do not always make the best project managers. Therefore, the job of project manager should not necessarily be awarded to the most successful technician. Project management requires a moderately high level of maturity, experience, and data-processing knowledge; it does not necessarily require a background of extraordinary technical accomplishments. In fact, the planning, scheduling, project documentation, and other "administrative" tasks project managers must perform are frequently unpalatable to people who are star technicians.

The best choice as project manager is a person with *data-processing maturity,* that is, someone who has not only the requisite technical and project management knowledge but also has a balanced, rational approach toward systems development, the end user, the project team and EDP management. Given a choice between technical expertise and maturity, the latter is probably more important, because a project manager can "hire" the appropriate technical expertise for a team, but, in most instances, a technical expert cannot "hire" a project manager to run the project.

Bite the Bullet Now, Not Later

Time is rarely made up in the succeeding phase of any project. Nor will system features temporarily sacrificed in the interests of meeting a schedule ever be re-added prior to project completion. In fact, a mis-estimation of a development step is usually a sign that succeeding development steps were also mis-estimated. After all, the same group of people using the same assumptions were probably responsible for all the estimates.

It is *always* in the best interests of *all* parties to renegotiate system schedules and/or features as soon as schedule slippage becomes serious (i.e., +20% over schedule or over budget). If this is done, a number of happy results in an otherwise unhappy situation might occur:

- The end user may be forgiving because he or she was quickly and honestly informed.
- The slippage may be neutralized by increasing project resources, where appropriate, and renegotiating commitments with the end user.
- The end user may minimize losses because the problem was detected before major commitments and expenditures for conversion assistance, clerical overtime, and other cutover activities were made.
- A forthright attitude on the part of management in admitting mistakes encourages people at all levels of the EDP organization to do likewise. Conversely, fear of admitting error will cause self-serving misinformation to become the rule rather than an exception.

Monitor the Technical Aspects of the Project

Major technical considerations are too important to be left to technicians. This does not mean that management above the project leader level should be involved in day-to-day technical matters. Middle-level management is generally not in a position to make significant technical contributions (nor should it). However, management should participate in key technical decisions that seriously affect resource allocation, development schedules, the ease of future systems maintenance, and the relationships between EDP, the system, and the end user. Issues of primary importance to EDP management are covered in detail in Chapter 7.

A word of caution: it is sometimes tempting for managers, particularly those with a strong technical background, to meddle in systems design. This should be avoided. Imperfect knowledge of system requirements and technical features, which is the best a manager above the project leader level can hope for, is a poor basis on which to make technical judgments. There is a fine line between *questioning* and *doing*: the manager should encourage conformance to good design techniques by judicious questioning; the project leader and his or her team should be the doers.

Insist on Well-Written, Complete Documentation

A manager should be very sceptical about any "complete" piece of work that lacks supporting formal documentation. Many well-designed and potentially useful systems were difficult to develop and even more difficult to maintain because of inadequate documentation.

It is very tempting for project leaders to announce the "completion" of general design without a published, approved report; it is tempting for systems analysts to consider program specifications complete before they are subjected to peer review (or, worse, before they are even completely written); and every seasoned project leader has experienced the "90% complete" syndrome of optimistic programmers. Systems development is, to a large extent, a methodical, rational process. It is a blend of complex human and technical factors. The orderliness of the process can only be maintained through careful documentation. Therefore, no step in the development process is finished until both the deliverables *and* the supporting documentation are completed.

A corollary to the documentation rule is: "if it has not been reviewed, it is not complete." First, the product and the documentation must exist. But then, sometimes even more importantly, the product must acquire the stamp of approval from the person who bears responsibility for it. There can be a very wide gap between "existence" and "approval," particularly in controversial documents such as user requirements definitions that are heavily dependent on a subtle network of understanding between users, managers, and systems analysts.

Men and Months Are Not Interchangeable

Frederick Brooks, in his book *The Mythical Man-Month*,[1] postulates that one of the most prevalent errors in project management is the attempt to add additional personnel to late projects. The naive hope is that adding people will somehow put a project back on track. Indeed, Brooks claims that adding personnel may actually cause project schedules to slip even further, because it necessitates educating the new people, which takes time away from the original project team members, and disproportionately increases the complexity of communication between project team members.

Training is always necessary when adding people to a project because, no matter how skilled and experienced additional team members may be, a certain amount of project-specific knowledge must be absorbed before an effective contribution to the project can be made.

Increased communications is caused by training needs and by the "social" nature of systems development projects. The increase in communications that takes place as the size of the project team increases is described by the formula

$$\frac{n(n-1)}{2} = X$$

[1]Frederick P. Brooks, Jr., *The Mythical Man-Month*, Addison-Wesley Publishing Company, Reading, Mass., 1975.

where n is the number of team members and X is the communications complexity factor for project teams of different sizes.

The communications impact of adding new people is described below.

Communication between a two-person team (Joe and Bob)

Joe ⟵———————⟶ Bob

Using Joe and Bob as an example of the smallest possible development team, we derive a communications complexity factor of 1. This is done by factoring the number of people on the project into our formula (i.e., $n = 2$):

$$\frac{2(2-1)}{2} = 1$$

Communication between a three-person team (Joe, Bob, and John)

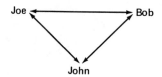

The addition of John to the project team, a 50 percent increase in personnel, caused a 300 percent increase in the communications complexity factor. The formula for a three-person team is

$$\frac{3(3-1)}{2} = 3$$

Doubling a five-person team

A more realistic example is the doubling of a five-person team. Compare the communications complexity between five and ten people working on the same project:

- A five-person team consisting of Joe, Bob, John, Mary, and Louise has a communications complexity factor of 10:

$$\frac{5(5-1)}{2} = 10$$

This is illustrated by the following communication pattern:

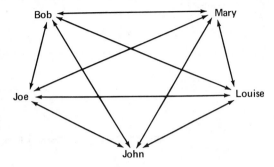

- A ten-person team will have a communications complexity factor of 45:

$$\frac{10(10-1)}{2} = 45$$

Therefore, doubling the size of a five-person team increases communications complexity almost fivefold.

In some respects, this theory is simplistic and does not accurately represent the real world. It has the following limitations:

- The figures in the examples represent the "worst case." That is, they assume the need for an equal degree of communication between all team members. In a real-life development project most tasks require extensive communication with key people but relatively little communication with others. Therefore, the validity of the communications complexity factor may be exaggerated.
- Communications complexity should not be confused with total project time or effort. If communicating takes 10 percent of the average team member's time, even a fivefold increase in the communications complexity factor will increase total project time by less than 50 percent.
- Brooks' theory rests on the assumption that most systems development projects are not significantly partitionable; they cannot be subdivided into smaller tasks that require no communications between people working on each task. In reality, some development tasks *are* partitionable. They can be subdivided in such a way as to reduce the necessity for interaction between people to a very low level. Most systems development tasks fall between the two extremes illustrated in Figures 4–2 and 4–3. In Figure 4–2, the task will take two months to complete, regardless of the number of peo-

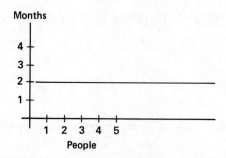

FIGURE 4–2. A Totally Nonpartitionable Task

ple assigned. In Figure 4–3, elapsed time can be reduced in proportion to resources assigned (within reasonable limits). Thus, one person would require five months to complete the project, two people would require 2.5 months, and so on.

In addition to the arguments stated in Brooks' man-month theory, an increase in the size of a project team can cause the nature of a project to change and may result in an entirely new set of problems:

- The level of project documentation may no longer be adequate.
- The formality and degree of project control (e.g., frequency of meetings and status reports) may have to be increased.
- The reporting structure, both within the project and between the project staff and the end user, may need to become more formal.
- Project members with a low tolerance for paper work may be less successful on a large team than on a smaller team.
- The project manager may have to be replaced if she or he is unwilling to spend more time on management activities and less time on solving technical problems, or if she or he simply lacks the experience to manage a larger project.

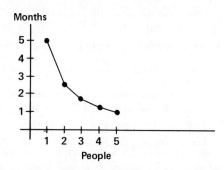

FIGURE 4–3. A Totally Partitionable Task

- The overall quality of work may suffer through loss of a unified technical approach to the product. This may result from personnel changes and the disruption of original task definitions. For example, it may be important for one person to design a series of closely related system components rather than to distribute design responsibility among several people.

Respect Murphy's Law: "If Anything Can Go Wrong, It Will!"

One of the most pervasive causes of project failure is unjustified optimism. The notion that "everything will go well" underlies many project estimates but is, in fact, the most insidiously faulty assumption in data processing. The complexity and technological newness of much that goes on during system development results in a great deal of uncertainty. In addition, the interdependent nature of data-processing tasks and deliverables predisposes each task in a sequence to be affected by the probability of failure of each preceding task. This chained-probability effect can be illustrated by assigning a 90 percent success factor, or, conversely, a 10 percent probability of failure, to each of the following events:

Event 1: Correct interpretation of user requirements.
Event 2: A systems design based on user needs.
Event 3: Programs written according to program specifications.
Event 4: Programs working according to program specifications.

The probability of failure of each of these events has a cascading effect. A simplified version of the appropriate chained probability formula is $X - P(X) = Y$. It represents the success rate of the project where

P = probability of failure of each task independent of other tasks

X = probability of success of the previous task

Y = cumulative probability of success after the completion of each task

In our example, the 90 percent success factor will produce the following results:

- Probability of success of event 1: $1 - 0.1(1) = 0.90$
- Probability of success of events 1 and 2: $0.9 - 0.1(0.9) = 0.81$
- Probability of success of events 1 to 3: $0.81 - 0.1(0.81) = 0.73$
- Probability of success of events 1 to 4: $0.73 - 0.1(0.73) = 0.66$

Our initial 90 percent success factor has been reduced to 66 percent by the cumulative effect of the probability of failure of each event. Although in real life it is very difficult to predict such probabilities, the lesson is clear: the failure of dependent tasks or events has a cumulative effect.

Fight for Reality of Expectations

One of the most frustrating problems facing the project leader is how to deal with unrealistic expectations of end users. It is frequently insoluble at the project leader level. Often, user commitments are made or sanctioned at higher management levels without consideration of project realities. These commitments may severely affect the ability of project managers to develop technically sound systems within reasonable time frames.

The EDP manager is responsible for providing an environment in which some measure of professional excellence can be brought to bear on the development of systems. This is good management in that it nurtures a competent staff and is conducive to developing high-quality systems that will make end users happy. Unfortunately, an EDP manager rarely starts with a clean slate. More often than not he or she inherits someone else's mistakes and unrealistic commitments. The choice then is to temporarily alienate users by force-feeding them the unpalatable truths of soon-to-be-missed schedules and unimplemented system features or to somehow make compromises in systems quality that will keep the wolf at bay. It is extremely tempting to make the latter decision. Not only does it cause fewer immediate problems with end users, but it ensures the short-term survival of the EDP manager, who is often hired precisely because a predecessor did not meet commitments.

Once the decision is made to compromise, the die is cast:

- Resources are borrowed from projects that are in the beginning stages of the system life cycle to enable currently due projects to be completed on a crash basis.
- Resources utilized in this fashion are not effectively used because both the borrowing and the lending projects suffer disruptions and increased training and communications costs.
- When the lending projects come due, they will also have to borrow resources and the cycle will be perpetuated.
- Technical quality suffers. Therefore, a disproportionate amount of maintenance will be required. This will further reduce the availability of resources and will exacerbate resource shortages.
- Users will not be happy with the system. It is generally better to provide a quality system late than to provide a shoddy system on

time. Poor quality will be remembered long after on-time delivery is forgotten.

- Noncritical tasks such as documentation will not be completed in the rush to implement the system. This increases future maintenance problems. In addition, if time for documentation is factored into time estimates for future systems, end users will legitimately ask why these activities, unimportant before, are suddenly so important. Shortcuts invariably produce attitudes on the part of the user that make it increasingly difficult to sell realistic schedules in the future.

- EDP morale and skills suffer because a crisis environment becomes the norm rather than the exception. This unnecessarily exhausts data-processing people and leads to poor programming, documentation, and testing habits caused by continued shortcuts and unreasonable time constraints.

The EDP manager and his or her project leaders must work hard to infuse a sense of reality into user expectations. If this is not done, the credibility and effectiveness of EDP will surely suffer.

In a Crunch, Reduce System Scope, Not Quality

A system that performs a limited number of functions well and requires a minimum of maintenance is invariably preferable to a more ambitious system that suffers from frequent malfunctions and requires extensive maintenance. Although it is tempting to opt for a reduction in quality in order to retain originally promised system features, this is not a wise alternative. Setting priorities for systems features, a necessary part of systems planning, enables the project leader to negotiate fallback positions with the end user that will result in the retention of key features that will not unacceptably compromise the integrity of the system.

Avoid Paralysis By Analysis

"The road to Hell is paved with good intentions" accurately describes what happens when data-processing people attempt to produce the "perfect" system. Decisions are interminably postponed because no one is sufficiently sure of the answers; nothing is ever finalized because no one wants to take responsibility for taking a guess; and development does not proceed—or proceeds too slowly—because there is no sense of when to stop analyzing and start designing.

The key fact is that it is impossible to accurately predict which features should be designed into a system and how those features should be implemented. This is particularly true if the business problem addressed by the system has never been automated. Features that appear critically important during system definition may, in fact, be underutilized when the system goes into production. Conversely, marginal features may prove extremely useful. Therefore, the design process should not be unduly extended to accommodate every conceivable possibility. It is more important to implement a system that accommodates 90 percent of the user's needs than to jeopardize the schedule by trying for 95 percent.

HOLDING SUCCESSFUL MEETINGS

Project managers may spend as much as 50 percent of their time in meetings and conferences. It is, therefore, appropriate to discuss guidelines for holding successful meetings as a subset of project management.

Meetings are held when it is more effective to meet with people than to communicate by memo or on an informal, one-to-one basis. There two types of meetings:

- *A one-way information meeting.* This is an announcement-type meeting in which one or more speakers impart information to a large, essentially mute audience. This is not a give-and-take situation and, except for a few perfunctory questions at the end of the meeting, there is no feedback to the speaker. (Of course, there may be emotional feedback in the form of blank stares, grunts and groans, stunned silence, or cheering.) Examples of one-way information meetings are stockholder meetings, political rallies, and organizational announcements.
- *A two-way information meeting.* This is a mutual information or problem-resolution meeting in which all members are free to participate and in which extensive information flows in all directions—at least theoretically.

Some meetings have the characteristics of both one- and two-way communication. Examples are announcement meetings with a limited audience where participation is encouraged and formal presentations to small groups of people where participation is encouraged but occurs in a very structured fashion.

Most business meetings fall into the two-way information category. Therefore, the comments that follow apply to that type of meeting.

Agenda

Every meeting should have a specific purpose, and this purpose should be reflected in the agenda. The agenda should state the projected length and purpose of the meeting, specific goals to be accomplished, and topics to be covered. If participants are expected to make special preparations for the meeting, the agenda should be distributed in advance. Otherwise, it can be handed out at the meeting.

The importance of the agenda is not limited to the fact that it represents an orderly blueprint for the conduct of the meeting. The creation of an agenda forces the meeting chairperson to carefully think through the reasons for holding the meeting.

Preparation

People are expected to arrive at meetings prepared. If specific preparation is necessary, assignments should be made sufficiently in advance of the meeting to allow reasonable preparation time. It is not realistic to distribute a 250-page document on Monday and expect it to be read in time for a Tuesday meeting.

Promptness

On-time arrival at meetings is not trivial. Because meetings represent an inordinate percentage of a manager's time, 10 minutes of waiting time per meeting can easily mean the loss of one or more hours of productive time per day. The best way to encourage on-time attendance is for the chairperson to arrive a few minutes early to prepare the physical environment (e.g., chairs, overhead projector) and to start promptly without necessarily waiting for all participants to arrive. Starting meetings without habitually tardy people sometimes encourages prompt attendance.

Minutes

Someone should always record the significant events that transpired during the meeting. Meeting minutes should be concise, and their accuracy should be continually validated during the meeting. A good set of minutes contains the following:

- Date and place of the meeting.
- Starting and ending times.
- Names, titles, and organizational affiliation of all attendees.
- Synopsis of topics that were discussed.

- Major decisions that were reached.
- Open items for the next meeting.
- Significant disagreements.
- Specific actions to be taken, by when, and by whom.
- Date, time, and place of the next meeting.

Minutes of the previous meeting should always be distributed prior to the next meeting.

Number of People

An effective interchange of ideas generally cannot take place between more than 10 or 12 participants. This is true for the following reasons:

- The physical presence of more than 10 or 12 people reduces the time that can be devoted to discussing each person's ideas and views.
- Shy people tend to be even shyer in large groups than in small. Therefore, it is more difficult to elicit their participation. Conversely, aggressive people who dominate a meeting are easier to repress in small groups than in large ones.

Leadership

Every meeting should have a chairperson. Without a leader, meetings soon degenerate into chaotic, purposeless talkfests. It is the chairperson's responsibility to elicit effective participation from meeting members, to make sure the meeting is conforming to the agenda, and to ensure that the meeting fulfills the purpose for which it was held. The meeting chairperson is the most important participant because he or she sets the tone for the meeting and, therefore, substantially influences the meeting's effectiveness.

Seating

The seating position of each participant relative to every other participant and to the meeting chairperson can play an important psychological role. For example, a meeting to resolve differences between two warring factions may be more successful if members of each are intermingled rather than arrayed on opposite sides of a conference table.

A participant's proximity to the chairperson may be interpreted (or misinterpreted) as a sign of favoritism. Sovietologists carefully examine photographs of the dais in front of Red Square during the annual May Day parade in Moscow for clues to who is in and who is out in the Soviet hierarchy. Likewise, a manager formally announcing the promotion of a person to project leader will generally place that person next to her or him. Proximity can also be a sign of support. When a politician's aide is in trouble and the politician chooses to publicly defend him or her, the aide is generally placed next to the politician as a visual symbol of support.

Timing

The early part of the meeting should be devoted to discussing the minutes of the last meeting and should establish the purpose and tone of the current meeting. Short topics should generally be covered first because this increases the probability that the meeting will achieve at least some concrete results. Controversial topics should either be left for last or should be covered toward the middle of the meeting. The argument for leaving sensitive topics until last is that controversy can cause anger to contaminate noncontroversial topics that could otherwise be covered quickly and objectively. The argument for discussing controversial issues in the middle of the meeting is that this allows a cooling-off period so that participants can end the meeting on friendly terms. The choice depends on which is more important: amity at the end of the meeting or an atmosphere of tranquillity during the meeting itself.

A Discussion Guide

Following are some hints for successfully conducting meetings:

- Draw out shy participants through strategic questioning and by listening attentively to what they have to say. Remember, silence does not necessarily represent a lack of good ideas. Defend junior and less knowledgeable, less confident participants from unjustifiably severe and tactless criticism. If you don't, you may lose a potentially valuable source of ideas.
- Stay on target. It is altogether too easy to stray into topics that do not contribute to achieving the meeting's goals.
- Keep a balance between directed and nondirected discussion. The point of a meeting is to achieve quality solutions as well as to fulfill meeting objectives. To do this, a certain amount of "wandering" must take place, but it should always be judiciously guided and channeled toward the topic at hand.
- Do not disparage ideas. Constantly remind meeting participants that there is no such thing as a stupid question or a dumb idea.

- If two participants have a superior-subordinate relationship, do not ask the boss for an opinion before you have questioned the subordinate; otherwise, the subordinate is likely to be influenced by the boss's opinion.

Ending the Meeting

All meetings should end with a summary and verification of major decisions that were reached, actions that must be taken, and the specific people who are to take these actions. Without this kind of explicit restatement and mutual agreement, even the most productive meetings will often result in confusion and inaction.

Discussion Questions

1. What is a "project"? How are planning, scheduling, and control concepts used to ensure successful project completion?
2. Choose three management considerations described in the chapter. How would you put them into practice in the "real world"?
3. What role should the project leader play in ensuring the technical excellence of a new system? What is management's role?
4. Briefly describe Frederick Brook's theory of what happens when manpower is added to a late project. Do you agree?
5. What are the qualitative changes in the project environment that can be triggered by substantially increasing its size or scope?
6. Give a tangible example of how problems or missed schedules at the beginning of a project can have a cascading effect on the success of the remainder of the project.
7. How can seating arrangements and the sequence of controversial topics potentially impact the success of a meeting?
8. Discuss the role of the chairperson in a meeting. How does he or she keep the meeting on target and elicit constructive dialogue?

5

THE SYSTEM LIFE CYCLE

SYSTEM LIFE-EXPECTANCY FACTORS

Every EDP system is a complicated web of hardware, software, and application programs designed, maintained, and used by people. Both technology and people's needs change. Therefore, it should not be surprising that EDP systems, like living organisms, pass through a cycle of development, maturity, and decline.

Technological changes make yesterday's hardware and software increasingly difficult to maintain and increasingly awkward to interface with newer products. This is partly a matter of planned obsolescence and partly a genuine incompatibility between old and new concepts. Technological changes also commonly result in price-performance improvements that make current products more attractive.

Changing end-user requirements necessitate an increasingly heavy systems maintenance burden. This makes older systems lose their cost effectiveness, usually after their development costs have been capitalized. User requirements may change so dramatically that a system cannot be modified to accommodate needed changes.

The life expectancy of a typical applications system (not including development time) is about 7 to 10 years (see Figure 5–1). Particularly volatile systems may die sooner; stable, well-designed systems may live happily into their teens. Life expectancy is dependent on many factors specific to the system and to its environment. Some of these factors are as follows:

- Volume increases
- System change volatility
- Resource availability
- Soundness of the initial design

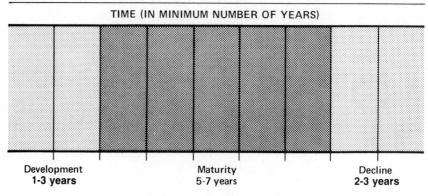

FIGURE 5–1. System Life Cycle

- Technical advances
- Management attitudes

Volume Increases

Increased volumes can cause input or processing bottlenecks that make a system less responsive to the end user and more time consuming to operate. This performance degradation, particularly in teleprocessing systems, is difficult to predict because it is generally nonlinear. That is, a relatively small increase in transaction volumes can cause system responsiveness to decline very dramatically. For example, a 10 percent transaction volume increase from 5000 to 5500 transactions per day can double, triple, or even quadruple the response time an end user experiences on a terminal. Complicating the situation even further is the fact that response time can vary from day to day depending on other work being processed concurrently. A 10 percent transaction increase on the lightly loaded night shift may have no discernible effect; a 10 percent increase during prime time, particularly on the day the payroll is run, may prove disastrous.

In addition to the degradation of response time, the storage capacity of computer mass-storage devices can be exceeded by volume increases. This is generally caused by the growth of master files beyond the capacity of the storage media allocated to the system. A common solution to volume increases is to increase storage and/or computing power. This is done by adding more disk drives, upgrading the speed and storage capacity of the central processing unit, increasing input-output channels, and expanding the capacity of the communications system. In addition, software changes and performance "tuning" can mitigate some of the impact of volume increases. Another solution is to move competing applications and unnecessary system components to other computers.

These solutions may be effective in the short run. However, the expandability of any configuration is eventually constrained by the limits of its architecture. If volume increases continue past this point, there is no choice but to switch to a different family of computers. This switch may necessitate so many application and operating system changes that a total redesign is more cost effective than continued tinkering with the old system.

System Change Volatility

System modifications necessitated by changing user requirements affect the life-span of a system. User requirements change because of changes in company procedures, reporting requirements mandated by the government, industry practices, and improved ways of running the business.

The nature of application systems is such that modifications beyond a certain point cause a system to become more cumbersome and inefficient. Although initial changes may improve system performance and may increase the usability of the system, continued changes generally destroy its "conceptual integrity". This term was coined by Frederick P. Brooks[1] to describe unity of concept and singularity of purpose in computer systems. Some systems never achieve conceptual integrity: they attempt to be all things to all people and, in consequence, fail to satisfy any logical set of requirements with distinction. But even systems that do achieve a measure of integrity may, under a constant stream of changes, lose their original purpose and thus begin to perform the functions for which they were originally designed with less and less efficiency.

Availability of Development Resources

Generally, the cost effectiveness of maintaining a system ceases long before resources are applied to its redesign. The tendency is to postpone redesign until a system becomes almost totally unresponsive to user needs. Until that time, resources are simply not made available, in spite of the theoretical cost benefits of developing a new system.

---

[1]Frederick P. Brooks, Jr., *The Mythical Man-Month,* Addison-Wesley Publishing Company, Reading, Mass., 1975.

Unavailable resources may be computer test time, user personnel, or, most commonly, EDP people who can be freed from other tasks to develop the new system.

Soundness of the Original Design

By and large, carefully conceived and soundly executed systems enjoy a longer life-span than poorly designed, hastily implemented systems. The most critical factors are how well a system meets the needs of its users and the degree to which the system can accommodate changes. The ability to make changes is dependent on the following:

- Good documentation
- Modular design
- Conceptual integrity
- Maximum use of tables and parameterization

Good documentation increases the efficiency with which changes can be made. Modular design results in smaller, less complex, more easily maintainable program modules. Conceptual integrity results in the elimination of marginal system functions. The use of tables and parameterization enables changes in processing to take place without disturbing program logic.

It must be noted, however, that some of the factors that contribute to future ease of maintenance also have negative aspects: they increase the complexity of program libraries, may reduce operational efficiency, and increase the initial costs of systems development.

Technical Advances

The availability of superior hardware and software may, in and of itself, shorten the life-span of an otherwise satisfactory system. An excellent example of this is the rapid spread of minicomputer-based on-line applications that provide a dramatic increase in responsiveness to the end user. These relatively inexpensive alternatives to batch or manual systems have caused the untimely demise of older but perfectly adequate batch systems.

Our perception of what is "adequate" is, of course, highly colored by our awareness of what is available in the marketplace. Before two-speed windshield wipers were available on cars, people managed with one speed. Today, only two-speed wipers are considered acceptable. So it is with computer systems. The need for new systems is largely governed by the state-of-the-art.

Management Attitudes

Some companies pride themselves on their pioneering experimentation with new products, avant-garde concepts and state-of-the-art technology. Other organizations are cautious and conservative. They innovate only after new products can no longer be ignored; that is, the old ones are no longer available and the new ones have been thoroughly tested by more adventurous organizations. A computer system that would be considered hopelessly inefficient and outdated by one organization may still be in its prime in a more conservative environment. This is not to say that one or the other attitude toward change is superior; they are simply different and will have a bearing on the longevity of computer systems.

DEVELOPMENT

Development Chronology

System development consists of seven steps:

- Preliminary investigation.
- Feasibility study.
- General design.
- Detail design.
- Program development.
- Installation.
- Postimplementation audit.

Various textbooks and system life-cycle methodologies refer to these steps by different names and sometimes group them into different categories. For example, Arthur Andersen's development methodology refers to the preliminary investigation as the "Hi-Spot Revue." The feasibility study and part of general design are circumscribed by the terms "System Design Objectives" (SDO) and System Requirements Definition (SRD) in, among others, Systems Development Methodology 70 (SDM70), a commercially available system life-cycle methodology. General design and parts of detail design are known as "System External Specifications" (SES) by SDM70. The important fact is that individual tasks and end products are, by and large, the same, regardless of terminology.

Not all development steps are strictly necessary to build a computer system. Minimally, a computer system must contain working computer programs. Therefore, the only absolutely necessary steps are program development and implementation. However, meaningful and effective program development presupposes design work; this makes general and detail design an implicit part of the development process. The preliminary investigation and feasibility study are necessary if we wish to determine the "do-ability" and cost effectiveness of the system (generally a good idea). A postimplementation review is needed to compare an operational system to its original specifications.

Ideally, all seven steps should be followed: the preliminary investigation and feasibility study help ensure that the system in question is worth developing; general and detail design provide an orderly framework within which to define a system that will solve the business problem; program development and installation make the system a reality; and a postimplementation review determines if the system has met its original design objectives.

It would be a mistake to consider each development phase a discrete step with no overlap into the following phases. Because system development is a complex, confusing, and imprecise process, misunderstandings, omissions, and imperfect knowledge all contribute to the difficulty of designing a neat system with well-defined demarcation points between phases. The systems development process consists, therefore, of a series of overlapping tasks that flow into each other.

In addition, different parts of a system may be in different stages of development at the same time, particularly after the general design phase has been completed. The desirability of proceeding in this overlap fashion is determined by the dependencies between components. For example, if component B is dependent on A, both components should probably be designed together or component A should be designed first, even if implementation is not concurrent.

Relationships between Development Steps

A rough one-to-one correspondence can be postulated between analysis/design activities and programming/installation activities. That is, the preliminary investigation, feasibility study, general design, detail design, and postimplementation review steps consume roughly half of total system development personnel resources. Programming and installation use up the other half.

Typical elapsed times, people commitments and percentage of total effort represented by each development step for a medium-sized project are illustrated in Table 5–1. The rationale for these figures can be understood by reading Chapter 6.

TABLE 5–1. Comparison of Development Steps

Development Step	Elapsed Time (months)	Number of People Needed	Percentage of Total Effort
Preliminary investigation	1	1	1
Feasibility study	2	1	2
General design	6	4	18
Detail design	6	6	28
Program development	10	6	45
Installation	2	3	5
Postimplementation review	1	1	1
	28		100%

MATURITY

Maturity is the phase of the system life cycle within which a system reaches its full potential. Maturity can be divided into a short period of acclimatization, followed by a longer period of normal system use. Three factors serve as good indexes of how a system is progressing through its period of maturity:

- *Change volatility.* The volume of changes needed to make the system function at a reasonable level of effectiveness and efficiency.
- *System effectiveness.* The degree to which the system meets the needs of the end user. Effectiveness, like beauty, is largely in the eyes of the beholder (i.e., the user).
- *System efficiency.* The degree of technical quality the system enjoys, that is, its maintainability, ease of operation, rational resource usage, and data integrity.

Figure 5–2 illustrates the relative level of each of these factors throughout the system's period of maturity and decline.

A successful system evolves through its period of maturity by passing through a relatively short start-up stage and a longer period of normal use.

Start-Up

The start-up stage is characterized by user euphoria, unrealistic expectations, disappointment, fear, confusion—a mixed and contradictory group of emotions and attitudes.

Euphoria is caused by sudden, dramatic benefits to the user department, for example, the ability of the computer to print invoices that, for many years, were laboriously prepared by hand. Even though many systems produce no immediate, dramatic benefits (indeed, many systems suffer from unreliability and other problems during start-up), the expectation of benefits is important.

Unrealistic expectations result from the tendency of users to demand every possible (and impossible) benefit from a new system. It is as if immediate payment is demanded for all the time and trouble the user went through to get the system implemented. Unrealistic expectations exist in inverse proportion to the experience the user has had with computer systems. A first-time user does not really know what to expect and, therefore, generalizes from the initial experience and expects either more than a system can realistically deliver or becomes unjustifiably pessimistic. A more seasoned user understands that neither an initially happy experience nor great difficulty at start-up are necessarily harbingers of future results and, therefore, tends to have less extravagant expectations.

Disappointment sets in after it becomes clear that the system will not be equally successful in dealing with each business problem addressed; that, in fact, the system may have serious deficiencies. Euphoria and unrealistic expectations almost invariably doom the user to a period of disappointment.

Fear will be experienced by individuals in the user department who feel threatened by the new system. This threat may be seen as the elimination or downgrading of jobs, or simply as change; after all, people become accustomed to routine ways of doing things. A new system throws old ways into jeopardy, and no one really knows at the beginning of a system's useful life what effect these changes will ultimately have on the people who work with the system.

Confusion is bound to exist for a period of time because, no matter how good documentation is and how well trained people are, serious mistakes will occur. At start-up no one knows for sure what effect these mistakes will have on the system. In addition, new situations will occur that, due to people's lack of experience, must be resolved in an ad hoc fashion. Confusion should disappear after a system has been in use for several full processing cycles.

The three indexes of how the system is moving through its life cycle will have the following characteristics during the start-up period.

Change volatility is high. A large number of changes are needed to enable the system to perform according to specifications. Most of these changes consist of resolving problems that invariably appear only after a system is in full production. In addition, certain "absolutely essential" features will have been left out and others may have been misinterpreted or misdesigned. These must be implemented before the system produces maximum benefits. System enhancements beyond original specifications should be discouraged during this period of high change volatility for two reasons:

- The confusion and chaos that accompany system implementation are not a good environment within which to attempt functional enhancements. People have their hands full just trying to make the system work.
- Accurate judgments about the viability of current system features and the desirability of proposed changes cannot be reached during the initial period of production. Time is required for the system to become stable, to function properly, and to enable users and EDP personnel to become familiar with it.

The level of effectiveness and efficiency is not high but begins to improve. Although some significant benefits may accrue immediately, a system does not reach its full potential until everything works smoothly:

- The incidence of system failure is low.
- The user interacts effectively with the system.
- The user learns how to use the information produced by the system to best advantage.

Because none of the preceding are true during start-up, the system will not reach peak effectiveness until the period of normal use.

Normal Use

If the installed system proves to be a success, the second stage of maturity, normal use, will be characterized by user acceptance, realistic expectations, smooth operations, and peak benefits.

Acceptance is reflected by a willingness on the part of the system's users to accept the system on its own terms. Invariably, every system produces surprises—some pleasant, some not. Features that were considered indispensible during system design may turn out to be of marginal value. Conversely, features that were added almost as an afterthought may prove to be immensely valuable.

Some features never work right, perhaps because of inadequate turnaround time, inaccurate input, poorly designed programs, or organizational problems. During normal use, the user learns to take advantage of unexpected benefits and to live with system shortcomings. The original promises and concepts on which the system was based are forgotten, and the system is now accepted as it is.

Realistic expectations result from the experience of using a system, working with it, and enhancing it to increase effectiveness. This enables both user and EDP personnel to judge the kind of improvements that can be made to the system within reasonable time and resource constraints. Complex portions of a system may prove to be very difficult to modify without causing problems in other parts of the system. Other changes may be trivial from a technical standpoint but may prove difficult to implement because of internal company politics, training problems, or union regulations.

Smooth operation occurs after everyone has been trained, major problems and traumas have been resolved, and people have had the opportunity to work extensively with the system under various conditions. Most problems that will occur have already occurred at least once and are therefore more manageable than they were during start-up.

Peak benefits occur during the normal-use stage. The system is stable, people have learned how to use it, and sufficient time has passed for some of the system's indirect benefits to become visible. In an inventory-control system, for example, customer satisfaction levels may increase, inventory carrying costs may decrease, and more effective purchasing decisions may be possible. If peak benefits are not achieved during the normal-use stage, the system is either unsuccessful in achieving the desired benefits or there is an extraordinarily long lead time between implementation and meaningful results.

All the life-cycle indicators should be at their peak during what should be a long period of normal use: *change volatility* is low because the system is functioning smoothly and to the satisfaction of the user. *Effectiveness* is at its peak because the user is reaping maximum benefits. *Efficiency* is high because the system has been tuned to function at its peak level of operational efficiency.

DECLINE

A system's period of decline is characterized by technological obsolescence, the inability to meet changing user needs, increasing maintenance costs, and declining efficiency.

Technological obsolescence is caused by the availability of hardware and software that can do the job faster and cheaper. Since an existing system frequently cannot be modified to take advantage of these new components, the only alternative is the development of a new system. Although new technology is important, it is not usually the primary cause of system decline.

The inability to meet changing user needs almost always is. The world changes. New government regulations, new union contract provisions, competitive pressures, and changes in the industry all put pressure on data-processing personnel to make the system conform to new realities. Some system changes are easily absorbed. Others are prohibitively expensive. When the changes that cannot be made accumulate to a critical level, the system becomes ineffective.

During its period of decline, overall system *maintenance costs* rise. *Change volatility* increases dramatically, but then declines rapidly. This is caused by a great increase in needed maintenance followed by a reluctance to perform maintenance because of low payoff. Increased maintenance needs are caused by a combination of declining system performance, which necessitates constant tinkering with the system to make it perform adequately, and an increasingly large gap between the capabilities of the system and user needs. Over time, every system accumulates a backlog of system modifications that cannot be made at a reasonable cost. Eventually, the potential benefits of these unmet demands rival the benefits the system actually produces.

A conflict occurs because users bring more and more pressure to bear on EDP to keep the system at maximum usability, while EDP is increasingly reluctant to commit resources to maintain an inefficient, increasingly ineffective system. Eventually, a point is reached when all parties agree that a new system must be developed. The addition of resources to maintain the old system is counterproductive, because it reduces the resources available to develop the new system. When that point is reached, maintenance is reduced to a bare minimum, and the change volatility curve drops rapidly.

System *effectiveness* and *efficiency* in the declining years of its life cycle decrease. This is caused by the "needs gap" mentioned pre-

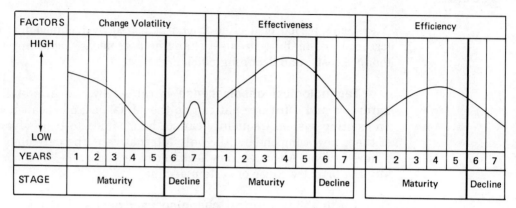

FIGURE 5–2. Levels of Change Volatility, System Effectiveness, and System Efficiency

viously and by layers of modifications that reduce the operational efficiency of system components. The growth of master files and increased transaction volumes also contribute to the system's decline: files must be frequently reorganized, file access becomes slow and cumbersome, and large transaction volumes cause inordinately long production run times.

Discussion Questions

1. Discuss the major reasons why EDP systems decline.
2. How can the soundness of a system's original design contribute to a longer life?
3. Give an example of technical advances that have caused otherwise adequate systems to become obsolete.
4. Compare the staffing levels typically needed in each major step of the systems development process.
5. What is the progression of change volatility, system efficiency, and system effectiveness over the lifespan of a typical application system?
6. Describe the characteristics of the system start-up stage. How do these characteristics change as the system goes into its period of normal use?
7. Discuss the main symptoms of a system's decline.

6 THE STEPS OF SYSTEM DEVELOPMENT

The system development process consists of the following steps.

- Preliminary investigation
- Feasibility study
- General design
- Detail design
- Program development
- Implementation
- Postimplementation audit

The relative importance of each step and the time and resources each step normally consumes are described in Chapter 5. A detailed description of each step is presented next.

THE PRELIMINARY INVESTIGATION

The purpose of the preliminary investigation is to define the general extent and scope of the business problem, determine if additional work is warranted, recommend the next step, and prepare a memorandum or short report documenting these findings. Typically, the preliminary investigation consists of three tasks:

- Interviews with user and EDP personnel.
- An inspection of relevant files, procedures, and EDP systems.
- Preparation of a memo or brief report that includes the following:
  —A description of the business problem, its scope, and implications.
  —The range of possible solutions.
  —A recommended course of action.

The preliminary investigation should require one person less than one week to complete. It should adhere to this constraint as closely as possible in order to minimize systems research into unprofitable areas.

Three alternative courses of action can result from a preliminary investigation: terminate all work on this project (the problem is trivial or is not soluble through automation); proceed to a full-scale system design (the project is clearly justified or, more likely, is politically mandated); proceed to a feasibility study (the project may be justified).

A recommendation to perform a feasibility study may be made if a business problem has been identified, the problem is nontrivial, and it appears to be amenable to a computer solution. (Although the development of manual systems and procedures as a solution to business problems is important, our main emphasis is on computer-supported solutions.)

An Identifiable, Nontrivial Business Problem

Vague, disconnected "problems" cannot necessarily be distilled into a set of conditions suitable for systems analysis. If a specific problem or problems cannot be revealed in the course of a short investigation, a specific set of problems may not exist. Resolution of the problem should be important to the organization. If the problem can be resolved by 6 hours of clerical activity per month, it is probably trivial.

Amenable to Computer Solution

At this stage, we probably do not know if a computer solution is cost effective; however, we may have a strong suspicion if a computer system can be developed to address the problem. Business problems not amenable to computer solution often have the following characteristics:

- *They require extensive human intervention and judgment.* If the steps needed to perform a process are extremely complex and subject to many exceptions based on human judgment, the process may be difficult, if not impossible, to computerize. The portion of the process that *can* be computerized may, in fact, be trivial.

- *They are essentially political,* that is, are caused by mismanagement, poor human relations, or other factors over which EDP has no direct influence. Business problems that are political are dangerous and frustrating to address with computer solutions for several important reasons. First, computerization per se will not eliminate the basic problem; therefore, a large expenditure of time and money may cause little discernible benefit. Second, a computer system implanted in an environment suffering from management and personnel problems may not be properly and conscientiously administered. This leads to disenchantment with the system and with EDP in general. It results in a loss of reputation for the EDP department through no direct fault of its own.

Preliminary Investigation Report

A preliminary investigation culminates in the preparation of a report that has the following characteristics:

- It is geared to the end user, not the technician. Its language is nontechnical and stresses the *business problem* rather than the *technical solution*.
- It clearly and succinctly answers the question, should we proceed with a feasibility study?
- It is *specific* in that its focus is on a specific problem or situation; it is *general* in that it avoids detailed proposals for the resolution of the problem (detailed solutions are time consuming to develop and are usually inaccurate at this level of knowledge).
- It is short and to the point; it does not digress from its immediate purpose and does not discuss topics more appropriately covered in other documents.

THE FEASIBILITY STUDY

The purpose of a feasibility study is to recommend to management whether or not a specific project should be undertaken. It results in the development of a feasibility study report whose conclusion is generally a yes or no recommendation; however, the feasibility study report can also be written in such a way as to qualify a decision and recommend alternative solutions depending on the assumptions management wishes to make.

The feasibility study report, like any other business document, should be precisely written, clear, and geared to its audience. Systems analysts who author feasibility studies sometimes forget that their audience includes user personnel who are not familiar with data-processing jargon. The report should be understandable to a person acquainted with the business problem but not familiar with the technical wherewithal needed to solve it. Sometimes a degree of oversimplification is, therefore, unavoidable. Technical data and detailed explanations can be placed in an appendix or under separate cover.

In addition to avoiding jargon, the report should stress *results* and *benefits,* not technical features. The user's primary concern is to effectively solve the business problem at a reasonable cost; the technical details of its solution are of secondary importance.

Another characteristic of a good feasibility study is a balance between generality and detail. The degree of detail should be just sufficient to enable a decision to be made on the project. Anything more than this should be left for the general design stage.

The use of extensive visual aids is also recommended. Descriptions of current and proposed procedures, which are important elements in any feasibility study, are ideal candidates for illustration. These processes are frequently very difficult and awkward to describe without the use of flow diagrams and other illustrations.

The contents of a feasibility study report are discussed in the following paragraphs.

Purpose and Scope of the Study

The purpose and scope portion of the study consists of a brief discussion of the reasons the feasibility study is being undertaken. It should impart to the reader a clear, concise picture of the problem being studied and the situation that prompted the study and that makes it important. For example, in a labor-intensive company a feasibility study for a system that could potentially increase the productivity of labor should be identified as such. It will probably be of greater interest to management than a study dealing with less critical company activities.

The scope of the feasibility study should indicate the geographic areas, functional areas, organizational units, subsystems, and organizational levels specifically included and excluded from the study.

Assumptions and Constraints

This section describes the basic assumptions on which the study of the business problem was based and the constraints within which potential systems solutions must function. It may also outline the assumptions and constraints of the feasibility study itself, such as unavailability of certain types of data needed for the study and organizational considerations that precluded the analysis of certain alternatives.

Assumptions and constraints may be categorized as follows:

- *Organizational.* These include fixed reporting structures, staffing levels, job descriptions, skill levels, resource availabilities, and political factors within the user area and within EDP. For example, long-standing animosities between departments that must share a system should be diplomatically stated and will probably influence the recommendations in the feasibility study.

- *Functional.* These are user-oriented constraints and assumptions related to data volumes, system responsiveness, needed support procedures, and system development-time limitations. For example, mandatory year-end system cutover requirements and the need for additional user personnel should be stated in the study.
- *Technical.* These are the constraints and assumptions that affect the availability, size, and technical characteristics of system hardware and software components. If the study is done with the knowledge that budgetary considerations preclude hardware upgrades and the system under study requires a significant upgrading of computing power, this fact should be stated and the study may result in a no-go decision.

Description of the Current System

A description of how the functions addressed in the study are currently being performed is important because it places the feasibility study recommendations in perspective. It also provides up-to-date information to members of user management who may have lost touch with how certain important functions are performed in their department. It is not uncommon for managers to learn, for example, that activities they thought were being faithfully performed are no longer done or are being done in a radically different fashion. Conversely, functions that were not previously performed may currently be done without the knowledge of management. In either case, a description of the current system provides a meaningful context in which to judge the wisdom of developing a new system.

Functional Requirements

Functional requirements define the user-oriented objectives of the system. This section of the feasibility study answers the following questions:

- What must the system do for the user?
- With what degree of responsiveness?
- Within what error and performance tolerances?

These questions are generally answered in terms of output requirements, report turnaround time, inquiry and update response times (in the case of teleprocessing systems), data accessibility, timeliness of file updates, error rates, and the types of information the system must gather and manipulate. It also mandates the system's ability to process the projected volume of batch and teleprocessing transactions.

Proposed System Description

This section contains a brief narrative and a high-level diagram or flowchart illustrating the major inputs, outputs, and processing steps required by the system. The system description should convey an accurate picture of the general types of files in the system, the contents of key reports, and the major data elements that are required. No attempt should be made at this time to define the technical characteristics of data elements, construct report formats, write program descriptions, define access methods, or prepare detailed data element definitions. A very common error in the development of feasibility studies is to spend too much time defining the exact characteristics of the system. The degree of detail in a feasibility study should never exceed the degree of detail needed to make a go or no-go decision.

Cost-Benefit Analysis

This is a comparison between the projected development and operating costs of the system and the benefits thereof. A large amount of guesswork is unavoidable during the feasibility study phase. However, a greater level of accuracy and specificity should be expected during general design.

The cost-benefit analysis is probably the most difficult and, despite its importance, the most inaccurate exercise in the entire feasibility study, because at this point there is insufficient knowledge of system development costs, operating characteristics, and potential user costs and benefits.

At best, the cost-benefit analysis is a means of comparing the cost effectiveness of various systems in order to develop rational priorities. At worst, it is a straitjacket that deters an organization from developing needed systems because they are not cost justified for a specific department in the short term. The worth of a system is invariably in the eyes of the beholder, and EDP systems, like advertising programs, are sometimes needed regardless of their cost. Can anyone really prove, for example, that airline reservation systems are cost justified? Yet no major airline can function without one.

Alternatives

There are always alternative approaches to a business problem. Some may not be organizationally palatable, realistic, or cost effective, but they exist nonetheless. Any feasibility study which claims that a system *must* be developed or *must not* be developed is incomplete. It should always present one or more alternatives to its recommendation and should indicate the approximate cost difference or trade-off between the recommendation and the other alternatives.

One alternative that is always available is to do nothing. Its cost is the continuation of the business problem that prompted the feasibility study. Sometimes that cost may be lower than the cost of developing a solution. Another alternative may be improvement of the present system through program modifications, if it is a computer system, or through the development of effective manual procedures if it is a manual system.

Although it is not usually necessary to present as much detail on the alternatives as on the recommended solution, the alternatives should still be described and their advantages and disadvantages stated.

Development Plan and Resource Requirements

This section contains a general development schedule and an approximation of resources needed to implement the system. The development plan includes major milestones such as user approvals, completion of general design, completion of program specifications and completion of system testing. It should establish a realistic framework of expectations in terms of elapsed time needed to develop the system and should, therefore, remove the temptation to make informal commitments that cannot be honored. (Once an overly optimistic schedule is advanced, it is extremely difficult to counteract it with a realistic schedule.)

Resource requirements should also be estimated. They constitute an extremely important part of the feasibility study because they define the extent to which both EDP and user resources must be committed in order to make the project a reality.

Recommendations

A feasibility study does not fulfill its main function if it does not contain clear, well-supported recommendations. Recommendations can be of three types: binary, if-then, or value.

A *binary* recommendation simply declares the proposed solution to be the best solution. Or it rejects a computerized solution as impractical, ineffective, or too expensive.

An *if-then* recommendation presents several alternatives and qualifies each alternative based on specific assumptions. For example, if a 15 percent annual growth in sales is assumed, an expensive, sophisticated order entry system may be recommended. On the other hand, a recommendation to enhance the old order entry system may be made if sales are expected to increase by only 5 percent.

A *value* recommendation consists of the assignment of numerical values to each alternative. Factors such as cost, flexibility, responsiveness, and maintainability are assigned weights based on their importance. Each alternative is then judged by these factors, and a numeric total is developed for each alternative. The advantage of this approach is that is presents management with a choice of ranked alternatives rather than simply a yes-or-no decision.

Management Summary

If a feasibility study is over ten pages long, a management summary is necessary. A frequent mistake made by systems analysts is to assume that managers have nothing better to do with their time than read feasibility studies. In real life, a manager may spend only 5 percent of his or her time thinking about the system and may not wish to read the complete feasibility study. Therefore, it is wise to condense the salient points of the study into a one- or two-page summary that succinctly expresses its tenor and conclusions. This is also a good technique for gaining quick approvals from managers, who may merely become confused if forced to read a long document.

Appendix

This section of the feasibility study should contain explanatory and supporting material that is too lengthy, detailed, or technical to be included in the main body of the study. An appendix is particularly important if the technical level of the audience varies widely. Thus, a nontechnical manager can read and understand the main body of the report and, at the same time, a technical person can delve deeper into the subject by reading the appendix.

GENERAL DESIGN

The purpose of the general design phase is to develop a high-level design of the entire system, including hardware, software and manual subsystems, in sufficient detail to allow program specifications to be written, major procedures to be identified, and major hardware components ordered. As in the preliminary investigation and feasibility study, care must be taken to ensure that a sufficient level of detail is maintained without overdesigning.

The degree of detail required should be sufficient to permit management to make an informed decision as to the technical and financial soundness of the project and the extent to which the system meets user requirements. The completion of this phase represents the last practical point at which major design and functional requirements changes should take place. It is the last chance for the user to cancel the system entirely. Although systems development can be terminated at any point, the personnel and time already invested make such a move difficult for management to justify after the general design has been accepted.

The general design report is the vehicle by which the results of general design tasks are documented and presented to EDP and user management. Although mounds of working papers are a by-product of general design, the report is the only formal document for this step of system development.

The general design report must be sufficiently comprehensive to give the user a clear outline of the system, the benefits it is intended to provide, and the approximate cost of development and maintenance. At the same time, the design report should provide EDP technical people with enough information on how the system will satisfy functional requirements to enable preparation of detailed technical specifications.

The general design process usually ends with a formal presentation to user management. This is followed by a period of redesign to make needed system design changes and correct oversights. If the user has been closely consulted throughout the general design process, nothing in the final report should be of great surprise. However, since not all key user levels are equally involved in the design of the system, some changes should be expected.

Responsibility for completing the general design usually rests with a senior-level systems analyst assisted by one or more less experienced analysts. A significant amount of interaction is required with user personnel and EDP operations.

Responsibility for approving system design and initiating the detail design phase rests ultimately with user management. However, the report should never be submitted to the user without prior approval by EDP management.

The major tasks that constitute General Design are described next.

Verify Major System Objectives

If the feasibility study report was accurate in its identification of the business problem and its description of the proposed system's goals, completion of this task merely requires transcription (and, perhaps, some elaboration) of information from the feasibility study report. Frequently, however, new objectives evolve during general design. For example, the presence of data for the primary user may enable the production of information for another department as a by-product of the main system. The inclusion of a new user changes the scope of the original system.

Refine System Assumptions and Constraints

The general design process results in a more detailed level of knowledge about what is needed to make a system effective and the limitations under which system development and operation will take place. In addition, assumptions and constraints may well change between the feasibility study and the end of general design. For example, the acquisition of certain hardware and software components may have been authorized in the interim.

Both changes to and elaborations of feasibility study assumptions and constraints should be included in the general design report. System assumptions and constraints, even those of a technical nature, should be described in terms that will be meaningful to the end user and should be no more than six pages in length. If the assumptions and constraints section is longer than this, too much emphasis is being placed on technical considerations, which should properly appear elsewhere in the report.

Develop User-Oriented System Requirement Specifications

This task translates general, high-level system objectives into specific, detailed performance specifications that include the following:

- Frequency of master file updating.
- Turnaround time for reports.
- Response time for display terminals.
- EDP and user personnel needed to operate the system.
- Degree of accuracy of various system files and reports.
- Balancing, audit, and other system controls.
- Environment specifications (temperature, humidity, fire protection, office and desk space, etc.).
- Security and privacy features, particularly adherence to privacy guidelines and protection of sensitive data from destruction.
- System restart and recovery provisions.
- Expansion and growth requirements.
- Data cleansing and purge requirements.

The level of detail and relative importance of these performance specifications varies from system to system. Government agencies, insurance companies, and mailing list businesses may be particularly sensitive to data-security considerations. Firms that require timely and accurate inventory information may stress fast turnaround, short response times, and file accuracy. Accounting systems require a high degree of auditability and may, therefore, stress system controls, audit trails, and effective balancing procedures. A profitable, fast-growing business may be very interested in system expansion potential; however, a stable, no-growth firm with thin profit margins may wish to minimize system operating costs. The requirement specifications must, therefore, stress those aspects of the system of greatest importance to the end user.

Identify Major Hardware and Software Components

Frequently, a new system will require hardware upgrades, conversion to a new operating system, or software that must be acquired from outside sources. Special, custom-built features may also be needed for TP switching hardware, data-collection terminals, and other equipment.

Needed hardware and software components must be identified as early as possible because lead times for their development, delivery, and installation are frequently quite long. In addition, the implementation of the support environment may further extend lead time. For example, a new operating system may require extensive modifications to current application systems.

If the hardware and software configuration of the new system is not substantially defined by the end of general design, the new system is in danger of not being operable when completed. The following items should receive particular attention:

- Teleprocessing capacities, networks, equipment, and protocols.
- Main-frame computer hardware.
- Operating systems and utilities.
- Simulation and other software needed to develop the system.
- Application package capabilities (if application programs are to be purchased from an outside vendor).
- Delivery schedules.

Once hardware and software needs have been identified, their satisfaction can proceed in a cost-effective manner. Sufficient time is available to negotiate the best terms and to select the most competent vendors. This is far better than being forced by short lead times into rush decisions that are invariably expensive and less likely to satisfy system needs.

Develop a High-Level Schematic

A high-level schematic describes the functions and relationships of each major system component. This includes both manual and automated processes. The high-level schematic should emphasize the *functions* that are performed rather than the specific *methodology* involved in their execution. End users should be comfortable with the way ideas are presented in the schematic. Program names, job steps, arcane data-processing symbols, and other technical exotica should be avoided in favor of a clear, understandable picture of how system components fit together and what they do, even if this results in some oversimplification.

A high-level schematic is important because "one picture is worth a thousand words." Important decision makers in the user department may prove less than attentive in reading the general design text but may contribute important comments and ideas when presented with a system schematic.

Describe System Outputs

The only information in a general design document that is really meaningful to some end user personnel is report and display terminal screen layouts. This is particularly true when a total understanding of the system is not required by a person reviewing the general design document. The only information that is relevant to such a person is specific outputs that she or he will be working with. From these, the person can deduce the kind of information that will be available in the master files, the frequency with which information of interest will be updated, and the convenience with which the information is formatted and presented.

Most end users can relate to outputs. Even if a person has never worked with display screens or computer-printed reports, their resemblance to familiar manual documents and forms serves to reduce the difficulty of understanding a computer system.

As with the high-level schematic, some simplification, particularly with respect to formatting and heading conventions, may be acceptable in the interests of user understanding. For example, the use of make-believe information in the body of the reports may be more effective than the EDP-oriented convention of using 9's and X's to denote numeric and alphanumeric data. A strong case can also be made for not using standard computer report facsimiles: first-time computer users may find it easier to understand a typed, 8½ by 11 report that closely resembles memos and other documents with which they are familiar. For information on software that assists in the development of report and screen facsimiles, see Chapter 7.

Describe Key Files

The heart of any data-processing system is the skill with which master files are designed and the accuracy with which these files reflect user needs. This is, therefore, one of the primary activities of the general design phase. If critical files are inadequately or inaccurately specified, detail design cannot proceed. The following information about system files should be developed during general design:

- General file contents; that is, the generic category of data that will be stored in each file (e.g., employee biographical data, job description data).
- Specific data elements of particular importance to the system (e.g., total year-to-date dollar volume for each customer on the customer information file).
- File keys and access methods (e.g., the inventory file will be loaded and accessed by a record key based on the current stock number).
- The "logical" design of the data base if the system is under the control of a DBMS. The relationships between segments or records in the data base must be identified.
- File volumes (e.g., the customer history file will contain 100,000 customer records with an average of 5 orders per customer representing an additional 500,000 records).

This information has a substantial impact on the final shape of the system, the resources needed to operate it, and its responsiveness to user needs.

Update the Cost-Benefit Analysis

This task is of particular importance if the scope and complexity of the system have changed significantly between the feasibility study and the general design. Even if no major change has occurred, our greater understanding of how the system will work now enables us to estimate systems development and operating costs more accurately.

Despite the advisability of repeating the cost-benefit analysis, this is not done for most systems. Since a decision to proceed with development has already been made, time spent on refinements to the cost-benefit analysis is not considered necessary. This is unfortunate, because a realistic assessment of system costs is an invaluable aid in preventing misunderstandings about the resources the system is consuming.

Develop a Work Plan for the Remaining Phases

The general design report or an attachment thereof should present the end user with an estimate of when the system can be completed. This is important because the elapsed time required to develop a data-processing system may influence system costs, feasibility, and effectiveness. For example, new government reporting requirements may necessitate start-up of a new system sooner than it can be developed in-house. The purchase of applications software may, therefore, be the only way to satisfy the requirements stated in the general design. This, of course, affects development costs and the responsiveness of the system to user needs.

A word of caution: estimated completion dates should be developed with great care and should always be couched in qualifying language. It is altogether too easy for the end user to remember the date on which the system was to be completed but conveniently forget the tasks his people were charged with accomplishing in order for the completion dates to be met. The following guidelines should be considered when preparing schedules:

- Always subdivide the development schedule into easily understood, measurable milestones. Do not simply present one date at the end of the installation phase and ignore milestone dates in between. Stress the criticality of meeting individual milestone dates in order for the final date to be met.
- Insist on the right to adjust the final turnover date based on milestone slippage, particularly if that slippage is due to delays on the user side of the project.
- Qualify the final date as well as all milestone dates by clearly specifying the subtasks that must be completed in order for schedules to be met. And, of course, identify the parties responsible for these subtasks.
- Achieve agreement on schedules and milestones with all parties that will contribute to or affect the project. This should include computer operations, software, conversion personnel, end users, and the applications development staff.
- Do not ignore or underestimate the importance of nontechnical needs that must be met in order to place a system into production.

Many systems have languished because of union disputes, the inability to hire qualified user personnel for clerical functions, and other organizational difficulties.

- Always make your schedule contingent on sign-offs achieved by a certain date. Remember, a delayed sign-off on the general design document invalidates the estimated completion dates for subsequent phases.

- If estimating is a particularly sensitive issue, perhaps because of past disputes or failures to meet schedules, the general design document can avoid the subject altogether by simply presenting worker-day figures that are not translated into elapsed times. This may be a welcome approach to the EDP department but is invariably frowned upon by the end user, who wants to know, "When will my system be done?"

In addition to time estimates, milestones, and other schedule data, the work plan should include a preliminary conversion and implementation plan. This can be an extremely important part of system planning. It is not uncommon for conversion costs to represent as much as 50 to 60 percent of total development costs when very large manual or computer files must be purged, modified, reformated, and loaded into the new system.

If new hardware or facilities are to be implemented, their installation should also be included in the work plan. The timing of hardware deliveries, site construction, personnel movement, and personnel training on new equipment are crucial elements in the success of an installation.

Achieve User Consensus

The achievement of user consensus should be an on-going task that takes place during the entire design process. After the general design report has been issued, a series of meetings is held with users during which questionable portions of the document are discussed, changed, and clarified. These meetings may be punctuated by rewrites and redesigns, which are discussed at subsequent meetings. The end result of this process is a formal sign-off of the general design report by both EDP and user management. The document now represents a picture of the proposed system as mutually agreed upon by all parties.

Although this task culminates in a formal sign-off, informal agreements on portions of the general design must be reached throughout the general design process. If this does not happen, a problem may exist between EDP and the end user: either there is antipathy between the parties, or system designers may not be spending enough time with the user. In either case, management action is warranted. However, if close cooperation exists, the general design report will not contain any great surprises, and consensus will be achieved without undue difficulties.

DETAIL DESIGN

The purpose of this step of system development is to define all portions of the system to the point where computer programs can be written and processing steps can be implemented. Most detail design activities are begun during general design (or earlier) but do not result in their ultimate level of detail until the detail design stage.

Detail design of individual system components sometimes overlaps succeeding steps in the development process. For example, installation of subsystem A can proceed concurrently with program development of subsystem B and detail design of subsystem C, as long as these subsystems are sufficiently independent to preclude possible system inconsistencies.

Following are descriptions of the tasks that result in the development of key detail design deliverables.

Define Data Element, Files, and Data Bases

During general design, major system files and their contents were identified and described. During detail design these files and data elements are defined in sufficient detail to permit development of programming specifications. The documentation produced by this task should, in fact, be included in program specifications. If the system is under control of a DBMS, data-base schemas and subschemas must also be developed, and the physical design of the data base must take place.

File, data-base, and data-element design should receive maximum exposure to peer and user review procedures. (Also see Chapter 7.) This "social aspect" of the design process, particularly with respect to elements and files, is of great importance because the knowledge required to design elements, files, and data bases transcends knowledge of specific parts of the system; therefore, the advice and opinion of user personnel and analysts whose combined view encompasses the entire system is invaluable.

Unless data-base, file, and data-element design successfully includes most user and technical requirements, much time and effort will be wasted during program development to retrofit needed features. The degree of skill with which the definition process takes place is, therefore, a critical aspect of system development. It should be carried out with meticulous attention to detail.

Prepare Detailed Input and Output Specifications

During general design, major system inputs and outputs were identified. That process must now be taken one step farther: each field on each input file, screen, and output report must be identified and described in sufficient detail to enable program coding.

Input data validation rules must be defined and source documents designed. Instructions must be developed to cover source document preparation, keying, input retention schedules, and report usage. It is important to develop these instructions during detail design because their development occasionally results in the discovery of system features or requirements that were omitted during the general design step.

Design Program-to-Program and Information Flows

The overall processing scheme for the system was developed during general design. However, no attempt was made to identify individual programs and how they relate to each other. Detailed program-to-program flow charts must now be prepared to enable development of program specifications.

Programs that comprise each functional piece of the system such as the update process, the report-generation component, and the input edit, must be identified and the relationships between programs must be defined. Descriptions of these relationship should include the following:

- The formats and characteristics of records passed from program to program.
- Field values that can be assumed on input to each program, especially record-type codes and other identifying information.
- Program-to-program controls, switch settings, and tables.
- Values passed from program to program via job control language.

Information flow diagrams, which are user-oriented versions of program-to-program flow charts, may be useful for understanding the system when processing is particularly complex. The emphasis is on the flow of functional information into, through, and out of the system, as opposed to the flow of machine-readable data between programs.

Design System Controls

The development of system controls requires the definition of features and processes that ensure the integrity of data and of system components. These controls affect every aspect of system operation from receipt of source documents to the production of reports. They must ensure the following:

- Effective balancing and error-correction mechanisms are present to detect, trace, and, if possible, resolve errors.
- Preventive measures are implemented. These include periodic file backups, retention policies, and security provisions.
- Appropriate input, master file recovery, reconstruction, and fall-back procedures exist in case of system failure.

System controls cannot be designed in a vacuum. They must be developed in close consultation with the end user, the auditing department, and computer operations. End-user information is needed to determine the output balancing procedures that will "prove" the correctness of processed information. Auditors are familiar with various industry, government, accounting, and internal policy regulations that mandate the establishment of specific system controls and audit provisions. Operations is consulted to gain familiarity with existing backup, recovery, security, and other policies that govern system operations. Application-specific controls can be designed within this context.

Write Program Specifications

This is probably the single most time-consuming task in detail design. Its deliverables, program specifications, are necessity for the commencement of program development. Following are guidelines on how the program specifications task should be performed.

- Inputs, processes, and outputs relevant to a specific program must be understood before the development of specifications for that program can commence.
- The level of detail that is desirable in program specifications depends on the policies of the installation and the skills of the programming staff. In general, specifications will approach a "pseudo-code" level when the staff is less experienced. Otherwise, the emphasis should be on the "what" rather than the "how". For more information see the program documentation section of Chapter 7.

- For systems operating under the control of a data-base management system, the subschema or "view" each program has of the data base is included as part of program documentation.
- Close contact should be maintained between the designer and the user department when developing program specifications. This will ensure that the resulting programs reflect end-user requirements.
- Program specifications and program coding should not, as a normal policy, be done by the same person for a specific program. The intensity of understanding that is achieved when one person does the whole job, and the resulting speed with which the program can be completed, are largely negated by the poor documentation and lack of peer review that inevitably accompany a one-man show. A person responsible for writing a program "from scratch" will rarely take the time to develop good formal specifications. Even when adequate specifications *are* developed, peer review of program specifications is difficult. By definition, the programmer "understands" the specifications, so there is little to review.

Design Forms and Procedures

The design of forms and procedures needed to support an EDP system is often the most neglected aspect of systems development. It is considered by many skilled analysts to be dull, unglamorous, and not worthy of attention. This is unfortunate. Frequently, the most troublesome bottlenecks and most persistent problems in the day-to-day operation of a system are input procedures and other steps needed to integrate computer programs with the human beings who will work with the system.

Poorly designed source and other forms lead to inaccurately filled out data, keying errors, time-consuming data verification and training problems. Awkward manual procedures are difficult to administer, are prone to carelessness (or even sabotage), and create morale problems among end-user personnel ("the computer people don't pay attention to our problems").

To facilitate thoughtful, efficiently designed forms and procedures, the forms design process must start early in the development cycle. The detailed design of input forms should begin as soon as input transaction records have been defined. Manual balancing, audit, and other user instructions should be developed as soon as the reports and algorithms on which these procedures are based have been defined. Since reports, files, and computer processing steps are defined in their ultimate level of detail during the detail design step, this is the logical time for manual procedures and forms to be developed.

One additional note: The publication of forms and the implementation of manual procedures frequently takes longer than expected. Negotiations with forms vendors, the development and execution of training programs, and other related tasks can be an
agonizingly slow process. Therefore, the temptation to leave these activities until last should be resisted.

Review Schedules and Work Plans

Each major step of system development should result in a schedule
and work plan for each succeeding step. Since accurate time estimates and schedules are very difficult to develop, they should be updated constantly, and user and EDP management should be presented with updated schedules during each development phase.
Changes in milestone dates and resource requirements are of particular importance and must be brought to the attention of EDP and
user management.

Specifically, three work plans must be developed during detail
design:

- A detailed schedule for the program development step.
- A general schedule for the installation step.
- A conversion schedule (see the conversion plan task).

The schedule and work plan guidelines presented in the general design section and in Chapter 4 should also be followed during detail
design.

Review Hardware and Software Requirements

Changes in hardware or software components needed to implement
the system should be identified no later than detail design. Compatibility of vendor-supplied products should also be reviewed and delivery schedules revalidated. Significant changes in hardware or software costs must be brought to the attention of EDP management
and, if the user is paying for these components, to user management.

Prepare Test, Conversion, and Certification Plans

The development of subsystem, system, and parallel test plans must
commence well in advance of actual testing. Subsystem and system
testing, known generically as integration testing, is the process of
verifying that the "fit" between programs is correct. Integration testing is an extremely important part of system development and it can-

not be done haphazardly. A great deal of thought and planning should go into identifying system features to be tested and the kinds of test data that will enable testing to take place.

Although planning for the system test can begin during general design, the individual transactions that will constitute the test data itself cannot be coded until all the features and processes of the system are known in detail. However, the test plan should not be postponed past detail design because a great deal of time may be required to think through all the possibilities to be tested, to create the test data, and to implement the procedures needed to perform system tests. These procedures include finding the appropriate hardware and software configuration to do the test, if the organization does not yet have its own EDP installation, and implementing the manual and computer procedures needed to check test results.

Plans for parallel testing and conversion should also be prepared during detail design. Parallel testing consists of operating both new and old systems concurrently in a production mode and comparing results. Because much preparation may be required to perform parallel testing, planning should begin as early as possible. Conversion planning is also extremely important. As stated in the general design section, the cost of converting data from the old system to the new can be as high as 60 percent of total development costs. Data-cleansing programs may be required, high clerical costs may be incurred for data transcription, and a very long installation cycle may be needed to integrate old data into the new system. Unfortunately, conversion planning is often put off until it is too late. Chaos and missed deadlines are the result.

In addition to test and conversion plans, certification procedures must be defined during detail design. These procedures consist of a set of standards by which test results can be judged in order to decide if the system can go into full production.

All test, conversion, and certification planning should be done in close cooperation between EDP and the user.

Update System Documentation

As the development of the system proceeds, we gain more accurate knowledge of costs, system characteristics, and development schedules. Much of this new information is different from what we expected during general design, but is not particularly significant in its overall impact on the project. However, some new information may have an important bearing on our allocation of resources, on the results the end user can expect from the system, and on the time frames required for the system's completion. Documentation that is particularly vulnerable to important system changes and that must, therefore, be updated during detail design is the following:

- *System objectives, constraints and assumptions.* Changes to the basic scope of the system, the constraints under which it will operate, and the assumptions leading to its development must be clearly presented to the user and to EDP management. See the description of the general design step for more information.
- *Performance specifications.* Sometimes the development of the detail design for a system leads to changes in performance expectations. Performance that seemed achievable during general design may not prove feasible after detail design has commenced.
- *Schedules and work plans.* This is the most volatile part of the general design report and is invariably inaccurate by the time system development is in the detail design phase. Therefore, schedules and work plans must be updated during each stage of the development cycle.
- *Cost-benefit analysis.* As in general design, the costs of developing and operating the system, as well as its expected benefits, can take on a different hue as the system nears completion. If any part of the analysis begins to show a negative variance of 25 to 50 percent, user and EDP management should be notified and possible fallback positions should be discussed. The most common fallback strategy is to postpone or abandon system features of marginal importance to the user. The availability of sound fallback positions is determined to a large extent by the degree to which major functions can be tied to independent system components.
- *System features.* Certain system features may be proposed to the end user without a firm grasp of how these features are to be implemented. This should not be the case with the pivotal, critical features that constitute the heart of the system: we *must* be certain that these can be successfully implemented. However, general design invariably includes a "wish list" of desirable but not critical features that, if possible, will be implemented during the initial phase of the system. These noncritical features can sometimes be abandoned or postponed if they are found to be infeasible or if their implementation will seriously delay completion of the system. The decision to abandon or postpone should not be made unilaterally; the end user must be consulted and system documentation must be updated. The user should also be consulted before making changes to reports, screens, and input documents. These changes may appear trivial to EDP people but can have a profound impact on the end user.

- *Organizational and procedural requirements.* Technical constraints encountered during detail design may result in the need for unanticipated user organization changes. An example of such changes is the growth of a relatively simple input procedure into a complex process needed in order for effective data validation to take place. The new procedures may require full-time data-entry clerks rather than the part-time attention of persons with other responsibilities as envisioned during general design. Such a change may require the creation of a new section in the user department or may even mean the removal of the data-entry function from the user, a change that can alter the entire concept of the system. System changes that may result in organizational or political shifts must always be discussed with the user. Changes in the logistics of report delivery, quality control, batch balancing, and the like, must also be discussed with users.

- *Hardware and software requirements.* The need to acquire or install hardware or software that was not specified in the general design must be documented and presented for approval. Any significant increase in the hardware and software budget obviously indicates an important system change.

Obtain Sign-Offs

The general design phase culminated in the preparation of a general design report containing all the features, costs, schedules, and so on, that were defined during general design. This provided the end user with a comprehensive document that could be debated, altered, and, finally, approved.

The "products" of detail design are more fragmented. Normally, a single comprehensive report is not issued. Rather, detail design results in the preparation of many documents such as file layouts, data-element definitions, and program specifications. Therefore, it is easy for significant information to escape the end user's notice. Care must be taken to ensure that user sign-offs have been achieved on all important documents. In addition to user sign-offs, appropriate internal sign-offs are required for system features that affect operations, systems programming, and other parts of the EDP organization.

Deliverables Checklist

Specific deliverables that result from the detail design step are listed next. For additional information see Chapter 7.

Data-Element Definitions

- Description and use.
- Legal values or ranges.
- Validation rules.
- External and internal (storage) length.
- Type (numeric or alphanumeric).
- Precision (number of decimal places and rounding instructions).
- Sign.
- Source (input, derived, or calculated).

File Specifications

- Purpose and use.
- Record contents and layouts.
- Record and block sizes.
- File organization method.
- Physical storage sequence (if appropriate).
- Access method.
- Physical media (disk, tape, card, other).
- Retention schedules.
- Approximate number of records.

Data-Base Definitions

- Subschemas.
- Element, record, and file level security definitions.
- Relationships between data-base components (e.g., between data elements and records).

Input Specifications

- Source document layouts.
- Keying instructions.
- Input card, magnetic media, and display screen layouts.
- Input retention schedules and disposition.

Output Specifications

- Report descriptions (frequency, use, distribution, etc.).
- Report layouts.
- Screen layouts.
- Output distribution.
- Retention schedules.

System Flow Diagrams
- Program-to-program flow sequence.
- Data and control information passed between programs.

System Controls
- Backup and recovery procedures.
- Error-detection and correction procedures.
- Balancing steps.
- Security and privacy specifications.
- Fallback, recovery, and reconstruction specifications.
- Auditing provisions.

Program Specifications
- Specifications for each program, module, and utility that is part of the initial system implementation.
- Program test specifications.
- Integration of data-base subschemas with program specifications.

Manual Procedures
- Diagrams and flow charts.
- Manual procedures narratives.
- Forms.

Schedules and Work Plans
- Detailed work plan for program development step.
- Work plan for the installation step.

Hardware and Software Specifications
- Required hardware.
- Required software.
- Delivery and installation schedules.
- Site-preparation plans.

Test, Conversion, and Certification Plans
- Certification requirements.
- Subsystem test plans.
- System test plan.
- Test-data definitions.
- Plans for parallel testing.
- Conversion plans.

Updated General Design Documentation

- Design specifications (files, reports, display screens, etc.).
- Work plans.
- System objectives, constraints, and assumptions.
- Performance specifications.
- Required hardware and software components.

User Sign-offs

- Report and screen layouts.
- Forms.
- Manual procedures.
- Revised cost-benefit analyses.
- Work plans and schedules.
- File and data-element definitions (as appropriate).
- Test plans.
- Changes to the general design report not covered by the above.

PROGRAM DEVELOPMENT

The purpose of the program step of the system development cycle is threefold:

- Code and unit test all programs in the system.
- Perform system (integration) testing.
- Complete all support activities needed to prepare the system for installation (documentation, training, forms and procedures design, etc.).

The one and only deliverable of the program development step is a fully tested system that is ready for production or for parallel testing with live data. Major program development tasks are described next.

Code Programs

This task consists of the design and coding programs from specifications developed during detail design. Care should be taken to ensure that the programs reflect the intentions of the systems designer as stated in the specifications. Since there is always a risk of ambiguity and misunderstanding, frequent communication between programmer and analyst must be maintained. (In some EDP installations, system designers code and test their own programs in order to avoid this problem. However, this approach also has some disadvantages, which are discussed earlier in this chapter.)

Programmers should be encouraged to ask questions and offer suggestions. This results in fewer misunderstandings and, thus, better programs. It also uncovers the design contradictions and missing pieces that accompany the design of any system. The important thing is to identify problems before they are programmed into the system, and this can only be done by attentive programmers who are encouraged to communicate with systems analysts.

Close cooperation between programmers and analysts is also valuable because significant efficiencies can sometimes be achieved through design changes that do not affect the functional aspects of the systems. Programmers are usually best qualified to suggest such changes but will not do so unless there is an interested audience.

Test Programs

Program or unit testing is the process of testing individual programs or program modules. It should be done by the programmer, with an occasional assist from the analyst.

An experienced programmer must be able to develop all the test data needed to test an individual program from information provided in the specifications. Sometimes, however, test data are developed independently of individual programs and shared by all programmers working on the system.

It should be noted that all possible conditions can never be tested within reasonable time and money constraints, nor do they need to be. Certain conditions must be assumed as "given." For example, a file update program must assume that the edit programs performed appropriate data validation on input transactions. Thus, most conditions that passed muster in the edit component usually need not be retested downstream. But sometimes there is little obvious distinction between possibilities that must be tested and those that need not be. This is where close cooperation with the analyst is imperative. Because the analyst has a broader picture of the system than the programmer, he or she knows where errors are most likely to occur and which errors are most detrimental to system integrity.

The analyst should be shown test results as soon as the program works well enough to produce output that reflects the programmer's basic understanding of program specifications. It is not wise to wait until the program is letter perfect. The programmer may have misunderstood a portion of the specifications, and this misunderstanding is best corrected as early as possible. The completion of unit testing enables the tested program to participate in system or integration testing.

Perform System (Integration) Testing

This task entails the testing of each system component in series, that is, as a member of a system rather than as an individual entity. Generally, test data are processed through the entire system and the outputs of programs along the way are compared to expected results. This procedure ensures that individual programs work in concert with other programs. If they do not, one of two situations exists: unit testing was faulty and did not unearth bugs that cause this program to work improperly; or there was a logic error in program or system specifications that caused an improper fit between programs.

System testing cannot be performed without a good deal of forethought about the exact conditions that need checking, the type of data needed to test for those conditions, and the exact characteristics of the files and reports at each point in the system. This requires the preparation of a comprehensive test plan as described in the detail design section. Primary responsibility for system testing rests with the designer. Although the designer is assisted by programmers who write individual programs, only the systems analyst's knowledge of the total system makes it possible to properly plan and execute the system test plan.

Complete All Documentation

Although this task is not functionally related to program development, it is generally performed at this time. Ideally, the bulk of all documentation except some portions of program documentation, should be completed during general and detail design. However, since changes inevitably occur between design and program development, people generally wait until programs are written before completing all documentation. In addition, items such as user instruction manuals are not on the critical path until training or installation time; therefore, they tend to get completed toward the end of the system development cycle.

The final design of all forms and the development of detailed procedures needed to operate the system are also frequently left till last. However, care must be taken to allow sufficient lead time to design, order, and receive special forms in time for system installation.

Train Personnel

Personnel training should be undertaken early enough to ensure proper skill levels by the time the system is installed, but not so early that the students to forget what they learned. The program development phase is a good compromise between premature and last-minute training.

Training programs should insure the following:

- User personnel know how to input, correct, and analyze data that are fed into the system.
- EDP operations personnel know how to operate the system, back up its major files, perform appropriate input and output quality control, and distribute reports.
- User management and other personnel know how to use system reports and other outputs.

To accomplish these training goals, clear, comprehensive manuals must be developed, and training classes geared to the appropriate personnel levels must be taught. For more information on education and training, see Chapter 8.

INSTALLATION

The purpose of the installation step of system development is to convert master files and other data from the old system to the new, perform parallel testing, and place the new system into production. The deliverable that results is a fully working production system. The circumstances surrounding each system installation are unique. The complexity of the process and the length of time needed to accomplish it will vary greatly. However, the following activities commonly take place.

Convert Files and Procedures

Some systems have no predecessors and begin life with no existing master files. Data that will constitute system files will be collected starting with "day one." In this situation little or no conversion is necessary.

At the other extreme is the installation of a system that requires the conversion of large, complex files and a phased integration with its predecessor. This situation requires an extensive commitment of resources and can represent over half of all development expenditures for a system. Large, complex conversion programs may be necessary, and installation may require several years to fully complete.

The installation of most systems falls between these two extremes. Generally, some master file creation takes place, even if the file is a nominal "start-up" file with only a few records. Also, since most new systems emulate existing manual or automated functions, some cut-over procedures must be performed. These procedures may include the use of files especially developed for conversion purposes and the use of temporary procedures that serve as a bridge between the old and new.

Perform Parallel Testing

Parallel testing is the most accurate indicator of system integrity available to the development team. It should, therefore, be performed whenever it is possible to repeat functions that are being performed by the old system and to compare the results. Not all functions can be paralleled, because the old system may produce results that cannot be emulated by the new system, and vice versa. Nevertheless, every effort should be made to verify each component by testing it in parallel with its functional twin in the old system.

The following should be taken into consideration when planning for and performing parallel testing:

- Expected results should be carefully documented. Obviously, no accurate comparisons can take place unless we know precisely what to expect.
- Care must be exercised in making sure that comparisons are valid. This is done by predicting and documenting potential test result discrepancies that will be caused by processing differences between the two systems. An example is error checking that weeds out suspect data in one system but not the other.
- Parallel testing should be performed using "live" data; presumably all appropriate tests using specially prepared test data have already been done during unit and integration testing.
- Actual production conditions should be maintained to as great an extent as possible. Data entry, operations, and supporting manual functions for the new system should approximate the conditions that will exist when the system becomes operational.
- All differences between actual and expected results should be investigated until a satisfactory resolution is achieved. Production cannot begin until all differences have been reconciled.
- Close cooperation should be maintained with the end user at all times, because the user is knowledgeable about expected results and can save time in the investigation of differences; the user frequently knows what events may have triggered deviations from expected results.
- Parallel testing should be carried on through at least one full proc-

essing cycle. For example, parallel testing for a monthly payroll should commence at the beginning of one month and should continue until the beginning of the next month. This ensures that special and transitional processing that normally accompanies a "break" from period to period is working properly.

- Processing results from the old system are not necessarily correct. The implementation of a new system sometimes brings to light error conditions that have existed since the original system was installed. A difference in results that stubbornly resists explanation may, in fact, be caused by previously undetected problems.
- Sometimes parallel testing must continue for several processing cycles before user acceptance is achieved. Parallel testing may also be stopped and then restarted in order to allow time to correct system errors.
- Parallel test sign-off should be received from user, systems development, and EDP operations management. If testing is rigorously performed, the agreement to use the system should be a natural outgrowth of testing activities. However, system acceptance can be conditional; that is, parts of the new system can be placed into production while other parts are still in various stages of integration or parallel testing.
- User acceptance need not mandate the complete dismantling of the old system. The old system can sometimes be retained as backup until sufficient confidence in the new system is developed and the user is persuaded to relinquish the previous system.

Begin Production

After user acceptance has been achieved, production can begin. Following is a checklist of all completed activities, tasks, and milestones that are prerequisites to system start-up.

- All testing is complete.
- Documentation is finished.
- User and EDP personnel are trained in the use of the system.
- All software and hardware are in place.
- All appropriate user sign-offs have been received.

POSTIMPLEMENTATION AUDIT

The purpose of this step of system development is to determine the degree to which the system has met its original expectations and the degree to which it meets generally accepted design and performance standards. It results in the preparation of a report to EDP and user management. Postimplementation audit of a specific system should not be confused with an EDP management audit, which is described in Chapter 13. However, there may be some overlap between the postimplementation audit and the systems audit described in that chapter.

Most organizations do not routinely perform a postimplementation audit. This is a mistake. First, a postimplementation audit should not be a costly process; one or two months of effort by one person is usually sufficient. Second, the audit can provide valuable information that can be used to improve the planning and design of future systems. Specifically;

- It tells us how close we were in estimating the time and resources to do the project.
- It exposes design flaws that can be avoided in the future.
- It identifies gaps between promises and deliverables. Postimplementation audits for several different systems may show, for example, that the response times a user can expect on terminals are chronically exaggerated by system designers.

If an internal EDP audit staff exists, the postimplementation audit should be performed by members of that staff. Otherwise, the audit should be done by a systems analyst who was not involved in the project or, preferably, by an outside consultant. Directions for carrying out the audit should be shared by EDP and user management. Under no circumstances should the audit be directed by the project leader who was responsible for system development.

The audit should be performed after the system has been installed and has had time to settle down. It is not wise to do an audit until all the major components of the system are in working order and until the end user is comfortable with the system. A good rule of thumb is that the postimplementation audit should be performed 6 to 9 months after a system has been installed. The following tasks are normally performed as part of the audit.

Compare Promises to Deliverables

This task requires familiarization with the historical documents related to the system: the feasibility study, general design report, and various memoranda generated during system development. A comparison is made between system features that were promised by the historical documents and features that were actually delivered as part of the finished product.

The analysis is accomplished by developing a list of promised system features and comparing this list with actual system outputs. Operational characteristics such as response and turnaround times are also analyzed and compared to original specifications. In addition, the fidelity with which user data entry, report usage, and clerical functions follow the original intent of the system is determined. This is important because a system audit is a two-way street: it evaluates the user's interaction with the system as well as EDP's skill in delivering a quality product.

A comparison of promises with deliverables should not, however, be used as the ultimate gauge of the system's effectiveness. The features that comprised the original specifications may not always represent the ultimate best interests of the user. A system that is different from its original specifications may, in fact, be more responsive and effective than one that slavishly adheres to originally promised features. The bottom line is always user satisfaction.

Monitor Operational Performance

The purpose of this task is to determine system efficiency. It consists of analyzing job accounting statistics, reading operator logs, and observing system operation. Job accounting statistics are collected by software that monitors the use of various computer resources such as disk space, core storage, and CPU cycles. It identifies use by application and produces appropriate statistical reports. Operator logs indicate the frequency of reruns and serve as a guide to the diligence and accuracy with which operations functions are performed.

Observing a system during production is important because it enables the audit team to probe behind the statistics. Watching operators run a system and data-entry clerks key input data provides a far more complete story than do error rates and rerun statistics alone. It indicates the degree of skill and dedication with which the system is run. Observation is particularly important when the system is highly interactive with the user. An example is when the user department has access to master files via display terminals or has data-entry responsibility. In that case, observation should be used to check terminal response times during various periods of the day and the speed and apparent accuracy with which data are keyed in.

Evaluate the Quality of Information

Accurate, timely information is the lifeblood of any system. Without quality information, all other system benefits are of little use. Therefore, a very important part of the post-implementation audit is to determine the timeliness of system response to recordable events, the degree of accuracy with which these events are recorded, and the timely, understandable presentation of information to the user.

Responsiveness to events is gauged by determining the average time between the occurrence of an event and its reflection in the system. For example, the batch daily updating of an inventory file that services a 24-hour storeroom operation will occur an average of 12 hours after the fact if additions and withdrawals from stock are evenly distributed over time. If activity is heavily concentrated during the morning hours, system data will be more timely if updating is performed at midday because most activity has taken place very recently.

The correctness with which events are recorded is determined by examining error rates on edit and file maintenance reports and by observing the keying habits of data-entry clerks. Massive errors may indicate that data are not being captured accurately at the source, that the design of the system does not encourage accurate data entry because it did not take into consideration the needs of data-entry personnel, or it can indicate training or management problems in the data-entry department. An additional step that should be taken is to verify the accuracy of data that are used infrequently by the end user. An example is record status and dating information. Utilities or specially written programs may be used for this purpose.

The timeliness and convenience with which important information is presented to the end user can be gauged by analyzing system reports for clarity, by observing the ease with which recipients use reports, and by noting the lead time between the recording of an event and its appearance on the appropriate report or accessibility on a terminal display screen.

An evaluation of system quality is incomplete without extensive user interviews. If users complain about data accuracy, timeliness, or method of presentation, there is surely a problem. Of course, failure to use system data can also be an indication of poor training, animosity, or other reasons that are not explicitly stated by the user.

Evaluate Security, Privacy, Backup, and Recovery Provisions

This task is important for two reasons: (1) it helps determine if currently used security, privacy, backup, and recovery procedures are adequate, and (2) it verifies that these procedures work properly.

The evaluation of security and privacy features in a postimplementation audit is generally limited to determining the ease with which unauthorized access or destruction of master files can occur and the impact of privacy legislation on this application. A thorough analysis transcends individual applications. See Chapter 14 for additional information. Backup and recovery procedures are frequently short changed during system testing. Therefore, their viability may never be determined unless they are tested during the postimplementation audit. This should be an important part of the audit.

Determine the Adequacy of System Documentation

Quality of documentation has an important effect on the maintainability and ease of operation of a system. Because documentation is commonly not considered critical, its development tends to be postponed until the last possible moment. In some cases, documentation is not completed until considerably after system installation, and sometimes it is never completed. The postimplementation audit should, therefore, verify the following:

- An up-to-date user instruction manual exists and is used.
- Systems and programming documentation is current and follows installation standards.
- Concise, well-written operating instructions exist and are used by computer operators.

For a description of what constitutes good documentation, see Chapter 7.

Interview Users

Contact with users is an important part of each task in the postimplementation audit. Yet it is surprising how often audits are done by examining paper work but ignoring the actual users. The analysis of files, reports, job accounting statistics, and the like is never a substitute for asking the user, "Are you satisfied?" This question must be phrased in such a way as to encourage meaningful answers, and it must be asked of many people, not just top management, who may have little idea of how the system is used or how effective it is. Of particular importance is the inclusion of people who are directly involved in using and operating the system, but who were not the key decision makers responsible for its development. People who mandated the system or who were responsible for its development will be less than objective in their response.

Prepare the Postimplementation Audit Report

The postimplementation audit culminates in the production of a report whose audience is user, EDP development, and EDP operations management personnel. The report should contain the following information:

- *A description of major changes from the original design.* The stress should be on conceptual and functional changes rather than on technical changes.
- *System problems.* This should include system responsiveness, documentation gaps, inadequate reports, poor error handling, and other problems that were discovered during the performance of the audit. An attempt should be made to rank or otherwise indicate the severity of each problem.
- *Plans for the future.* This should cover plans EDP and the user department have for the resolution of known problems.
- *Recommendations.* This should include suggestions on how problems uncovered in the audit should be corrected. Detailed problem solutions cannot always be defined until the audit report is read, evaluated, and approved. Therefore, the recommendations section may contain a number of general suggestions, such as further investigation of specific problems or more user training.

The postimplementation audit should result in the following:

- A plan for resolving major problems uncovered in the audit.
- Recommended changes in project estimating techniques, design standards, and other factors that may have contributed to system problems.
- An educational effort designed to support the preceding.

Discussion Questions

1. What is the purpose of the preliminary investigation? What two factors disclosed during the investigation would result in a recommendation to proceed with a feasibility study?
2. Identify the nine major components of the feasibility study report.
3. What is the purpose of the general design? Discuss the major tasks that must be performed.
4. Why is it important to update the cost-benefit analysis during general design?
5. Compare the level of detail that is required during general design with the level of detail needed for detail design. Use the development of files, data elements, and reports as examples.

6. Can detail design overlap other stages of system development? Under what circumstances?
7. What are the major tasks associated with program development?
8. Describe the installation step of system development.
9. What is the purpose of the postimplementation audit? What information should the audit report contain?

7

SYSTEMS DEVELOPMENT CONSIDERATIONS FOR MANAGEMENT

This chapter covers five topics that profoundly affect the development, usability, and maintenance of EDP systems:

- Standards
- Documentation
- System design practices
- Productivity aids
- Management of system maintenance

EDP standards and documentation are closely related. Most standards have documentation requirements associated with them and, conversely, much documentation is prepared according to standards. Effective standards and documentation contribute to the orderliness, consistency, maintainability, and ease of use of EDP systems. Sound system design practices contribute to the quality and longevity of systems. Productivity aids are tools that help programmers and analysts develop quality systems. Management of systems maintenance is important because in most mature EDP installations, programmers and analysts spend well over half of their time maintaining current systems. This represents a substantial, sometimes unnecessary, drain on EDP resources and, therefore, deserves management attention.

DEVELOPING AND ENFORCING STANDARDS

A standard is a statement of approved rules and conventions followed in support of a particular objective. It is important that a standards program normally contain provisions for varying degrees of enforcement and permanence:

- *Standards* are compulsory rules that are relatively stable.
- *Guidelines* are suggested but not compulsory ways of doing things.
- *Technical bulletins* are temporary standards that address conditions too volatile for permanent inclusion into a standards program

In this chapter, standards will be discussed in their broadest sense; that is, no explicit differentiation will be made between degrees of enforcement and permanence.

Standards are important because they represent our only assurance of continuity and consistency in developing, maintaining, and operating EDP systems. EDP attracts people with a wide diversity of skills, backgrounds, attitudes, and educational levels. Personnel turnover is extremely high. The relationships among hardware, software, and applications systems, as well as between EDP staff and users, is complex and highly interdependent; and the rapidity of technical innovation is startling. Therefore, there is no practical way that even the smallest EDP installation can function effectively without the continuity and stability that standards contribute to an organization.

Unfortunately, standards development and enforcement is a difficult task. It is difficult to sell programmers and analysts on the need for following standards. Although they pay lip service to standards, EDP people dislike organizational control of their creative activities. In addition, standards are useless unless they are followed. Enforcement must rely heavily on incentives, because standards that are highly unpopular will simply be ignored, a fact that no amount of policing will correct. Therefore, standards must be developed, sold, and enforced in such a way as to make their use largely voluntary.

Finally, the development of standards is a staff activity. It does not contribute directly to the profitability of the EDP department. Therefore, standards development must not cause an immoderate drain on EDP resources. The difference between too much and too little can only be defined within the context of the specific environment. Standards covering the following areas normally carry the highest payoff for an installation:

- Systems development methodology
- Documentation standards
- Technical rules
- User relations
- Internal EDP procedures
- Project control

- Computer operations
- Naming conventions

Development of standards for these areas is discussed next.

Systems Development Methodology Standards

The standards with the most far-reaching implications are those that define the procedures, documents, and key decision points in the systems development process. These standards reflect the philosophy of the EDP department and, to a large extent, can shape the technical quality and responsiveness of the final product.

A general description of the methodology to be followed is the first step in establishing standards in this area. This is done by describing each system development life-cycle phase, identifying its deliverables, defining the tasks needed to achieve those deliverables, and identifying the organizational units responsible for the completion of each deliverable. The general description of the system development methodology should not be longer than several pages.

The methodology section should mandate sign-offs for the following:

- Basic features of the system.
- Data-element definitions and file contents.
- Report and screen layouts.
- Schedules and work plans.
- Cost-benefit analysis.
- User procedures.
- Test results.
- System acceptance.

It is important to stipulate in the standards that agreements on many of these issues must be reached several times during the developmental cycle. As development of the system progresses, we achieve greater levels of detail in our design and become increasingly cognizant of the exact shape and texture of the system. This is particularly true with respect to data-element definitions, file design, report and display screen layouts, and user procedures.

In addition to achieving a progressively greater level of detail during design, we gain a better understanding of the time frames and resources required to complete the system. Therefore, standards should stipulate the preparation of new work plans, schedules, and cost-benefit analyses as systems development progresses.

Descriptions of documents needed to support systems development methodology standards can be found in the documentation section of this chapter and in Chapter 6.

Documentation Standards

Standards for written documents represent one of the most important aspects of a standards program. Documentation enables continuity in the development and maintenance of systems. In addition, documentation is used to prove that a required action was taken or a proscribed action was avoided. Without such proof, the enforcement of standards is difficult. Specific documents and forms that should be included in a standards program are described in the documentation section of this chapter.

Technical Rules

Most medium and large EDP installations require conformance to technical rules that govern design and programming activities. These rules enhance our ability to develop better code and, conversely, forbid technical practices that result in inefficient or difficult-to-maintain programs.

Following are examples of technical rules:

- The mandatory use of one computer language, such as COBOL, for the development of all application systems. This standard may be promulgated in order to minimize the cross-training needed to maintain systems and to ensure the use of a language that is most appropriate to the environment.
- Restrictions on the use of on-line file updating. Since this type of processing can be very expensive in terms of computer resources, on-line updating may be limited to systems where access to the latest information is absolutely essential.
- Mandatory use of structured programming, top-down design, or other techniques in order to maintain a consistent approach to systems development. (Also see Productivity Aids.)
- Use of standard subroutines, macros, and utilities for date validation, error checking, opening and closing of files, and so on.
- Conformance to standard report and screen production and formatting techniques. This may include the use of generalized report pro-

grams to produce reports, the use of standard headings, and the mandatory production of totals and record counts.

- Development and use of predefined file backup, purging, and history spooling techniques. This helps ensure adequate file backup and orderly file growth.

User Relations Standards

Standards dealing with user relations generally cover request procedures, sign-offs, commitments, and relationships between EDP and its clients.

Request procedures deal with the methods, forms, and protocol required to initiate, evaluate, process, and, if accepted, implement a user request. Since maintenance activities consume a large part of an EDP installation's time and resources, a consistent procedure in this area is desirable. Request procedures normally stipulate the following:

- Forms and protocols used to initiate and process requests.
- Approvals that are needed for request evaluation and implementation.
- Lead times needed to respond to requests.
- Groups within the EDP department responsible for processing various types of requests.

Sign-off or approval standards specify the organizational units that must approve work done by the EDP department and the tasks that are subject to this approval. Key approval points in the development of a system are described in Chapter 6.

Commitments standards describe the personnel and other commitments a user is expected to make when a new system is being developed or an existing system undergoes major changes. These commitments usually take the form of liaison and other user personnel to work on a full- or part-time basis with EDP, budget commitments (if any) that must precede development efforts, and clerical support to be provided by the user in the development of the system.

User/EDP relationship standards identify EDP contact points for user questions and problems. They also specify the process by which questions are answered and problems resolved. For example, they identify the EDP organizational unit to contact in case of display terminal failure and describe the procedure for requesting a training class for data-entry clerks.

Internal EDP Procedures

Internal EDP procedures describe the formal interactions that are required between development staff, operations, the data-base administration function, and EDP management. Of particular importance are the following:

- Procedures for the erasure of datasets.
- Procedures for designing and implementing data bases.
- Rules governing access to computer facilities.
- Interaction between programmers and technical support personnel.
- Internal sign-offs required before a feasibility study, general design report, or other document can be distributed to the end user.

In addition, the EDP department will probably need to maintain policies and procedures regarding absences, work shifts, disciplinary procedures, and other subjects that have no direct bearing on the EDP function. These non-EDP standards are not relevant to this discussion.

Project Control Standards

Project control is one of the most important internal procedures. Standards dealing with project control are primarily, but not exclusively, designed to satisfy the internal needs for the effective management of EDP activities. Project control standards generally deal with three aspects of project management: project planning, time reporting, and status reporting.

Project planning standards describe the activities that must be performed and the documentation that must be produced when developing work plans and schedules. Work plans are updated during the course of the project and may include critical path networks, task descriptions, and resource and time estimates.

Time reporting standards specify the frequency, format, and procedural rules for reporting time expended on various projects and tasks. Time is generally reported in a way consistent with the organization's accounting practices. Other time subdivisions and categories may also be used to make time reporting more meaningful to EDP management. In fact, sometimes two time reporting systems exist, one for developing accounting information and another for providing meaningful data to EDP. In small installations, time reporting may be done on a manual basis. In medium and large installations, internally developed or commercially purchased project accounting systems are frequently used.

Status reporting standards describe the formats and frequency of documentation that must be submitted to track the progress of various EDP activities. These status documents usually include Gantt charts or other visual representations of a schedule and a narrative report describing the progress of the project. The latter usually includes activities and accomplishments during the current period, problems encountered, tangible products produced, and goals for the next period.

For more detailed information on project planning, time reporting, and status reporting, see Chapters 4 and 8.

Computer Operations Standards

Computer operations standards describe the procedures and documents needed to place a system into production and to enable operations to successfully run the system. Operations standards normally cover the following:

- Turnover documentation and required sign-offs.
- Operations documentation (run books).
- Lead time needed to secure approvals and to place a system into production.
- Test procedures to be followed by operations prior to placing a system into production status.
- Library and data-set management.
- Computer usage protocols.

Turnover documentation and sign-off standards describe the forms that must accompany a request to place a program or file into production and define the approvals that must be secured.

Operations documentation (the run book or operations manual) describes, in detail, the procedures computer operators, I/O control clerks, and other operations support personnel must follow in operating the system. Operations documentation is described in detail in the documentation section.

Lead times needed to secure approvals and place a system into production are frequently specified explicitly in standards. This helps prevent unrealistic expectations on the part of development personnel regarding the time period within which a system can become operational after "everything is working." The lead time needed to place a system into production is intended to provide operations with sufficient time to allocate files, inspect operations documentation, verify that the job control language to be used in production is correct, and train operators in the operation of the system. As might be expected, validation and sign-off procedures are one of the major causes of friction between development people, who are under pressure to place the system into production, and operations personnel, who need accurate run instructions.

Test procedures used by operations may also be described in operations standards. These test procedures are not intended to ensure that the system produces and manipulates information consistent with its specifications; that is the job of development personnel during unit, system, and parallel testing. Rather, operations testing certifies the system's conformance to operations documentation and verifies that the job control language needed to run the system is correct, that restart and recovery procedures work, and that the applications programs successfully interface with production hardware and software components. This is particularly important when unit and system testing was not done at the installation where production will take place.

In addition, operations may also crash test the system; that is, they may intentionally induce hardware and software failures in order to determine if the system works in conjunction with operating system components needed to enable recovery.

Program library and data-set management standards are critically important in maintaining the integrity of production data sets and programs. In addition, they ease the bottlenecks that invariably result from a failure to monitor and control the proliferation of data sets. Library and data-set management standards address the following issues:

- The approvals needed to scratch data sets of various types.
- Procedures programmers must follow in requesting space allocations for test data sets and programs.
- Program and data set naming conventions.
- The features of the installation's library management software that should be used.

Computer usage protocols are standards that describe test time allocations, timesharing rations, test priority schemes, rules governing the number of print lines allowed for test runs, and other machine-oriented protocols governing program development and maintenance.

Naming Conventions

Naming conventions are an extremely important part of any standards program. The proliferation of data sets, programs, data bases, jobs, and data elements will result in chaos and confusion without the predictability of standard names.

Naming conventions should cover the following system components:

- Data elements
- Files
- Data sets
- Data bases
- Reports
- Jobs, job steps, and procedure
- Macros
- Application programs
- Installation-written utilities
- Data definitions (DDs)

Who Should Develop Standards?

There are three ways an EDP installation can acquire the standards it needs:

- Purchase a standards package from a commercial source outside the company.
- Assign or hire one or two full-time individuals to develop and maintain standards.
- Develop and maintain standards by a committee whose members represent systems development, operations, and staff areas within EDP.

The first two methods require a minimum of involvement on the part of line EDP personnel. The third method requires considerable involvement. All three have merit and are widely followed. All three also have serious drawbacks. The approach to be used in a specific EDP installation will depend on the size of the installation, the skills and experience levels of people in the installation, and the budget available for a standards program. Following is a description of each approach.

Packaged standards. The advantage of this approach is that, if the standards in the package do not require extensive alteration, it represents the highest-quality alternative for the least amount of money, within the shortest time period. Most prepackaged standards programs include all the forms and procedures needed to develop and maintain systems. The forms can be printed with the logo and the forms numbers of the organization and usually contain a level of detail that is more than sufficient for any standards program. Such packaged standards are relatively inexpensive and their quality is at least as high as standards developed in-house.

Unfortunately, the packaged approach has some disadvantages:

- Forms and standards contained in a commercial package are aimed at the widest possible audience; therefore, custom features required in an individual installation must be developed in-house. If substantial modifications are made, the cost benefit may be lost.
- Commercial packages tend to be all-inclusive because a commercial package must cover the widest possible ground and because the developers of these packages seem to operate under the notion that sheer volume has sales appeal. Therefore, an EDP department with limited standards needs may be paying for forms and standards it does not need.
- Packaged standards are normally selected by a small committee without much involvement from the EDP department at large. Therefore, standards that are acquired from outside often enjoy less support than standards that were developed internally and were extensively studied and discussed.

Standards developed by experts. This theory postulates that one or more people on the EDP staff who have an inclination toward this kind of work should have the full-time job of developing, updating, and enforcing standards. If such people are not available in-house, consultants may be hired. This approach is faster and more efficient than standards by committee and, frequently, the quality of the work is higher. The job gets done expeditiously because responsibility is vested directly in one or more individuals who can devote all their time exclusively to this task.

There are several disadvantages to this approach. As with packaged standards, there is very little direct involvement from the EDP staff. People tend to dismiss the standards as unrealistic because they are created without the consultation of those who must live with them. Enforcement is thus even more difficult than it would be when wide agreement is reached.

In addition, people who volunteer, or are volunteered, to do standards as a full-time job are usually staff, as opposed to line, people. Staff people are frequently better writers and planners than line people. But they are also further removed from the realities that standards must address. Therefore, standards written by staff people tend to be overly detailed and rigid and cover ground that does not need covering in a standards program. Asking a staff person to write standards is like asking a lawyer what to do about a neighbor's noisy dog. The lawyer may recommend a fat lawsuit, just as the EDP staff person may recommend a needlessly extensive standards manual.

Standards by committee. The main advantage to this approach is that it forces key people in the EDP organization to think seriously about standards, become involved in their development, and, once agreement is reached, wholeheartedly support those standards. The committee approach requires the part-time involvement of five to ten individuals who represent every major interest and function within EDP. This committee elects a chairman; establishes ground rules for voting, committee membership, and the like; and develops priorities for the creation of needed standards. Individual members, with some help from technical writers or from their own staffs, then write standards and present them in committee. The standards are discussed and modified to satisfy the major interests represented on the committee.

If the committee enjoys strong management support, if its members are carefully selected, and if they take their work on the committee seriously, the committee approach works very well. Standards will be developed more slowly than with the other approaches, but they will more accurately represent the everyday realities of the department and will enjoy greater support.

The disadvantages of the committee approach are that its work can degenerate into power struggles between opposing viewpoints, responsibilities can be shirked because of other duties, and a general do-nothing atmosphere can result. In short, the committee approach represents all the advantages and disadvantages of developing products by consensus.

Major Standards Issues

The most difficult aspect of developing and enforcing an effective standards program is the successful resolution of competing viewpoints and the achievement of a healthy balance between the following:

- The attempt to control too many aspects of EDP versus insufficient coverage.
- Too much detail versus insufficient detail.
- Overly rigid enforcement versus weak enforcement.
- Standards development by consensus versus standards development by management fiat.

The compromises that result will, to a large extent, determine the effectiveness of the standards program. Here are some suggestions on how to achieve a good balance.

Too much versus insufficient coverage. Standards have little virtue in and of themselves. The fact that a procedure, document, or technique is "standardized" does not necessarily make it better or more efficient. On the contrary, generalization, which is what any standard is, rarely serves the specific instance; rather, it is intended to make the overall EDP function more effective and more efficient. For example, an individual program that can be written using the language, file access methods, and other techniques most directly suited to the task at hand will almost always (by definition) be a better program than one written in conformance to a prescribed programming language and technical conventions. However, an installation containing 200 or 300 highly individual programs is chaotic and difficult to manage.

Standards coverage should be extended only into those areas where conformance of the specific instance to general policies provides an overall benefit that outweighs the advantages of specificity. *The burden of proof should always be on the side of justifying the existence of a standard, not the other way around.* It is extremely difficult to establish where the line should be drawn. Although areas that can, potentially, be covered by a standards program appear to encompass practically every EDP activity, caution is advised in selecting the specific topics to be standardized.

Too much versus not enough detail. The purpose of standards is to describe what is expected, not to instruct people in the skills required to produce the expected results. Care must, therefore, be taken to ensure that standards do not evolve into textbooks on programming, systems design, and human relations. The level of detail should be just sufficient to precisely explain the task, procedure, or form to be followed and should always focus on specific issues rather than generalities.

Overly rigid enforcement versus weak enforcement. How rigidly should standards be enforced? As mentioned previously, standards may be considered a generic category of rules and procedures necessitating varying degrees of enforcement. Guidelines may be suggested ways of doing things. Technical bulletins may be mandatory but transitory; they may, for example, stipulate program testing procedures that are only in effect until a new hardware configuration is installed. Standards, as a specific category, are permanent and mandatory. Enforcement should, therefore, vary depending on the category. In general, it is more important to have a small number of standards, and to enforce them, than it is to have many guidelines that are not enforced.

Standards by consensus versus standards by management fiat. This issue is addressed in the section dealing with the theories of who should develop standards. The trade-off is between the inefficient process of developing standards by committee and the development of standards by decree, in which a small number of people write standards based on management's ideas of what is needed. The trade-off is between telling people how they should be conducting EDP activities and allowing people to define their own rules through a committee approach.

In a mature EDP environment where a high level of experience and data-processing skills is available and overall EDP goals are appreciated, the committee approach works well. In a young installation where EDP experience and skill are not widely available, the standards-by-decree approach is most practical.

Characteristics of an Effective Standards Program

Following is a synopsis of the major characteristics of most successful standards programs.

Management commitment. Management commitment is the single most important element in an effective standards program. The only way a standards program can succeed is with strong, visible, consistent management support. Without this support, there is a 100 percent guarantee that even the most carefully developed program will fail.

Since people are judged by the quality and timeliness of the products they produce, their natural tendency is to circumvent any requirements that do not have a direct positive impact on the production of that product. Standards rarely have such an impact. Therefore, top EDP management must resolutely insist on the implementation of programs and systems that meet standards. This is not easy to do. There are great pressures to grant exceptions in order to complete projects as quickly as possible.

However, if EDP management consistently demands adherence to standards, even for rush projects and in crisis situations, users and computer people will realize the necessity of following standards. The extra time required for sign-offs and the preparation of various documents will be built into schedules and will be accepted as part of the normal work of the department.

Wide involvement. The surest way to gain support for a standards program is to demand that key people devote time to the development and maintenance of standards. The comments and suggestions of people who will actually use the standards should also be encouraged.

It is axiomatic that participation and consensus lead to a greater degree of voluntary compliance than does the establishment of standards by management decree. Therefore, the ideal vehicle for the development of standards is the standards committee as described in the previous section. After people have argued the issues and have reached a consensus, their strong support can be legitimately expected.

Sensible coverage and degree of detail. Coverage and degree of detail should be kept at a level consistent with the needs of the organization. Care must be taken to ensure that standards developers do not standardize every imaginable activity and write standards in unnecessary detail. The burden of proof should always be on the expansionists and elaborators. As Mies van der Rohe, the great architect and father of the lean, functional school of modern architecture, remarked, "less is more." What he meant was that the absence of clutter, unnecessary ornamentation, and nonfunctional architectural features results in better buildings. This philosophy should also apply to standards and should be taken to heart by everyone charged with their development.

Strong enforcement. It is better not to have standards than to have standards that cannot be enforced. Care must be taken to develop standards that are reasonable and can be adhered to without undue hardships. If a standard requires a significant amount of what is perceived of as unnecessary or extraordinarily difficult effort, it will be ignored. Or, in some instances, the form but not the substance will be adhered to, which may be worse than total noncompliance. Standards, like laws, depend on a wide degree of voluntary compliance.

Clear, concise English. Standards are not intended for light entertainment. Nevertheless, their language and writing style need not be obtuse, boring, and inelegant. Again, Mies van der Rohe's dictum of "less is more" is applicable to standards language: don't say in 20 words what can be said in 10. If a simple word or sentence will serve, do not use its complicated equivalent. Avoid buzzwords, meaningless generalities, and "bureaucratese."

Currency. A standards program cannot be frozen in time. The computer environment changes, technology progresses, organizational needs change. So must standards. If they are not updated in a consistent and timely fashion, standards will fall into disuse. There-fore, the people charged with developing standards must be con-stantly on the alert for changing conditions that require addition, deletion, and modification of existing standards.

EFFECTIVE DOCUMENTATION

Documentation consists of written material that records events, pro-poses actions, or serves an instructional purpose. An orderly series of documents is the only way a modern organization can successfully cope with the complexities of data processing. Documentation enables us to perform systems development, maintenance, and computer op-erations tasks in a consistent fashion. It is a critical tool for manage-ment control of EDP.

The documentation used to support EDP activities is normally categorized as follows:

- Systems documentation
- Programming documentation
- User documentation
- Operations documentation

These areas cover the development, maintenance, and operation of computer systems and are described next.

Systems Documentation

The purpose of systems documentation is to present an overview of how the system functions, to impart an understanding of how system components interact, and to describe how the system interfaces with users and computer operations. It contains file descriptions, report layouts, functional and system flow schematics, and other documents that describe the system as a whole. In addition, systems documen-tation includes memos and other documents that provide information about the history and evolution of the system.

The primary audience for systems documentation is systems an-alysts. However, programmers, managers, and even user personnel may need occasional access to systems documentation. Programmers may need to become familiar with the context within which program changes are made; managers may need to become familiar with the history and functions of systems under their direction; and user per-sonnel may need to gain an understanding of how the system performs the functions that result in the products received from the system.

The information that constitutes system documentation is described next.

High-level system description. People who are closely involved in systems development or maintenance sometimes forget the fact that a high-level overview is needed in order to present system details in a meaningful context. Therefore, a high-level flow chart or box diagram, accompanied by explanatory narrative, should always be included in system documentation.

Overview information can be extracted from the general design report. However, care should be taken to ensure that no major functional revisions have been made since development of the report. A high-level system description should be included in user and operations documentation, as well as systems documentation.

Project history. Project history documentation consists of the following:

- Memos.
- Miscellaneous reports and studies.
- The original preliminary investigation, feasibility study, and general design reports.
- Project schedules and task lists.
- User requests.

The project history file is an indispensable source of information about a system. It tells the story of how the system evolved, the motivations and politics behind various design decisions, and the original goals of the participants. As with other historical data, an intelligent reading of the project history file enables us to deal with current situations through an understanding of the past.

File, report, and screen layouts. System files are used at many points in a system. Therefore, they should be described centrally in the systems documentation files. In practice, it is extremely difficult to control the proliferation of file layouts, even when automated documentation techniques such as word processing exist. Copies of file layouts and descriptions appear in people's desks, in the operations run book, in programming documentation, and in user manuals. Some of this proliferation may be legitimate and justified. Generally, however, it should be discouraged.

A copy of report and screen layouts should also be kept in the systems documentation file. They are a key to understanding the system as a whole because they provide descriptions and visual examples of the end products the system produces. Report and screen layouts may, in some cases, be kept in both systems and program documentation. The advantage to this approach is that programmers can more easily make program modifications when they have layouts as well as program code. The disadvantage is that two sets of documents invariably means that only one set gets updated when changes occur. A data dictionary can help alleviate this problem by centralizing report and screen information. Data dictionaries are described in the productivity aids section of this chapter.

Hardware and software environment. The computing environment under which a system functions should be described in systems documentation. This is particularly important in installations using a variety of computers and operating systems. Enough information must be provided to identify the general configuration of the hardware, communications network, and operating system software used by the system.

Data-element definitions. The definitions of data elements found on transaction files, master files, and data bases should be included in systems documentation and should include the following information:

- Data-element length in terms of internal and external storage characteristics.
- Data-element type: numeric, alphabetic or alphanumeric.
- Data-element description, including:
  —Narrative of how a data element is used.
  —Legal values.
  —Decimal placement and precision (e.g., rounded to hundreds).
  —Element category (e.g., amount field, narrative field).
- Where used. This may consist of a cross-reference table between elements and the files in which they appear.
- Data-element name as used in documentation, file descriptions, and user terminology (e.g., Payment Amount and PAYAMT).
- Data-element validation rules.

System controls. Editing rules, error procedures, balancing steps, and other system controls should be described. This information is necessary for an understanding of major system features and functions.

Glossary. If the system contains terminology that may not be generally familiar to systems analysts, a glossary should be included to reduce misunderstandings and to enhance precise knowledge of system functions. A glossary is particularly important for systems that support esoteric applications areas and for in-house-developed software.

Program Documentation

The purpose of program documentation is to enable problem resolution and maintenance activities to take place. Ideally, program documentation should be available 24 hours a day to facilitate emergency program changes. The effective control of program documentation is critically important because one of the most common causes of program failure and inefficient maintenance is poor documentation. Outdated program listings, inaccurate descriptions, and lack of a good revision log can cause serious problems.

The following information should be kept in the program folder (or on machine readable media) for each application program and carefully updated when program changes are made.

General information. General information includes the name of the author, the date the program was written, the programming language used, the purpose of the program, required parameters, files used by the program, and run instructions. This information usually consists of one or two cover sheets in standard format.

Partial system flow chart. It is helpful to know which programs immediately precede and immediately follow each program in the system. Therefore, a one-page flow chart that places the program in context should be included.

Program listing. This is the most critical component of program documentation. It is one element without which effective program documentation cannot exist. The listing of the current version of the program may be physically present in the program folder or it may be produced from the program library each time it is needed for reference purposes. The advantage of physical presence is that the listing is immediately accessible without dependency on computer availability to print the listing. The disadvantage is that there is no guarantee that the listing in the program folder represents the latest version of the program. This fact can only be verified by listing the program from the appropriate library. In addition to a current listing, a listing of the previous version of the program should also be available.

Job control language. Job control language (JCL) may be included as part of the program listing or it may be kept separately. In either case, it is needed in order to inform the programmer and computer operator of how the program is run in the production or test environment.

History of revisions. This is a record of changes that have been made to the program. Usually, the revision log is a standard form that is filled out each time a change is made. It describes the purpose of the change, the individual who requested the change, the programmer who made the change, and the date on which the change was implemented.

In addition to the change log, a listing of each set of changes should be included. This is important in order to enable previous changes to be "backed out" in case of problems, and is needed to verify that a set of changes has been made.

User Documentation

User documentation contains all the information needed by the end user to successfully interact with the system. It consists of a description of system inputs and outputs and defines user procedures needed to make the system work. User documentation may be contained in one or several manuals used by data-entry clerks, department managers, and other groups that interact with the system.

User documentation is normally prepared during the detail design, program development, and installation phases of the system development life cycle. The creation of user manuals is premature if done before detail design is completed and too late if done after system installation. The ideal time to develop user documentation is during program development. At that time, the design has been finalized but sufficient time remains before the system is to be installed. The following should always be included as part of user documentation.

System description. The high-level system description used in systems documentation can be used here. It should describe the purpose, major functions, and basic operational characteristics of the system in language the user can understand. Block diagrams are an appropriate part of a system description. However, care must be taken when using traditional EDP flow charts. All symbols should either be defined or should be self-explanatory to a layman; the level of illustration should not exceed several pages, and esoteric symbols that have little meaning to the user should be avoided.

Output descriptions. User manuals should always contain facsimiles and descriptions of reports and display screens. If possible, live data should be used on the examples. Output descriptions should include the following:

- Purpose of the screen or report.
- Sequence in which the information is printed or displayed.
- How the output is to be used.
- Balancing procedures.
- A description of each field that appears on the screen or report, including a clarification of all abbreviations and acronyms.
- Source of the data (i.e., the name of the file where the data originate).
- Frequency of production (i.e., how often are the data updated, printed and displayed).
- The specific user who is to receive the report or screen.
- Security considerations.
- Approximate number of report pages.

File layouts and descriptions are not usually included in user documentation unless processing of some files takes place in the user department.

Input instructions and formats. This portion of user documentation describes how the user should enter information into the system. The following questions should be answered:

- What forms must be filled out to enter data? To correct errors?
- How are input terminals (if any) operated?
- What data should be submitted?
- What types of data must be submitted in batches and how are these batches defined?
- What types of transactions can and cannot be submitted in the same batch?
- How should inputs be balanced and verified for accuracy?
- What input error correction procedures are used?
- Who should be contacted in case of input questions or problems?

Timing requirements. This section of the user manual deals with the timing of inputs, processes, and outputs. It indicates the frequency with which reports are produced and specifies the deadlines by which data that are to appear on these reports or that affect these reports must be submitted.

Timing specifications are particularly important in payroll, inventory, accounting, and other systems that require meticulous balancing and extensive audit trails. Users should be very aware of the cutoff points for entering time-dependent transactions such as payroll hours into the system. Complex timing requirements are best described through the use of charts that illustrate the relationship between various processing activities, and the hours, days, weeks, and months for which these activities are scheduled. A short narrative description should accompany each illustration.

Clerical procedures. Clerical procedures describe the manual activities that must be performed by the user in order to successfully interact with the system on a day-to-day basis. Clerical tasks may consist of filling out and batching source documents, balancing reports, correcting errors, and performing other activities requiring human intervention. Although most clerical procedure descriptions are usually placed into other user documentation categories such as input instructions, the clerical procedures section is an appropriate place to describe manual tasks that do not neatly fit into those categories.

Record-retention requirements. Every office accumulates documents that are outdated and no longer used. At the same time, important documents sometimes disappear. The purpose of developing retention requirements is to rationalize the process of keeping and throwing away. System-specific retention requirements of interest to the user should address the following issues:

- Audit trails (What source documents and reports should be kept in order to facilitate appropriate audit trails?).
- Back-up (What source documents and reports should be kept to facilitate recovery if computer files are destroyed?).
- Government regulations (What documents must be kept and for how long in order to satisfy government regulations?).
- Convenience (How long should people keep reports in order to be able to do their day-to-day work effectively?).

Operations Documentation

The purpose of operations documentation is to describe the procedures needed to operate application systems. It normally includes a system overview, a responsibility list, and descriptions of input, machine operations, and output processing. Although it is not system specific, a hardware and software inventory is also needed. Operations documentation is described next. For a detailed analysis of tasks associated with the operations function, see Chapter 12.

System overview. This is a high-level description of the system. It serves to familiarize operations personnel with the purpose of the system and imparts a perspective within which the operation of individual components can be learned.

Responsibility list. The key to quickly recovering from a system failure that cannot be resolved by a computer operator is to know who in the EDP organization to contact. Therefore, it is imperative that an up-to-date list of the titles, names, and organizations of people responsible for maintaining the system be included in operations documentation.

Input procedures. Input procedures must include instructions that cover the following:

* *Data entry.* Keying instructions are needed in order to enable the transformation of data on source documents into machine-readable form. Detailed, step-by-step instructions are needed to promote efficient keying and reduce errors caused by faulty input. Data-entry instructions usually consist of:

    —A narrative description of the keying process.
    —Sample source documents containing realistic data.
    —A source document layout indicating the positions on the screen, card, or record into which each element should be keyed.
    —Instructions for keying each individual element. These include zero filling, use of default values, legal values, and interpretation guidelines for hard-to-read entries.

* *Input disposition.* Specific input disposition instructions must be provided to instruct operations personnel on the treatment of

source documents and machine-readable input data after keying is completed. Disposition will depend on user and system retention requirements. In general, source documents are sent back to the organization responsible for collecting them. Input files are kept by EDP until a file update is successfully completed or until a complete system cycle is run.

- *Input control.* These batch-control procedures ensure that all source documents are received and that the information they contain is successfully keyed. Input control is normally done by comparing a physical count of source documents with the tally sheet that accompanies the documents, and by comparing the number of records produced by the keying operation with the number of source documents received.

Machine operations procedures. Machine operations procedures provide detailed instructions on how to run the system. They should cover all procedures from the time input files are received from the keying operation to the time reports and other output is produced. Documentation covering the following areas is of particular importance.

- *Run schedules.* Operations must be provided with information about when various portions of the system should be run. This includes input submission and output distribution deadlines, the sequence in which jobs should be run, and fall-back times and sequences in case of system failure.
- *Job control language.* An up-to-date JCL listing should always be included as part of machine operations procedures. The listing should be supplemented by clear job-to-job block diagrams that enable the operator to trace the operational flow of the system without the necessity of interpreting the JCL. The storage of JCL in program libraries is also recommended.
- *Special data instructions.* Many systems require special input of dates or other data by the operator at run execution time. The data that must be keyed in and the information on which it is based must be explicitly described in the machine operations procedures.
- *Set-up instructions.* These instructions include information that identifies the tapes and disks to be mounted, the type of printer paper that should be used, and labeling instructions for output files. Set-up instructions may also include the special data procedures described previously.

- *Error, Abend, Restart, and Recovery Procedures.* No system functions without occasional problems. Many of these problems can be predicted and procedures designed to minimize reruns, delays and the destruction of data. These procedures can be categorized as follows:

  —Error procedures cover application-specific conditions such as incorrect dates, transaction types, and field contents. These conditions are flagged by application programs and generally should not require operator intervention.

  —Abend procedures describe steps that must be taken to deal with "abnormal end-of-job" conditions. These conditions are described in appropriate software manuals, but additional applications-oriented actions must be documented in machine-operations procedures.

  —Restart and recovery procedures describe the steps that must be taken to restart a program in case of an abend or other condition and to recover transactions and/or master files that were lost during the course of the failure.

- *Back-up instructions.* Machine operations procedures should contain instructions for copying master files and supporting data at strategic intervals during processing. This may be done independently of specific applications (e.g., copying entire disk packs containing data from a variety of systems) or selectively by backing up files for specific systems.

Output processing procedure. This portion of operations documentation covers activities that commence with the production of outputs, mainly reports, and ends with the delivery of outputs to the user. Output processing for reports includes the following:

- *Bursting and decollating instructions.*
- *Distribution instructions.* This includes information on who should receive which copies of reports, when reports should be delivered, and what the delivery mechanism should consist of.
- *Report quality assurance.* Operations must participate in the verification of report accuracy. This includes checking for operations-oriented information such as records-in/records-out totals and applications-oriented information such as expected data volumes and characteristics (e.g., the reports should be about 100 pages in length and must contain 12 pagebreak headings corresponding to each company department).

Principles of Good Documentation

Effective documentation has the following characteristics:

- It is terse, relevant, clearly written, and makes liberal use of graphics. Words, phrases, and descriptions that do not directly contribute to an understanding of the subject are avoided.
- It is current. Documentation that is out of date may be more damaging than an absence of documentation.
- It is written with the audience in mind. Specifically:
  - —User documentation avoids "computerese." It is written in the business terminology of the end user.
  - —Programming documentation avoids arcane applications terminology that is not meaningful to programmers.
  - —Operations documentation avoids long-winded narratives that are difficult to follow under hectic machine-room conditions. It is directed toward people who are performing tasks that require substantial physical movement. Unlike systems or programming documentation, which is read by people sitting quietly at desks, operations documentation serves people who are busy manning the CPU console, mounting tapes, keypunching, and decollating reports. Therefore, it should be written and organized in a way that can be used in an environment of constant interruptions, noise, and physical movement.
- It is organized in an easy-to-update format and is subject to enforceable updating procedures. Documentation that is difficult to update will quickly become out of date and will not be used.
- It is centrally stored and updated. Change procedures are well defined and processed centrally, preferably with the aid of word-processing facilities and automated documentation tools such as text editors and data dictionaries (see the productivity aids section of this chapter).
- It is extensively cross-referenced. This is a particularly important characteristic for operations documentation, which is often used in situations requiring fast response to problems.
- It is segmented into independent components. A systems analyst, programmer, computer operator, data-entry clerk, or manager should be able to read a short passage explaining a specific procedure or component and understand that procedure or component without the need to read extensive introductory material. Therefore, documentation should always be structured with a view toward the maximum independence of each part.

SOUND DESIGN PRACTICES

Decisions regarding details of systems development are, or should be, the preserve of the designer working closely with the end user and the programming staff. However, data-processing and user managements have a legitimate interest in some aspects of systems design. They must monitor the technical features designed into the system to ensure that the following issues are adequately addressed:

- People orientation
- Efficient resource usage
- Maintainability
- Back-up and recovery
- Audit trails
- Flexibility and simplicity

These issues have a critical impact on the day-to-day usability and maintainability of the system. Verification that good design concepts and techniques are followed need not consume an inordinate amount of management time. Judicious questioning and perusal of key system documentation is usually adequate to determine if good design practices are being followed. Major areas of concern are described next.

People Orientation

Many systems fail because they are inordinately difficult to use. Unfortunately, systems analysts too often concentrate on the glamorous technical challenges of system building to the exclusion of people issues. For a system to work properly and to provide end users with useful information, it must achieve the following:

- Straightforward, uncomplicated data input.
- Understandable, easy-to-perform error-correction procedures.
- Meaningful, readable reports and display screens.
- A comfortable physical environment.

All these characteristics must be considered when designing a system and should be carefully monitored by EDP management before detail design is finalized.

Resource Usage

Perhaps the most important question that must be answered before a commitment to develop a system can be made is, "Do we have the resources to run the system?" These resources include storage space on peripheral devices, CPU capacity, and teleprocessing network facilities. Potential resource usage is difficult to predict. But it must be done in order to define the environmental parameters within which the system should be designed. EDP management can focus attention on the resources issue by taking several tangible steps:

- Each system, from the feasibility study to detail design, must be evaluated by computer operations. This will guarantee a critical view of computing resources the proposed system will use, because operations is the natural adversary of the development staff: its job of ensuring adequate computer power invariably becomes more difficult with each new system to become operational.
- Every system proposal must include an estimate of resource usage even if the estimate is difficult to prepare and is of limited accuracy. This will focus the attention of system designers on the importance of resource usage as a technical factor of system design.
- Adequate justification must exist for using system resources that are in short supply. For example, an installation that suffers response-time problems on terminals may wish to limit on-line processing to applications that are critically time dependent.
- Management policies for the conservation of computing resources should be formalized by inclusion in programming and systems development standards. This will further bring resource usage to the attention of the EDP staff.
- People, as well as computing power, are scarce resources. Therefore, the need for additional shift operators, clerks and other production personnel must be estimated.

Maintainability

System maintainability is achieved through sound system design and programming, as well as through good documentation. Management ensures maintainable programs by, first, identifying the design and programming practices that contribute to maintainability. They include the following:

- Modular or structured programming.
- Structured design.
- Widely supportable programming languages.

- Extensive commentary imbedded in program code when low-level languages are used.
- Comprehensive program documentation.
- Structured walkthroughs or peer reviews.

Next, the desired techniques must be formalized by incorporating them into EDP standards. Finally, standards that affect system maintainability must be enforced. The best enforcement mechanism is to develop a system of organizational checks and balances. Frequent interaction between peers, between various levels in the organization, and between different departments (e.g., operations and systems development) is the best insurance that techniques contributing to system maintainability will be observed.

Back-up and Recovery

No system should be placed into production without adequate back-up and recovery procedures. The adequacy of these procedures should be tested in the same manner as the system's functional characteristics. Insist on answers to the following five questions:

- What are the consequences to the user of different levels of system failure?
- How are destroyed master files re-created?
- How is an aborted file update restarted?
- How long does it take to accomplish the preceding two items, and at what cost in resources?
- Have all recovery procedures been tested in the production environment using files loaded with test data?

The answers to these questions will enable management to judge the cost effectiveness of back-up and recovery procedures and to obtain an idea of how well system recovery features have been designed and tested.

Audit Trails

Audit trails enable the user, EDP staff, and system auditors to trace what happened to a particular unit of input or to a computer process. Audit trails are important for purposes of documentation (e.g., financial accounting requirements) and for troubleshooting (e.g., backing out incorrect transactions).

The presence of audit trails needed by the user should be verified by the company's internal auditors and by system users. The presence of audit trails that support error correction must be verified by the EDP department. Following are examples of system features that support effective audit trails:

- Batch totals (e.g., a physical count of source documents and the number of input transactions they represent).
- Program-to-program records totals (e.g., the number of records read, added, changed, and deleted by each program).
- Before-and-after images (i.e., a "snapshot" of each master file record before and after it was updated).
- File maintenance details (i.e., information describing the transactions applied to master files during an update run and the effect of these transactions on master file records).
- Transaction logs (e.g., a record of each transaction and the time it was applied against a master file).
- Application-specific balancing information (e.g., check registers in a payroll system, total billing amounts in an accounts receivable system, ordered versus received amounts in an inventory system).

For more information on audit trails, see Chapter 13.

Flexibility and Simplicity

These two attributes are generally in competition. One is achieved at the expense of the other. System flexibility is developed either by building many functions into a system or by generalizing the system to accommodate extensive parameterization. In either case, a greater volume and complexity of code is the result.

The system designer is invariably faced with the job of achieving a balance between flexibility and simplicity. This is done by incorporating the most critical features of the proposed system and by weighing the relative importance of each additional feature against its implementation and maintenance costs. EDP management can support the effectiveness of this process by offering a detached and broad view that often does not exist at the designer or project-leader level. Intensive contact with the end user sometimes distorts an analyst's objectivity because he or she begins to view a system's goals and objectives exclusively through the eyes of the user. This builds a good understanding of the business problem and leads to sensitivity to user needs, but it can also cause the analyst to overburden the system with marginal features the user considers indispensable, but which are, in fact, trivial. An experienced analyst is always cognizant of the fact that system features must be balanced against cost.

PRODUCTIVITY AIDS

Much has been written about the need to increase the productivity of data-processing personnel. Various productivity improvement concepts and products have enjoyed wide popularity and have been intensively studied, analyzed and described. These concepts and products can be grouped into two general categories: development methodologies and software products.

Development methodologies are techniques that enhance the efficiency of the systems development process. Methodologies that can have a particularly important impact on productivity are structured or top-down design, structured programming, and structured walk-throughs. Of course, many other useful techniques exist. However, these three are currently of greatest interest because of the publicity, claims, and counterclaims surrounding their use. Productivity-enhancing software products can be grouped into the following overlapping categories:

- Design and documentation aids.
- Program development tools.
- Program and system maintenance products.

The development methodologies and software products that can play a major role in the enhancement of productivity are described next.

Structured Analysis and Design

The ideas underlying structured system analysis and design are not particularly new or profound. However, the methodologies taught by Yourdon* and others contribute a framework within which effective system development can take place. The key notion of most structured methodologies is that rational systems design requires the identification and definition of progressively lower level functions and components. The highest-level functions and components are defined first. They are then broken down into lower-level components. This process ends at the program or program module level.

---

*Yourdon, Inc., is a teaching and consulting firm which helped pioneer and popularize structured methodologies.

For example, a student registration system may have, as its top-level components, the development of class schedules based on anticipated course loads, real-time updating of these schedules, a modeling capability based on a student's desired courses, and the off-line printing of final schedules in mailers. The next level of detail encompasses individual modules that add a student to class, delete the student from a class, cancel a class, open a new section, reassign students, print individual schedules selectively, and so on. This level of detail is then followed by additional layers (e.g., the validation required to open a new class section). The process ends when individual programs and subroutines are defined.

Each level of detail is documented by a series of data flow diagrams and function charts. These identify the data entering the component, the functions or operations that the component must perform in order to satisfy the next higher level, and the output that must be passed to other components. Technical solutions such as batch versus on-line processing are not developed until the functional attributes of the system are known. Because top-down design necessitates the explicit identification and definition of all functions at each level of the system, the development of important processes is not overlooked. All (or most) needed functions tend to be designed into the system.

Top-down design does not necessarily result in faster systems development. Rather, its use may result in a better quality, more responsive, easier-to-maintain application system.

Structured Programming

Structured or "go-to-less" programming involves the use of subroutines to perform all the functions in a program. These subroutines relinquish control back to the mainline when they have accomplished their task and, hence, an entire program can be quickly understood by examining the mainline and accompanying comments.

In some respects, structured programming resembles the older concept of mainline coding. The difference is that structured programming represents a more comprehensive approach. It demands compliance with specific technical conventions, such as the use of the PERFORM statement (in COBOL) rather than unconditional branches, and has its own flow-charting and documentation conventions.

Although structured programming is not universally accepted, the experience of most organizations with it has been good. Structured programming has generally resulted in clearer, easier-to-maintain programs and represents a standardized approach to coding that can be enforced without excessive difficulty.

Structured Walkthroughs

A structured walkthrough is a peer-group review of a data-processing product or decision. The most common deliverables reviewed by this mechanism are system design documents, program specifications, and program code. The salient characteristics of walkthroughs are as follows:

- The purpose of walkthroughs is to subject EDP products to an evaluation process that results in the identification and correction of errors, inconsistencies, poor design, and lack of clarity. It can also be used to review hardware selection decisions and other major actions.
- Walkthroughs are normally attended by the developer's peers. In addition, staff people responsible for standards enforcement, training, data-base design, and other technical support functions may also be present. Generally, a person's manager should not be present at a walkthrough. The presence of management may stifle a free exchange of ideas and may give the impression that the walkthrough is a personnel evaluation technique. Walkthroughs are *not* designed for evaluating people; they are used to evaluate specific system components and processes.
- The purpose of a walkthrough should be fact finding, not fault finding. Comments should be objective and should directly address the issues under discussion.
- Walkthroughs should not be used as a forum for advocating specific technical solutions. Rather, walkthroughs should review the success with which the product meets it own internal criteria and the degree to which it meets reasonable design and coding practices.
- All serious disagreements are resolved "off line." That is, the walkthrough is not a problem-solving session; its purpose is to identify problems and discrepancies, not resolve them.
- Walkthroughs should be carefully orchestrated and tightly controlled:
  - —Attendees should be given walkthrough material to review in sufficient time to enable them to prepare adequately.
  - —Each walkthrough must have a moderator whose functions are similar to those of a meeting chairperson; the moderator directs the meeting toward the accomplishment of its goals. An additional task of the walkthrough moderator is the maintenance of an atmosphere of constructive criticism, a difficult achievement considering that the end result of the walkthrough is, by definition, an implied criticism of a person's work. The moderator can be any attendee capable of handling the job. Although the devel-

oper may not be the most objective party in the walkthrough, he or she is the logical choice because of close knowledge of the topic.

—The walkthrough should be planned to end at a specific time, usually not more than 2 hours after it starts. This discourages digressions.

• *In summary:* An essential ingredient for a successful walkthrough is the proper attitude on the part of all participants. Walkthrough participants should be concerned with error detection rather than error correction. The developer must have an open, nondefensive attitude in order to enable participants to critique the work fairly. She or he should welcome suggestions and encourage frankness. It is difficult to have such an attitude if it is felt that the developer is being evaluated by management. Therefore, the presence of managers should be discouraged.

The first two walkthroughs that are conducted during the development process are the functional or general design walkthrough and the detailed or internal specifications walkthrough.

The purpose of the general design walkthrough is to ensure that the high-level system design being evaluated meets the functional requirements of the user. This walkthrough takes place after a draft general design document has been produced but before this document has been given to the user for review. The following individuals may attend design walkthroughs:

• *Developer.* This is the person primarily responsible for developing the design.

• *Peers.* One or more system designers from outside the developer's project group.

• *Staff technical personnel.* These may include the data-base administrator, training director, and standards coordinator.

• *End user.* The presence of user personnel is optional. The user may be invited if an atmosphere of mutual trust and understanding exists and if the user is experienced in working with EDP systems. Otherwise, users should review the general design report only after it has been revised based on the walkthrough.

The second design walkthrough is held after the general design has been approved and the detailed design specifications for the system have been developed. The detailed design walkthrough answers the question, "Do the detailed technical specifications successfully address the functional needs identified in the general design document?" With the exception of the end user, the same individuals may participate in both the general and detail design walkthroughs.

Program specification walkthroughs are held in order to ensure that program specifications accurately reflect the requirements set forth in the detail design, and to ensure clarity, readability, and conformance with standards. The following individuals normally attend program specification walkthroughs:

- *Developer*. This is the systems analyst who wrote the specifications.
- *Peers*. One or more systems designers from other groups.
- *Programmer*. This should be either the programmer assigned to code this specific program or another programmer with approximately the same skill and experience level.
- *EDP technical staff*. This may include the training director, standards administrator, or other people who are responsible for providing technical direction to line project teams.

Code walkthroughs are held in order to ensure that compiled (but not yet tested) programs follow programming standards, conform to the functions defined in the program specifications, and are workable. Attendees at code walkthroughs are normally the following individuals:

- *Developer*. This is the programmer who coded the program.
- *Peers*. One or more programmers from other groups.
- *Systems analyst* (optional). This is the person who developed the program specifications. His or her presence may be helpful because of intimate knowledge of what the program must do. However, this knowledge may also bias the analyst's thinking toward a specific technical approach, which is not within the scope of the code walkthrough.
- *EDP technical staff*. This may include the training director and the person charged with standards enforcement. The presence of technical staff encourages the use of good coding practices and adherence to coding standards.

Software Products

Software products designed to enhance development productivity can be classified into design and documentation aids, programming aids, and program maintenance aids.

Design and documentation aids. The most popular design and documentation aids are text editors, data dictionaries, data-base design tools, and formating aids.

Text editors, such as WYLBER and IBM's SCRIPT, enable large quantities of documentation to be centrally maintained on a big main-frame computer. They have the following salient features:

- They enable documentation to be stored on disk and manipulated via display devices in much the same way as interactive program facilities allow on-line source code changes.
- Only those words, lines, and pages of documentation that require change are altered; everything else remains the same. This simplifies both keying and proofing. (The most common alternative is typing, which frequently requires retyping and proofing an entire page to correct a single error.)
- One official "copy" of a document exists centrally. Therefore, there is never a question as to which version of a document reflects the latest changes. This centralized control ensures greater accuracy than traditional typed documentation.
- Documentation can be made available whenever program testing occurs by simply requesting a printout of the needed data set. Typed documentation stored in filing cabinets may be much more difficult to access, especially when testing during odd hours. Text editors allow automatic page renumbering, the movement of lines, paragraphs, and pages from one part of a document to another, changing margins, and performing other useful formating tasks that are very laborious and time consuming without text-editing facilities.

Word-processing systems that use mini- or microcomputers also enjoy, and sometimes exceed, the features available with text editors. The primary difference is in the capacity of the hardware.

Data dictionaries and *data-base design tools* provide an orderly, automated method by which to define and maintain system attributes. Descriptions of data elements, files, reports, programs, and other components are stored and updated centrally. System changes can then trigger the reprinting of appropriate documentation. Dictionary software is often designed to support specific data-base management systems but can support conventional systems as well. Attribute information such as data-element descriptions and desired data-base file relationships is fed into the dictionary. It then performs error checking, searches for inconsistencies, and converts the data into a form that can be generated into control code needed by application programs and by the DBMS.

Unfortunately, most data dictionaries are passive; that is, they do not trigger changes in the environment. In contrast, fully active dictionaries, which do not currently exist in viable commercial form, affect the environment by serving as the input and trigger mechanism for attribute changes. An example of active interaction is when changes in data-element descriptions in the dictionary cause the automatic generation of new file descriptions in program libraries and recompilation of programs using the changed elements. The ideal, which is far from achieved, is the marriage of data dictionaries with program library software, word processing and text editor facilities, and interactive program development tools. Until this kind of interaction is achieved successfully, documentation will never fully mirror the environment.

Formatting aids assist analysts and programmers in the definition of display terminal screens and printed reports. Because of the character capacity of many display screens (almost 2000 in many instances), the process of interpreting a desired format to a computer program can be very tedious. In addition, the ability to see a proposed design on an actual display screen and the ability to change the headings and data areas on-line are a great help in developing a usable finished product. Reports can also be defined by the use of display screens. This type of design aid generates program code reflective of the report layout mirrored by the display screen.

Examples of currently available design and documentation aids are the following:

- SCRIPT, from IBM.
- WYLBER, from the University of Waterloo.
- UCC10, from the University Computing Corporation.
- MFS (Message Format Service), from IBM.
- PSL/PSA (Problem Statement Language/Problem Statement Analyzer), from the University of Michigan.

Program development tools. Program development tools are software facilities that reduce the repetitive aspects of program coding, assist in the definition and allocation of files, and help in testing and debugging programs. They reduce the extent to which common functions use original code for each new system and increase control over the quality of that code.

Program development tools can be loosely categorized into interactive programming tools, testing and debugging aids, application code generators, and macros and subroutines. In practice, most program development software overlaps each of these categories to some degree. Following is a synopsis of each.

- *Interactive programming tools.* This is probably the most significant and widely used programming aid. It enables programmers to change program code on-line on a display screen without the need to keypunch corrections. It assists programmers in defining and allocating files and, in some cases, is designed to support structured coding conventions. Interactive facilities also enable programmers to request tests and compilations via display terminals.
- *Testing and debugging aids.* These include the following:
  —Software that allows teleprocessing programs to be tested in batch mode. This enables program testing to commence even when terminals or other TP components are not available during the early stages of program development.
  —Utility routines such as tape compares and formated file dumps that support comparisons between the outputs of different computer runs. This is particularly important during parallel testing.
  —Program debuggers that enable batch or on-line tracing and stepping through of application programs. Checkpoints at critical junctures in a program can be built and instruction-by-instruction monitoring of program execution takes place. This enables programmers to check the results of each program instruction.
  —Dump shorteners and indicators that provide guidance in interpreting memory dumps. This is accomplished by eliminating unnecessary portions of the dump, by formating a dump into a more readable document, and by providing the programmer with an interpretation of what the dump indicates.
  —Test-data generators that enable programmers and analysts to create test data for unit and integration testing. This is done by specifying the desired test-data characteristics to the generator, which then produces variations of the data needed to perform program and system testing.
- *Application generators.* This is probably the newest category of programming aids. Application generators link together prewritten code for various common program functions. Therefore, a relatively small amount of coding on the part of the programmer results in the generation of large amounts of finished, debugged code. This can substantially reduce program development time. Application generators, or programming machines as they are also known, are still in their infancy and are capable of handling only the most commonly used functions.
- *Macros and subroutines.* Macros and subroutines are also used to perform commonly used program functions. Macros consist of standardized code permanently imbedded in the applications program; subroutines are called at execution time and do not reside

permanently in the host program. Subroutines are normally used to calculate dates, perform statistical calculations, and do other application-oriented tasks. Macros, which are generally used when coding in assembly language, perform housekeeping functions such as clearing or setting registers, clearing working storage areas, and opening and closing files. They are also used to find, read, and write records and perform standard error checking.

The advantage of using macros and subroutines is that their use avoids "reinventing the wheel" each time a piece of code is needed to perform a specific function. In addition, when only one, well-proved version of code is used, the probability of program errors is greatly reduced. Most macros are provided by computer manufacturers as part of their program (software) products. However, many are also purchased from software firms. Subroutines are generally developed in-house because they tend to be more application specific.

Although macros and subroutines appear to be similar to application generators, they are not. Application generators can perform much more comprehensive functions than macros and subroutines and are incorporated into an application system by an altogether different process: whereas macros and subroutines require a host or calling program, application generators generate the program itself, rather than a component of it.

Examples of currently available program development software, all available from IBM, are the following:

- TSO (Time Sharing Option)
- SPF (Structured Programming Facility)
- ADF (Application Development Facility)
- DMS (Development Management System)

Maintenance aids. Systems maintenance activities normally consume more than 50 percent of programming and systems analysis resources. Unless an EDP installation is very young, is experiencing a very high rate of growth, or is in the midst of a major upheaval, maintenance is the order of the day. The extent to which systems maintenance must be performed for any system is most heavily influenced by the quality of the system itself; that is, its ability to meet real (as well as perceived) user needs, its technical excellence, and its flexibility. These qualities can be significantly affected through the use of the methodologies and software products discussed in this chapter.

There is, however, another category of products that directly affects the maintenance process itself. Since these products are all used during development as well as maintenance, their inclusion in the maintenance category simply highlights their substantial impact in that area. Examples of maintenance aids are the following:

- *Languages and report writers.* Most applications systems are developed using a powerful "primary" language such as COBOL, Assembler, or PL1. These very comprehensive languages provide the programmer with the instruction set, operational efficiencies, and other capabilities needed to produce a quality product. However, once a system is functioning successfully, the EDP staff is invariably deluged with a variety of requests for specialized one-time as well as permanent new reports. The fulfillment of these requests can represent a significant drain on EDP resources. Therefore, rapid techniques have been developed. They consist of high-level languages and report generation software that enable programmers, and, in some cases, users themselves, to quickly produce needed reports. Languages and report generators such as RPG and Mark IV that were designed for producing reports enable programmers to define report contents, formats, and data sources more quickly and easily than conventional programming languages. Their use is of particular value for one-time reports that do not require extensive documentation and are not expected to meet high standards of operational efficiency. Although many report writers and languages started life with modest expectations, they are sufficiently powerful and flexible to use as the primary languages they were originally intended to supplement. RPG, ADPAC, and Mark IV, to name only a few, are certainly appropriate to use as the main development languages in many installations.
- *Query software.* This tool is normally used for accessing data-base records. It consists of English-language-like commands that are part of a DBMS-related high-level language called "command" or "user language." It is faster and more convenient to use for accessing data-base records than conventional computer languages such as COBOL. Specialized facilities designed to search a data base for records with specific characteristics (e.g., all grade 5 employees with foreign-language skills) are also available. Most data-base management systems are supplemented with query facilities.
- *Library software.* With the exception of operating systems, language processors, and sorts, library software is probably the most widely used software product. Almost every EDP installation uses either a vendor-supplied or commercially acquired librarian system. Library software enables programmers to store and manipulate source and object versions of their programs. These versions

may be for production use or for testing purposes. Version numbers and other information indicating the currency of various versions is maintained and is invaluable in ensuring the use of the proper program versions. Although library software does not have a direct impact on the degree of efficiency with which individual programs are written, its use during program development and testing considerably lessens the confusion that results from working with constantly changing versions of the same programs. Therefore, library software can be considered a programming as well as systems maintenance aid.

MANAGING SYSTEM MAINTENANCE

Unless an EDP installation is very young, most of the effort of programmers and analysts is devoted to maintaining existing systems rather than developing new systems. As Chapter 5 indicates, maintenance frequently continues even after development of a new system appears to be more logical than maintenance of the current one. The great expense of developing new systems, combined with the considerable investment most EDP installations have in existing systems, makes the subject of systems maintenance very important.

Most programmers and analysts consider systems maintenance less interesting and less prestigious than developing a new system. Therefore, EDP management is faced with the problem of making an inherently unpopular job as painless as possible. How is this done? Three alternative methods of managing system maintenance are described next.

Permanent Maintenance Team Concept

This method is based on the notion that the best approach to systems maintenance is to assign a group of programmers and analysts permanently to maintenance activities. System maintenance is interesting and challenging to some people. After all, maintenance can be a blend of playing detective and solving crossword puzzles. The task of pinpointing a problem and then researching and implementing the solution is satisfying to people who enjoy a fast problem-resolution cycle. Of course, not all maintenance involves interesting puzzle solving, and most EDP installations do not have many people who are attracted to permanently performing maintenance activities. Therefore, the use of conscripts is inevitable.

The practical result of the permanent maintenance team concept is that certain individuals are assigned to maintenance activities by virtue of their company loyalty and questionable competence. Although it is very true that every installation employs people who will never leave the company voluntarily, it is not ethical to take advantage of this to staff a thankless function. In addition, if the least capable individuals are assigned to maintenance, the quality of maintenance suffers.

On the other side of the coin, almost all EDP installations, particularly government installations and those dominated by trade unions, employ a number of people who refuse to learn new techniques or to upgrade their skills. Such people are best used to maintain the old systems they know and love.

The Take-Turns Concept

This method is based on the idea that maintenance is dull and, therefore, everyone should take turns doing it. It is equitable but does not take into consideration people's skills or preferences, as does the permanent team concept. In addition, it is difficult to implement because not everyone is equally capable of maintaining every system. Certain individuals have valuable rapport with specific users, and certain individuals have application experience for which there is no practical substitute. The take-turns concept also reinforces the notion that maintenance is an unpleasant chore. This is not a healthy attitude to foster.

The You Wrote It, You Maintain It Concept

This method represents the most efficient approach to system maintenance for new systems but is detrimental in the long run. Expecting the same people to perform both development and maintenance activities for a specific system is efficient and generally unavoidable in the early stages of a system's production life. System developers are always the most, and sometimes the only, qualified persons to maintain a new system. However, if carried to its logical extreme, this theory would sentence the most productive employees with the longest seniority to a lifetime of system maintenance. This is, in fact, what happens in many installations. Clearly, this method is best used with care.

Conclusions

The most effective approach to systems maintenance is to combine the most useful features of each of the preceding concepts. A good blend consists of the following:

- One-time reports may be developed by a permanent team composed of people who do not wish to or are not capable of engaging in new development projects. Programming for this effort might be done in Report Program Generator (RPG), ADPAC, or some other rapid language.
- People who enjoy maintenance should be assigned the lion's share of maintenance projects.
- Junior people and new employees can be rotated through temporary maintenance duty. Participation in maintenance projects is an excellent way to become acquainted with the techniques and systems in an installation.
- New systems should be maintained by their developers for no more than one year after implementation. After that, new people should be phased in.
- Most people should be given some new system development assignments. Exceptions to this rule should be rare.

Discussion Questions

1. Why are EDP standards important, and what major subjects should they address?
2. Identify three key areas that operations standards must cover.
3. Why are project control standards and naming conventions important?
4. What are the pros and cons of each of the following approaches to the development of standards:
   - Acquisition of standards package
   - Development by full-time standards writers
   - Standards by committee
5. Discuss major standards issues, such as the scope of EDP activities, that should be subject to standardization.
6. Name six characteristics of an effective standards program.
7. What are the major components of system documentation? Program documentation?
8. What is the purpose of user documentation?
9. Describe three design practices that contribute to the development of sound application systems.
10. Are the goals of system flexibility and simplicity in conflict? Explain.

11. How are structured walkthroughs conducted, and what is their purpose?
12. Describe three software products that assist analysts and programmers in developing and maintaining systems.
13. Why is the subject of system maintenance important? Describe three popular ways of assigning people to maintenance activities.

8

PERSONNEL MANAGEMENT

Should programmers and systems analysts be managed according to the same principles as accountants and salesmen, or are they somehow different? How are personnel requirements established? How should the EDP function be staffed? Is there a correct way to fire someone? What should EDP training and education requirements be?

This chapter attempts to address these and other personnel issues of specific interest to EDP managers. However, no attempt is made to comprehensively describe or review personnel management theories. Although three important theories, theory X, theory Y, and Maslow's hierarchy of needs, are briefly described in the appendix to this chapter, an exhaustive analysis is not within the scope of this book.

PERSONNEL MANAGEMENT IN AN EDP CONTEXT

What are the unique characteristics of managing programmers, analysts, and others who work with computers? Are EDP people different from architects, engineers, or plumbers? Are there peculiarities in the EDP profession that force us to treat its practitioners in a special way?

These questions cannot be answered with a simple "yes" or "no." However, some light can be shed on the subject by examining the major forces that have shaped the EDP profession and by looking at the actual behavior of data processors. The following historical factors have had a major influence on how people in the EDP profession view themselves and their craft:

- Very rapid technological change.
- A consistently high level of demand for personnel.
- An aura of mystery surrounding EDP activities.

It is important to stress that, of these historical circumstances, only the demand for EDP people continues unabated. Although technological innovation is proceeding at a very rapid pace, changes tend to be more "transparent" to the user than they were in the past; that is, major upheavals between generations of hardware and software are no longer tolerated. The aura of mystery that surrounded EDP in its early days is rapidly disappearing as more and more managers, particularly young college graduates, are exposed to formal training in computing and gain experience in managing computerized systems in their departments.

Rapid technological change, high demand, and the magic surrounding EDP activities have had the following impact:

- EDP people are generally more interested in the exciting things going on in their profession than they are in specific organizations. Therefore, appeals to company loyalty are rarely as successful in attracting and retaining competent EDP people as are opportunities to participate in technically challenging assignments.

- EDP people can afford to change jobs frequently because of high demand, and they cannot long remain in a technologically outdated environment because of the rapidity of change in their profession. These self-reinforcing factors virtually guarantee high personnel turnover.

- Constant change in hardware and software, as well as the development of computer applications in areas where little prior computerization existed, contributes to a high degree of technological uncertainty. Murphy's law, "If something can go wrong, it will," flourishes in the EDP business. Tasks that appear trivial to the inexperienced can, in fact, be agonizingly difficult and time consuming. This high degree of uncertainty contributes to the skepticism many data processors harbor about their ability to meet schedules. However, the self-serving myth, born in the early days of data processing, that EDP people are somehow not accountable to management for their performance or their productivity must be dispelled. No group of employees can be exempt from legitimate demands to perform in accordance with a set of reasonable standards. Data processors, like salesmen and engineers, must be held accountable for contributing to the goals of the organization.

- The nature of program testing and debugging sometimes requires unorthodox work schedules. This includes working nonstandard shifts and maintaining long periods of concentration. Therefore, management cannot always expect neatly packaged 9 to 5 work schedules from the programming department.

- The skills and educational levels of EDP people vary widely. Holders of Ph.D. degrees in computer science work side by side with graduates of programming institutes. MBA candidates work with high school graduates. Unlike lawyers and other certified professionals, there is a great deal of diversity in educational credentials and background among data processors. Thus some programmers may have a craft or union orientation while others may think of themselves as highly educated professionals.

- EDP is a relatively young profession. The average age of its practitioners is lower than the age of people in older, more established professions. In addition, high demand has pushed many young, inexperienced people into management jobs for which they are ill prepared. This dual problem of youth and inexperience causes friction between EDP and other organizations and requires extra attention on the part of management.

- EDP salaries appear exorbitant in comparison to salaries paid to people with similar credentials in the same age group in other professions. This is due exclusively to the shortage of qualified EDP people.

- Blacks and other minorities, as well as women, have found EDP to be more congenial in advancing their career aspirations than many other professions. Therefore, managers can expect some discomfort on the part of all-white or male-only groups when dealing with EDP. This may be a particularly serious problem in the development of applications in areas such as manufacturing where, because of union seniority rules, the majority of supervisors or foremen are older white males.

Cognizance of these factors is a prerequisite for successfully managing the EDP function. Management policies toward EDP may need to be somewhat flexible in the following areas:

- *Starting salaries*. Some positions in EDP may need to be staffed by people whose salaries exceed normal company guidelines. This situation will continue as long as a shortage of technical people exists.

- *Promotions and salary raises*. Since EDP people can afford high expectations owing to the great demand for their services, organizations may need to readjust their salary and promotion policies, particularly with respect to advancing less experienced technicians who are in their high-growth years.

- *Working hours, time off, and overtime policies*. The demands of system implementations and problem resolution frequently result in long working days, odd hours, and canceled vacations. Companies should be prepared to accommodate strange schedules and to compensate people with time off or overtime pay for extraordinary efforts.

In addition to flexible personnel policies, an attempt must be made to create an environment that is congenial to learning new skills, permits people to work with a variety of different systems, and provides rewarding career paths. These things are, of course, important in any functional area. However, they are particularly critical in the high-turnover EDP field.

ESTABLISHING PERSONNEL REQUIREMENTS

Perhaps the clearest way to describe the process of establishing personnel requirements is to assume staffing for a brand-new EDP installation. The EDP manager is always hired first because this clearly places the responsibility of establishing the department on his or her shoulders. Who should be hired next? The hiring chronology closely follows the systems development cycle. The new EDP organization must develop or acquire application systems and implement and operate them. This requires hiring systems analysts to design or select application systems, programmers to develop those systems, and operations support personnel (computer operators, data-entry clerks, I/O control personnel) to operate the systems. Of course, there is some overlap. For example, a programmer may be hired to help the analyst develop program specifications during detail design. If computer hardware is to be delivered prior to system implementation and program testing is to be done on site, a computer operator and data-entry person may be hired soon after coding begins. A common hiring chronology is illustrated in Table 8–1. The EDP manager must perform the following tasks to establish specific personnel needs:

- Prepare a list of necessary functions.
- Subdivide the functions into job titles.
- Prepare job descriptions.
- Grade job titles.
- Compare EDP to other organizations.
- Assign salary levels.
- Estimate staff size.

TABLE 8–1. Hiring Chronology and Task List for a New Installation

Title/Tasks	Time/Accomplishments				
	Installation Planning	Design	Coding	Implementation	Full Production
EDP Manager Establish development priorities, acquire hardware and software, establish personnel requirements, hire staff	x x x x x x x x x x x x x x x x x x x x x x x x x x x x x x x x x x x x x x x x x x x x				
Systems Analysts Design systems	x x x x x x x x x x x x x x x x x x x x x x x x x x x x x x x x x x x x x			
Programmers Code programs		x x x x x x x x x x x x x x x x x x x x x x x x x x x x		
Operators Operate computer			x x x x x x x x x x x x x x x x x x x x x x x	
Data-entry personnel Perform data entry			x x x x x x x x x x x x x x x x x x x x x	
Support staff Clerical, I/O control, library management				x x x x x x x x x x x x x x	

Preparing a List of Functions

The first step in establishing personnel requirements is to identify the functions needed to support an EDP installation. These functions generally include:

- Management
- Systems analysis and design
- Programming
- Computer operations (including input and output control)
- Data entry
- Clerical

In smaller installations some of these functions are combined: the EDP manager may be actively involved in systems design and even program coding; systems analysts and programmers may, in fact, be programmer-analysts; computer operators may be responsible for I/O control as well as operations. In large installations the basic functions tend to be further subdivided into classes based on level of supervision needed, skill level, and job complexity.

Subdividing Functions into Job Titles

Individual functions can be subdivided into specific job titles. For example, management consists of the EDP manager, middle-level group managers who are responsible for major EDP areas such as operations, project leaders who have first-line management responsibilities for project development, and supervisors who are in charge of ongoing activities such as computer operations and data entry. Table 8–2 illustrates a typical decomposition of functions into job titles in a medium-sized EDP installation.

Preparing Job Descriptions

The next step in establishing personnel requirements is to prepare job descriptions. The development of accurate job descriptions has three major benefits:

- Job descriptions enhance the EDP manager's ability to manage. They provide a context in which to train and assign employees and to reach an understanding with them on their performance.

TABLE 8–2.   Job Function Categorization in a Medium-Sized EDP Installation

Function	Job Title	Supervision Required	Job Complexity	Skill Level Required
Management	EDP manager	—	High	High
	Group manager	Low	Medium	High
	Project leader	Low	Medium	Medium
	Supervisor	Medium	Medium	Medium
Systems analysis and design	Senior analyst	Low	High	High
	Analyst	Medium	Medium	Medium
	Programmer/analyst	Medium	Medium	Medium
Programming	Senior programmer	Low	High	High
	Programmer	Medium	Medium	Medium
	Junior programmer	High	Low	Low
Computer operations	Senior operator	Medium	Medium	Medium
	Operator	Medium	Low	Low
	Junior operator	High	Low	Low
	I/O control clerk	High	Low	Low
Data entry	Senior data-entry clerk	Medium	Low	Medium
	Data-entry clerk	High	Low	Low
Clerical	Secretary	Medium	Low	Medium
	Clerk/typist	High	Low	Low

- Formal job descriptions are part of the objective standards needed to comply with equal-opportunity programs and to support union adversary procedures. Without a sound body of objective criteria by which to hire, promote, and fire people, a company is more vulnerable to grievance actions.
- Job descriptions enhance the EDP manager's ability to plan the department's personnel requirements. As in other forms of documentation, the process of developing job descriptions has a usefulness that transcends the document itself. It focuses attention on the kind of work people are expected to perform, their levels of responsibility, and the relationships between different jobs.

The preparation of job descriptions may, however, become a meaningless bureaucratic exercise unless careful attention is devoted to the quality of the product. Here are some guidelines in developing job descriptions:

- Do not over describe. In real life, the shape of each job is primarily influenced by the ability and personality of the job holder and by the needs of the moment, not the formal job description. Therefore, the description should be specific enough to convey the key elements of the job but not specific to the point of becoming quickly outdated and inaccurate. Negative comments, such as "the computer operator will not, etc.," should be avoided lest the "exception" proves wrong in the future.
- Avoid bureaucratese. Use standard English and avoid technical terminology. The purpose of the job description is to enlighten, not confuse.
- Do not turn the description into a "how-to" manual. Formal job descriptions are not a substitute for in-depth understanding of the job.
- Update job descriptions frequently. As with other types of documentation, the job description is intended to accurately represent actual conditions and events. Since job definitions change, so must formal job descriptions.

Grading Job Titles

After functions have been subdivided into job titles and job descriptions have been written, each job should be graded according to the complexity, skill level, and supervision required for its execution. This is an important step because these grade distinctions will be used to attach salary ranges to individual job titles.

Supervision required, job complexity, and skill-level classifications are somewhat subjective. They are usually categorized by a relative scale that compares job classes within a function. For example, the job complexity of work performed by both an EDP manager and a senior programmer may be high; the job complexity for junior programmers may be low.

Comparing EDP to Other Organizations

In addition to performing the analysis illustrated in Table 8–2, EDP functions and job titles should be compared to their equivalents in other departments. Table 8–3 illustrates a comparison between EDP and accounting. Such a comparison is important because it places the EDP function within the larger context of the host organization. It is a useful exercise for the following reasons:

- It helps identify organizational inconsistencies that may lead to inflated or undervalued grade assignments both in EDP and other functional areas.
- It places the EDP manager in a better position to defend his or her department's structure, grading system, and salary levels. Grade levels usually determine allowable salary ranges. Therefore, a pru-

TABLE 8–3. Job Titles by Grade

Grade	Title (EDP)	Title (Accounting Department)
10	EDP manager	Controller
9	Group manager	Section head
8	Project leader	Accounting supervisor
7	Supervisor	
7	Senior analyst	Senior accountant
7	Senior programmer	
5	Analyst	Junior accountant
5	Programmer/analyst	
5	Programmer	Accountant
4	Senior operator	
3	Operator	Clerk I
2	Junior Operator	Clerk II
2	I/O control clerk	
2	Senior data-entry clerk	
1	Data-entry clerk	Clerk III
2	Secretary	Secretary
1	Clerk/typist	Clerk/typist

dent manager assigns grade levels based on the salaries needed to staff functions. The comparison chart alerts the manager to the salaries other departments pay and enables him or her to justify EDP department salaries.

- It enables the EDP manager to better understand the organizational relationships between her or his department and EDP user departments. This is made possible by identifying similar job levels and functions in other departments.

Assigning Salary Levels

Salary levels are ultimately based on market conditions. In the short run, however, they are based on what the organization allows the EDP manager to pay the staff. At best, the marketplace and organizational constraints may agree on salaries. Unfortunately, this is frequently not the case. It is, therefore, important for the EDP manager to acquire the political and organizational skills needed to minimize the gap that often develops between organizational salary constraints and the salary levels the EDP manager needs to attract capable staff. Although pay is obviously not the only, or even the primary, factor in attracting capable people, it is often a basic prerequisite without which other attractions cannot be sold to job candidates.

EDP salary levels are influenced by the following factors:

- *Degree of job security.* The higher the level of job security, the lower the salary level tends to be. Highly volatile EDP jobs in consulting and service bureaus, for example, generally pay better salaries than similar government jobs or jobs with large corporations.
- *Geographic area.* Many people wish to escape the anxieties of living in urban areas. Therefore, idyllic rural locations often pay low salaries but still manage to attract a talented pool of people.
- *Industry.* Growing industries tend to pay more than industries in decline. They generally have more money to spend and may be more ambitious in their use of computers.
- *Prestige and experience value.* Prestige companies and industries may take advantage of their image to pay lower salaries. Firms offering exposure to challenging state-of-the-art systems may also be able to pay less for people willing to sacrifice financial rewards for challenging work.
- *Benefits.* Organizations that offer long vacations (e.g., universities), travel allowances (e.g., airlines), or generous retirement benefits (e.g., certain civil-service jobs) sometimes pay lower salaries. The difference is made up by a higher level of benefits.

- *Qualifications.* Firms that demand a high level of experience, education, and skill tend to pay higher salaries than firms that are satisfied to hire less qualified individuals.

A note of caution: The preceding are generalizations. Many exceptions exist, and market rigidities may invalidate certain premises. For example, highly unionized organizations may offer good benefits, a high degree of security, and pay high salaries; prestige firms may, in fact, pay top salaries (that may be part of the reason they are prestige firms); and individual firms in a notoriously low-paying industry (banks were once in this category) may offer top salaries in spite of the policies of others in their industry.

Estimating Staff Size

The final step in establishing personnel requirements is to estimate the number of people needed to fill each job category. Here are some guidelines:

- Analysts and programmers will be needed based on the number and complexity of applications being developed or maintained.
- Personnel needs for operations are contingent on the number of computers, the number of shifts, and the degree to which operations is involved in data preparation and output distribution.
- The need for systems programmers is a function of software complexity. Installations using data-base management software and sophisticated operating systems, for example, have the greatest need for systems programmers.

HIRING

This section attempts to answer the following questions:

- What are the sources of EDP personnel?
- What role should the personnel department play in the hiring process?
- How should desirable personnel qualifications be determined?
- How are effective interviews conducted?

Sources of Personnel

Most positions in the EDP department are filled by hiring from outside. However, some transfers may occur between different parts of the EDP department, and people may even be transferred from other departments within the host organization. The latter situation occurred with great frequency in the early days of EDP when outsiders with the requisite skills were difficult to find and firms trained in-house staff to work in EDP. Today, individuals with special application skills, such as knowledge of accounting or familiarity with inventory procedures, may be transferred to EDP and trained in systems analysis. Situations in which this is profitable are the following:

- When developing applications that require a high degree of esoteric applications knowledge that few data-processing people possess. A person who has a solid grasp of the applications area and who possesses analytical skills can usually be trained to work as a systems analyst.
- For projects that require a high degree of political and organizational sensitivity. Sometimes, people in line areas outside EDP can become valuable assets in liaison and systems work by virtue of their organizational connections and political abilities. In addition, EDP people who once worked in a functional area sometimes enjoy a higher degree of trust and credibility than "native" data processors because they are perceived as having a more user-oriented attitude.
- When organizational loyalty and stability are important. EDP people are notoriously peripatetic in their careers. They are not normally "company people" in the sense that their loyalty is more often attached to their profession than to the individual firm for which they work. Therefore, a long-time company employee who has proved himself or herself in another department may be a more suitable choice for participating in the development of some applications than a professional data processor.

The disadvantages of transferring internal personnel to EDP and training them in EDP skills are as follows:

- *High training costs.* It is expensive and time consuming to provide sufficient EDP training to make people professionally effective.
- *Inbreeding.* Every organization has a distinct personality and modus operandi that color the thinking of its members. A paucity of creative solutions to business problems may, therefore, result when insufficient new blood is infused into an organization. A new employee is more likely to present useful ideas that challenge the established way of doing things.
- *Questionable performance.* Sometimes individuals are transferred from one department to another because they are no longer wanted by the transferring organization. Highly skilled and energetic individuals are not easily relinquished by user departments.

- *Narrow experience.* The experience of internal personnel in the potential solution to business problems may be too limiting.

Outside sources of personnel are discussed below.

Personnel Agencies

Personnel agencies, or "headhunters" as they are sometimes called, are most useful during a sellers market, that is, a period when the demand for skilled data processors is very high in relation to the supply. They are also useful when people with specific skills are needed on very short notice. Good personnel agencies have a thorough knowledge of the marketplace. Through their extensive contacts, they are able to quickly compile a list of potential candidates for practically any position. In addition, they can save their clients the time and expense of screening and communicating with job candidates.

The disadvantage of using personnel agencies, other than commission costs (usually a month's salary for each person placed), is that if they are unscrupulous or unprofessional, as some are, they will fail to carefully screen candidates. In addition, there is always the danger that, just as personnel agencies entice people away from other organizations to fill your staff requirements, so they may raid your company on someone else's behalf. Although this is counterproductive for a personnel agency in the long run, it is widely practiced.

The most prudent course for a company that uses personnel agencies is to select one reputable agency and establish a long-term relationship with it through a contractual agreement. This minimizes the problem of stealing as the agency does not want to lose a long-term client. In addition, it gives the agency a strong incentive to be selective about job candidates because it is secure in the knowledge that it will not be upstaged by another firm.

Classified Advertisements

Classified advertisements are perhaps the most widely used means for finding employees. The following are suggestions for using the classified ads in the local newspaper or in trade publications:

- Don't be penny wise and pound foolish. If you are searching for highly skilled people, use the display classifieds, not the small print ads that people normally use to sell their lawn mowers. Many talented programmers and systems analysts never read the small print part of the help wanted section.

- Avoid endless lists of acronyms describing "required" experience (OS/VS, MVS, JES III, TSO, CICS, IMS). You will rarely find anyone who is experienced in all the specific hardware and software in your installation. Quality people who do not have all the qualifications but who should be interviewed may well be discouraged from applying if the ad gives the impression that they will not be seriously considered.
- Tell the truth. Potential applicants know what is reasonable to expect and will not feel well disposed toward your company if the first interview gives the lie to information in the ad.
- Whenever possible, do not use blind ads (i.e., ads in which the company name does not appear). Many people will simply not reply to blind ads. People assume that there is an unsavory reason a company will not use its name. So unless your reason *is* unsavory, for example, you are firing half of your staff and don't want the world to know about it, use your company name. Another, more benign reason skilled people may refuse to answer blind ads is that it shields the firm placing the ad from the responsibility of replying to each job inquiry. In fact, many firms who place blind ads do so precisely because they do not wish to be burdened by replying to each response.

Employee Referrals

This is the best source of qualified people. Friends, acquaintances, and professional contacts in the data-processing business represent the most consistently reliable pool of talent. The only potential problem with hiring professional acquaintances is clique building. Groups of people should not have more loyalty to each other than to the host organization. Clique building can have an adverse impact on the morale of the rest of the department.

College Recruiting

Colleges are an excellent source of promising but inexperienced programmers and analysts. Computer science, business, and mathematics students are generally the best candidates and can become productive after a relatively short training period. They are eager, have good academic credentials, and have not yet developed bad programming and work habits. In addition, salary costs for new graduates may be substantially below less well trained individuals with only two or three years of experience.

The best approach to college recruiting for most firms is to target one or two colleges with solid, but not necessarily renowned, computer science programs. A cadre of graduates can then be hired over a period of years through active recruiting and by word of mouth. Use of computer science students and faculty for temporary or summer assignments may enhance the company's image on campus. The disadvantage of college recruiting is that relatively few recent graduates have meaningful work experience.

Role of the Personnel Department

The personnel department has three basic functions that it should perform in support of EDP hiring:

- Coordinate and administer the logistics of the search.
- Screen candidates.
- Advise the EDP department on permissible salary ranges, job-level classifications, and other corporate policies.

The one function it should *not* perform is to dictate the job-related qualifications candidates need. Personnel departments are simply not equipped with the knowledge required to define such needs. The personnel department has expertise in writing advertisements, placing ads in newspapers, screening applicants, scheduling interviews, following through, and, if desired, carrying out the job offer. It should be used primarily for these purposes.

EFFECTIVE INTERVIEWING

Interviewing is an extremely important part of the hiring process. The skill with which it is performed will influence the amount of useful information received from a job candidate, the understanding that the candidate develops about the job, and the impression both parties are left with after the interview is over. Following are some useful pointers on how to conduct effective interviews.

Be Prepared

Read the candidate's resume *before* the interview, not during. The interviewer can and should refer to the resume during the interview; however, the general scope of the candidate's background and training should be absorbed before the interview begins. It is best to read the resume at the time it is received and to read it again just prior to the interview.

Be prepared to describe the job, the company, and the EDP department. Failure to do this in a clear, positive manner will result in confusion and lack of enthusiasm on the part of the candidate. In today's job market, the purpose of the interview is as much to sell the job as it is to screen the candidate.

Verify and Clarify

Remember, resumes are written in such a way as to present the candidate in the most favorable light, even if this requires stretching the truth or leaving a false impression. It is, therefore, necessary to ask specific questions about each important part of the resume and to request clarification of any vague statements or generalizations. Statements such as "participated in the design of . . ." should ring a bell; the "participation" may have been significant and important or it may have consisted merely of being on the distribution list for monthly status reports. Similarly, languages, hardware, and software listed in a resume should also be discussed. It is not possible to evaluate the candidate's experience just by reading the resume.

Ask about Job Changes

Diplomatically inquire about job changes, particularly if they have occurred frequently, and listen carefully to the answers; they may provide important clues to the candidate's personality. Be alert for the following:

- The professional victim who is always leaving a job because of organizational changes, personality conflicts, or political battles.
- The restless soul who always leaves because of boredom; such a person either has poor judgment in selecting jobs or (more likely) is incapable of sustained interest in his or her work.
- The opportunist who is constantly "trading up" in terms of salary and position. You can expect no company loyalty from this person.

Almost everyone may, at one time or another, change jobs due to personality conflicts, boredom, or for purposes of advancement, and many dynamic, aggressive individuals get fired at least once during their careers. The risk lies in hiring a person who always leaves jobs for the same reason, particularly when that leave-taking occurs frequently (every 1 to 2 years).

Ask Open-Ended Questions

Although many questions asked during an interview require specific answers ("How many years of COBOL experience do you have?"), many other questions should be couched in general terms. This gives the applicant a chance to voice opinions and present information that cannot be presented in the context of specific questions. Open-ended questions often reveal much more about a candidate than questions that require short, precise answers. The most appropriate open-ended questions are those that encourage the candidate to share career goals, describe outside interests, and explain motivations in seeking a new job. These things play an important role in how well the person will succeed in the new job.

Don't Do All the Talking

The interview is a two-way street: the candidate sells himself or herself and finds out about the job and the company; and the interviewer sells the job and the company and finds out about the candidate. It is, therefore, important for both the interviewer and the job candidate that neither party dominate the interview. However, since the interviewer is on his home turf, there is generally more danger that the interviewer will exercise too much control during the interview. Let the candidate talk!

Observe Behavior

The candidate may be nervous, tired, or having a bad day. However, as the interview progresses, the candidate should become increasingly more relaxed and self-confident. If not, this may indicate personality traits that conflict with the requirements of the job. Lack of eye contact, poor listening habits, continued interruptions, and other annoying social habits are not conducive to skill as a systems analyst. If these habits are continually exhibited during the interview, when the candidate is, supposedly, on best behavior, they will probably be very difficult to eradicate on the job.

Accept, at Face Value, Career Goals

The fact that a programmer wears Brooks Brothers suits and has a good grasp of business concepts is not necessarily an indication that she or he wishes to be a systems analyst or a manager. People do not always conform to stereotyped images. Many hiring mistakes have been made because interviewers have insisted on projecting their own version of what a person should want, instead of simply accepting the candidate's own assessment. Hence, if an individual tells you he wants no part of management, believe him. He is far more aware of his own desires and abilities than you are.

Instinctive Reactions Are Critical

Assuming the requisite modicum of talent and ability, the success or failure of an individual in an EDP job is at least as dependent on the ability to get along with peers, to feel comfortable in the environment, and to work effectively with a boss as it is on his or her own skills. Regardless of objective factors such as salary, position, working conditions, or even job challenge, if the "feel" isn't right disaffection will quickly set in. If there is no chemistry between the applicant and the people she or he will be working with, the candidate should probably not be offered the job, regardless of qualifications.

It should be noted that instinctive reactions transcend race, sex, national origin, and so on. They should, therefore, not be used as a justification to discriminate against members of a particular group.

Team versus Individual Interviews

Some companies conduct team interviews in which several interviewers participate at the same time. This saves time for both the candidate and the interviewer. However, team interviews also have disadvantages:

- The candidate tends to become intimidated. It is difficult enough to put a person at ease during the interview without giving the impression that several people are "ganging up" on him or her.
- The interviewers may compete with one another in asking "intelligent" or "incisive" questions and in impressing the candidate with their knowledge. This is especially true when there is a reporting relationship between the interviewers. This competition does not leave the applicant with a good impression.
- There is an inadequate opportunity for the candidate to express himself. After all, the greater the number of speakers, the less time there is for each speaker to express himself.

Who Should Participate in Interviewing?

The following people should conduct interviews:

- A technician who can gauge a candidate's level of technical expertise.
- A potential boss for whom the candidate may be working.
- A peer with whom the candidate may work.
- A person who is knowledgeable about company policies, benefits, and procedures.

How Long, When, and Where?

The ideal scheduling for a series of interviews should probably be two to three interviews in the morning, followed by lunch with a group of people from the company, followed by one interview after lunch. Additional interviews, if necessary, should be scheduled for another day, typically within one or two weeks. No interview should last longer than 2 hours. A series of interviews should never take up more than three-quarters of a business day. Time for lunch and coffee breaks should be generous.

The luncheon or dinner interview can serve a useful purpose. It enables busy people to get together without cutting into the work day, puts the participants at greater ease than they would normally be in an office environment, and provides insights into how people behave outside work. However, lunch or dinner can never be a substitute for the more structured, rigorous office interview. Therefore, it should be used as a supplement rather than as a substitute.

JOB QUALIFICATIONS

What is the relative importance of personality, intelligence, education, and experience as candidate attributes? Personality is used in this context to mean the ability to work well with people. It is important in direct proportion to the degree of interpersonal contact required for a specific job. Most jobs in EDP installations are fairly social. Therefore, candidates with an abrasive or unpleasant personality should be avoided unless they are very experienced and demonstrate high intelligence that will translate into substantial productivity. Although some technical work is solitary in nature and is suitable for people who have difficulty succeeding in a more social environment, many highly technical jobs in EDP require a great deal of contact with people. An example is teleprocessing problems resolution. This job requires not only a very high degree of technical skill and experience, but also the ability to deal with a wide variety of people: software programmers, applications programmers, systems analysts, computer operators, hardware and communications equipment vendors, and nontechnical end users.

High intelligence is desirable but not critical. Most activities in EDP do not require exceptional intelligence. They do, however, require patience, perseverance, attention to detail, and a reasonably pleasant personality.

How should educational qualifications be defined for EDP jobs? To what extent can experience compensate for lack of formal training and education? EDP jobs fall into three broad categories, each of which should have its own set of education and experience requirements: operations and clerical, programming, and systems analysis and management. They are described next.

Operations and Clerical

Most operations and clerical jobs in EDP are essentially repetitive and require the mastery of simple skills. These jobs include data entry, input-output control, program librarian, and computer operations. Although they do not naturally lead people into higher-skill-level jobs, operations and clerical assignments may lead to supervisory responsibilities. This is not to say that people holding such jobs cannot move into more challenging positions; it simply means that a move *outside* the basic framework of the job must be made in order to advance (computer operator to programmer, keypuncher to computer operator).

Operations and clerical jobs rarely require more than a high school education unless they are part of a career track that leads to an entirely different job. For example, in some companies computer operations was once considered a stepping stone to programming. Another exception is the computer operator who works in a large, sophisticated installation. Machine operators in such an environment frequently require as much skill as applications programming. Experience is not a significant factor in selecting people for operations and clerical EDP jobs except as an indication of maturity or stability. Computer operators, data-entry clerks, and other semiskilled individuals can generally reach peak efficiency within a few months on the job.

Programming

The major craft job in EDP is that of programmer. Programming requires great attention to detail, some communication skills, the ability to think abstractly, and the discipline to maintain a high level of concentration for fairly long periods of time. Formal education encourages and helps develop these abilities. However, except for knowledge of the programming language, most programming assignments do not directly depend on subject matter imparted in a college or trade school. Once a programming language is learned and the ability to use it is acquired, either formally or through on-the-job training, in-depth knowledge of the business problem being addressed is largely irrelevant. A programmer who writes high-quality inventory programs is equally capable of writing good accounting programs.

Unless programming is defined at the company as a temporary job leading to that of a systems analyst, and unless programmers do a substantial amount of analysis, educational requirements for programmers need not include a college degree. There are, however, two exceptions:

- *Scientific programmers.* Knowledge of the subject matter addressed by a program is more closely related to the act of writing the program when doing scientific work than it is when solving business problems. In addition, scientific programming may require an in-depth knowledge of calculus, differential equations, and other subjects that can rarely be acquired in a trade school or on the job. Therefore, educational requirements for scientific programmers usually include a college degree in mathematics, operations research, or some other scientific discipline.
- *Software programmers.* Some software programming projects, such as the development of compilers, the modification of operating systems software, or the development of teleprocessing software require a high degree of knowledge of computing or telecommunications theory. Such knowledge is usually gained only in a university computer science curriculum. Therefore, organizations that develop their own software (computer vendors, consulting firms, and software houses) usually require their programmers to have a degree in computer science.

Experience has four important effects on the productivity and skill of a programmer.

- It enables faster solutions to programming problems. Most programming projects fall into one of several broad categories: edit, on-line or batch update, report, and so on. Once a programmer has written a number of programs in one category, he or she can develop new programs in the same category with greater speed and accuracy.

- It shortens the learning curve for new languages. Each programming language has common characteristics with other programming languages. Even if programming languages are on very different levels (Assembly language versus COBOL), knowledge of one is always helpful in learning another. Therefore, a programmer with experience in, say, PL1, COBOL, and BAL is generally more valuable than one who is experienced only in COBOL.

- It shortens the learning curve for new software. Most organizations are continually acquiring new software. The latest version of an operating system, new utilities, data-base management systems, and new programming support aids are constantly being installed. The ability of programmers to successfully adapt to new software is partly a function of experience, because many similarities exist between different software products doing the same job. A programmer skilled in one brand of program library software, for example, is usually able to quickly learn the use and idiosyncrasies of another.

- It enables faster, more elegant, more correct use of complex programming techniques such as indexing and the use of subscripts. Learning about these features by reading a programming manual is not a substitute for experience.

A word of caution: "20 years of experience" can often mean "one year's experience repeated 20 times." This, obviously, is not the sort of experience to look for in a job applicant. References and careful interviewing can frequently screen out programmers (and analysts) with a fixation on doing things the way they were done 20 years ago. Beware of data processors who have never heard of structured programming, interactive program development, and other relatively new techniques.

A rule of thumb for required programming experience is 1 to 5 years if light experience is required, 5 to 10 years for medium experience, and over 10 years for heavy experience. Except for very specialized types of programming, diminishing returns set in after 15 years of experience. The reason is that the technical environment was so different in the early years of EDP that experience gained in the 1950s and early 1960s is generally not very useful in mastering the techniques of the 1980s.

Systems Analysis and Management

Systems analysts and managers deal with a wide variety of people, technologies, and application systems. Therefore, their training and experience must enable them to be creative and productive in a wide variety of circumstances. This usually demands cross training in other disciplines, most notably business, and requires communication skills and background that are usually acquired in college. Therefore, a university degree is generally required for systems analysts and managers.

As with programmers, 20 years of experience can mean one year's experience repeated 20 times. However, if the experience is varied, it is of greater value for systems analysts and managers than for any other category of EDP employees. The skills needed to be a good analyst or manager require years of experience to develop. In addition:

- Systems analysis and management are not as technology dependent as other EDP jobs, particularly programming. Systems analysis, in one form or another, has been practiced for as long as people have attempted to methodically solve problems. Therefore, a systems analyst's experience from the 1950s and 1960s is relatively more applicable to today's environment than is a programmer's vintage experience.

- Systems analysis, unlike programming, requires application-specific knowledge of accounting, manufacturing, inventory control, and other business applications. Although the operational characteristics and functional capabilities of these applications change from decade to decade because of changes in technology, the business problems they address do not change. Therefore, long-term experience, if meaningful, significantly enhances an analyst's value.

- Effectiveness in dealing with people is derived mostly through experience. It cannot be duplicated in classrooms, as many firms who overestimated the value of young MBA's have discovered.

In conclusion, long experience for systems analysts and managers may be an important asset.

EDUCATION AND TRAINING

There are three major education and training issues of concern to the EDP manager: the establishment of training requirements for the staff, the choice of training programs to satisfy those requirements, and her or his approach to educating non-EDP people in the organization to deal with computer systems. These issues are important because they affect the cost of EDP and the effectiveness with which computer systems are used.

Classroom techniques such as the use of training aids and class problems, optimum course length and class size, and the like, are of lesser importance to the manager. Therefore, these topics are not discussed.

Potential training needs should be based on the current technological environment at the installation and on the projected environment for the next 6 to 12 months. It is generally not effective to develop a detailed education program until software and hardware components have been selected and until standards and procedures have been stabilized. Unless the computer environment is known, little detailed planning for personnel education can take place.

The time period between the execution of a course and the on-the-job use of its subject matter should normally be less than 3 months. Unless the highly technical, detail-oriented subject matter of most EDP courses is used almost immediately, it will be quickly forgotten. Courses with a high degree of conceptual material may be an exception; they need not be put to use as quickly because concepts and general principles, if properly taught, are remembered longer than details.

Examples of courses that require fast conversion to practice are those that deal with teleprocessing monitors, programming languages, operating system internals, and the use of various program-support tools. Examples of courses with more conceptual material, and thus a lower need to quickly use the subject matter, are systems analysis, structured programming, data-base fundamentals, and technical writing courses.

Since most EDP organizations, as well as most profit-making enterprises, cannot afford to bankroll courses that do not quickly pay for themselves, most EDP courses tend to be short, highly technical, and quickly useful.

Establishing Training Requirements

The steps involved in developing the specific training requirements for an EDP installation are (1) develop a skills survey, (2) analyze its results, and (3) develop a training program based on those results. This three-step process is described next.

Develop a skills survey. The skills survey is given to application programmers, system programmers, systems analysts, first-level managers, and computer operators. It translates the EDP environment into the skills required to perform major EDP jobs and asks respondents to grade their skills and experience in the requisite areas. For example, if an installation mandates the use of COBOL, enforces structured programming standards, uses IBM's Time Sharing Option (TSO) for program development, and develops systems that utilize IMS, IBM's data-base management system, the questionnaire should list knowledge of these areas as necessary for effective applications programming. The listing of skills not directly and minimally necessary for the performance of a specific job should be avoided.

As with any questionnaire that is distributed to a large number of people in an organization, a kickoff meeting should be held to explain the purpose of the questionnaire, establish a deadline for its submission, and describe how it is to be filled out.

Analyze survey results. The first step in analyzing survey results is to screen responses for the purpose of reducing the number of exaggerated or self-serving claims. This ensures that replies are as objective and accurate as possible. The second step is to map the results in order to reveal the training gaps that exist among EDP staff. Training programs can then be developed to close these gaps. As new employees join the organization, their needs are analyzed using an up-to-date version of the survey; and, as the installation environment changes, education programs are modified to reflect those changes.

Develop the training program. The person responsible for implementing the results of the survey must rank training needs by immediacy and importance, select or develop appropriate courses, and schedule people into those courses based on the importance of their training needs. The immediacy and importance of needs depends on the nature and timing of various projects and activities in which people are, or will be, involved. For example, programmers assigned to develop an application system utilizing a data-base management system must learn data-base concepts, data-base programming techniques, and the use of supporting utilities. If the project is scheduled to commence in one month, data-base training is clearly immediate and important. The development of an internal training program versus the purchase of courses from outside is discussed in the next section.

The scheduling of people into training courses is based on course availability, the workloads of individual students, and an approximation of when each potential student is likely to put the course material into practice. As mentioned earlier, it is not effective to schedule people too far in advance of the time they will apply the subject on the job.

Types of Training Programs

The EDP manager is faced with the choice of developing and running internal training programs or sending staff to courses offered by computer manufacturers, consulting firms, software companies, or training firms. The manager may also choose to develop an elaborate formal program aimed at training people who are totally inexperienced in EDP. Finally, the EDP manager may send people to various self-improvement courses that are designed to increase employee productivity and morale by focusing on the development of positive mental and personality traits. The types of training programs an EDP manager can choose are described next.

Internal versus external. In the early days of data processing, there were not many facilities for training programmers, systems analysts, and computer operators. Most organizations relied on computer manufacturers to provide personnel for the development of computer applications and the training of internal staff. Applications development support and training was free; that is, computer manufacturers included these services in the price of their hardware.

However, in the 1960s IBM began to charge separately for education, applications support, software, and hardware. This caused the market for EDP education courses, as well as for non-IBM software and support services, to explode. For the first time, computer users had a wide choice of sources for training courses. They now had a financial decision to make: pay for external courses or develop in-house training programs.

Most medium to large EDP installations chose a mix of internal and external courses. The composition of the mix depends on the type and amount of training needed and on the size of the installation. Internal courses predominate in the following circumstances:

- The type of training required is easily available. Data processing installations that use programming languages, software components and system development techniques that are widely available have little difficulty finding people to teach the needed subjects.
- Training requirements are highly installation specific. Internally developed software, radically modified utilities, and esoteric application packages that are not widely used force training to be conducted in-house. Installation-specific standards must also be taught in-house.
- The amount of training required is high relative to the total number of people on the staff. An example is an installation with many

inexperienced programmers. Since externally taught courses are expensive, the high fixed costs of an internal education program may be justified if a large number of people need training.

- The EDP installation is large enough to staff a training department without exceeding 10 percent of its total personnel budget. Education expenditures greater than this are difficult to justify to management.

External courses are most appropriate in small installations where training needs are modest and do not justify the high fixed cost of operating an internal training program. External courses are also appropriate for training in state-of-the-art or newly marketed products. These generally require vendor training because the necessary expertise is not yet available at user sites.

Training courses offered by outside sources are frequently more polished, more thorough, and more effectively taught than internal courses, because internal education courses are often developed and taught by volunteers who may know their subject, but who have little experience in teaching.

However, internal courses tend to be more closely tailored to the needs of students and the specific organization. External courses must, of necessity, be based on the needs of the majority rather than on the needs of specific installations.

Because they are generally taught off-site, external training courses may foster a greater degree of concentration on the part of students. The interruptions that plague courses taught in the EDP conference room (telephone calls, emergency program problems, meetings) are not present in courses held off site.

Formal EDP education programs. Before the widespread establishment of EDP curriculums in colleges, universities, trade schools, and high schools, some large corporations and public agencies undertook the development of elaborate EDP training programs. In the forefront of this trend were, of course, the computer manufacturers. They had no choice: the skills and knowledge required to develop, promote, and maintain their products simply did not exist outside their organizations.

Other large firms did not wish to rely on the vagaries of the marketplace in their effort to recruit qualified people. In addition, they wished to indoctrinate new employees in company policies and modes of behavior. They believed that the loyalty, skill, and self-image developed by the training programs was well worth the very high cost. IBM was, and still is, a prime example. They have consistently managed to attract talented, aggressive people and have extracted a surprising degree of loyalty and tenure from them.

However, considering the high quality and availability of EDP curriculums in colleges and universities and the very high turnover rates in the EDP profession, it simply does not pay most companies today to hire bright, young recruits and spend 3 to 9 months training them at company expense. The only exceptions are large, high-technology EDP companies, such as IBM, and large, highly structured organizations such as major banks and accounting firms.

Self-improvement programs. Americans are obsessed with personal improvement. Hundreds of books are published annually that purport to teach us how to negotiate, how to look out for our interests, how to make a million dollars, and how to retain sexual vigor until the age of 90. Courses, retreats, and seminars that improve the body, mind, and psyche proliferate. Clearly, these programs have no direct effect on EDP technical skills. However, if the EDP manager feels that a course in, for example, interpersonal relations can help build better rapport between staff and end users, the manager may want her or his people to attend.

Courses such as speed reading, organizing time, or listening effectively may also be useful. They have limited objectives and enhance people's ability to perform day-to-day EDP activities. The student need not experience profound psychological or mental changes to use the skills they impart.

Unfortunately, most self-improvement courses that claim to change behavior patterns are of very limited effectiveness. They may cause superficial changes in the short term but their long-range impact is questionable. After all, "pop psychology" is never a substitute for psychotherapy, analysis, or other long, expensive, grueling journeys people undertake in search of a better self.

EDP Education for Non-EDP Personnel

Once upon a time, the friendly computer salesman would enroll the president of a company that had just bought a computer, or was thinking of buying one, in a three-day Computer Basics for the Executive course. This course would invariably be held in the plush world headquarters of the computer manufacturer, to which the company president would be whisked by private jet. The course would consist of a few dazzling, multimedia demonstrations of computing power, complete with sound effects, flashing lights, and other gimmicks; a few short, punchy lectures on how a computer works; cocktail parties attended by the computer manufacturer's top executives; fancy dinners in fancy restaurants; and, finally, a 4-hour "exercise" consisting of writing a COBOL program to read and print a deck of cards.

When the chief executive got home, well fed, impressed, and ready to sign a contract, he could look the EDP manager in the eye and say, "O.K., buddy, you can't pull the wool over *my* eyes; I know how the damn thing works!"

An exaggeration? Not by very much! At one time, EDP training for non-EDP people did not exist on a serious level. It was simply designed to sell hardware. But things have changed. People who acquire computers are not as easily fooled by dramatic displays of the computer's magic powers. They are better educated in computer technology, have more experience in living with computer systems on a day-to-day basis, and are wary of exaggerated claims and promises.

Although some EDP training for noncomputer people is needed, this training must be carefully targeted at people's immediate needs and must stress the tangible rather than the conceptual; it is fraudulent and dangerous to leave the impression that a three-day course in computer basics can enable the layman to understand the highly complex world of computing. A little learning is, indeed, a dangerous thing.

There are three groups of non-EDP people who need computer training: system users, system participants, and managers. These groups are not necessarily mutually exclusive; people can be members of more than one group.

System users are engineers, accountants, managers, and other people who *use* information from computer systems for decision making. They should be given application-specific training that stresses what the computer-generated data they receive means, how it is derived, and what its limitations are. They should be taught how to use their systems effectively. The only conceptual material about computers that needs to be imparted to system users is information on how different files are sequenced, how data are retrieved (e.g., keys and other look-up techniques), and what is involved in making changes to reports, data elements, and other system attributes.

System participants are people who must deal with a computer system on an operational level. They are generally clerks and secretaries who must enter, correct, or otherwise manipulate data that go into or come out of a computer. Users of word-processing systems are included in this category. The EDP training needs of system participants are also application specific. But, unlike system users, system participants must become familiar with the hardware and software characteristics that affect data entry and correction. For example, system messages appearing on a video display screen must be understood and the appropriate responses must be learned. This requires training in the use of terminals, as well as some knowledge of system software messages. In addition, system participants may need to learn about how files, records, and data sets are organized, the way look-ups are done, and other concepts needed to understand and maintain data on the system.

Managers who use computer services also have specific educational needs. Each manager must

- Learn how the computer systems used by his or her department solve, or don't solve, the business problems they address.
- Have an understanding of the key responsibilities and commitments involved in the development and operation of computer systems. Knowledge of who is responsible for what during the system development cycle, for example, is very important.
- Become familiar with the costs of doing business with data-processing organizations. A manager must pay for the computer system his or her department uses, either directly, as with an outside vendor, or indirectly through the organizational budget. The billing philosophy of the company and the relative costs of people, software, and hardware must be understood. Otherwise, the manager cannot make rational decisions regarding new systems development, the purchase of outside services, and the acquisition of departmental EDP capabilities.

PERFORMANCE REVIEWS

Formal performance reviews are normally the vehicle on which promotions, salary increases, and career strategies are based. Reviews are done at specified intervals, usually semiannually or annually, and consist of a critique of the employee's performance as reflected in answers and comments on a standard evaluation form. A discussion between the employee and his or her supervisor takes place at which the contents of the evaluation are discussed and an improvement plan for the next review period is formulated. In addition, professional goals are established, achievements are compared to the goals stated on the last review, and career paths are discussed. Unfortunately, the performance review is frequently done in a cursory fashion. It is never pleasant to criticize another person's work. Therefore, useful criticism is given short shrift, and the evaluation becomes a back-patting session during which raises and promotions (if any) are announced. This approach is neither fair to the employee nor is it an effective way of managing people. Ten key elements that comprise an effective personnel review are described next:

- *Regular time intervals.* Employee evaluations should occur at regular intervals not to exceed 1 year. Professional employees should be reviewed every 6 months. Once a schedule is established, based either on the employee's anniversary date or on a common review date for all employees (e.g., the end of each fiscal year), it should be scrupulously followed: evaluations are too important to be postponed because of project deadlines or other pressures. Reviews need not coincide with time periods within which salary increases or promotions can be granted. Semiannual reviews are recommended even when salary increases can only be made once a year.

- *Standard forms and instructions.* The review should be conducted within the framework of a standard set of questions and ratings. Common definitions of all terms, particularly rating categories such as "good," "superior," and "below average," should be published and the review should be based on those definitions. Unless all employees in a particular job class are evaluated using the same criteria, the review cannot achieve any semblance of objectivity.

- *Preevaluation discussions.* It is generally wise to discuss the evaluation with a third party before discussing it with the person being evaluated. This "review of the review" may serve to temper judgments that result from very recent experiences not reflective of the employee's total performance over the evaluation period. For example, a person with a mediocre track record may get unjustifiably high marks from a superior based on a good performance during the last month of the review period. Conversely, problems encountered during a person's last assignment should not blind the reviewer to good work done on previous projects. An additional reason for a third-party check is to ensure that the reviewer has developed the proper documentation to support the ratings, particularly negative ratings that can result in charges of racial or sex bias or in union grievances. The reviewer's superior should always be alerted to surprises (e.g., a highly thought of individual that receives a poor review, a mediocre performer who gets a good review), or any other unusual situation.

- *Specifics.* It is unfair and nonproductive to criticize an employee's performance in general terms. Specific events should be discussed during the evaluation, and the employee should be encouraged to analyze ways in which those events could have been avoided or mitigated. Specifics are important because they lead to concrete discussions rather than philosophical arguments. In addition, specifics underscore the importance of bottom-line performance.

- *Discussion of problems as they occur (don't wait until review time).* It is a mistake to avoid communicating with an employee until review time. Problems should be addressed as they occur. Therefore, a performance evaluation should present no great surprises to the person being evaluated. If management does its job, the review is little more than a recap and summary of discussions and critiques that have been occurring on an on-going basis.

- *A positive context.* Whenever possible, criticisms should be couched in a positive context. Although reviews that have no critical value should be avoided, so should evaluations that are thinly veiled inquisitions.

- *Candor.* It is extremely difficult to be candid about bad news. No one likes to tell a subordinate that some aspect of her or his performance has been inadequate. However, it must be done. Both the employee and the company deserve an honest, straightforward appraisal of the employee's work.

- *A spectrum of opinion.* Every person for whom the employee has done significant work should be asked to fill out an evaluation form. These comments should be carefully evaluated and discussed. Some organizations use multiple evaluation forms during the review itself in order to present the employee with the widest possible range of views on his or her performance.

- *Self-evaluation.* Quite often, an employee views himself or herself quite differently from how colleagues do. These contrasting images can cause misunderstandings and should be reconciled to as great an extent as possible. An evaluation form filled out by the employee gives the reviewer a notion of how the employee views himself or herself.

- *Objective performance measurements.* It is extremely difficult to establish specific standards by which performance of nonroutine jobs is measured. Keystrokes and error rates can be used to measure the performance of data-entry clerks; and units of production can be used for assembly-line workers. But systems analysis and programming are not very amenable to productivity measures. Attempts at establishing standards based on lines of code have been made. However, these standards are inaccurate and difficult to use because:
  —There is no relationship between program quality and the number of lines of code.
  —The number of lines of code produced by each programmer is not easy to track or define. For example, should maintenance changes or comment lines be included in the total?
  —The complexity of the programming problem cannot be measured by lines of code.

—Lines of code do not measure important intangibles such as persistence, willingness to work overtime to solve an important problem, and other traits that are the mark of a dedicated employee.

How, then, is the on-going productivity of professional staff measured? One useful tool is management by objective (MBO), a technique described in the appendix to this chapter. MBO enables on-going measurement of tangible accomplishments within a context of mutual agreement between employee and manager. This, in addition to overall program and system quality, is perhaps the best way of measuring the performance of programmers and analysts.

CAREER PATHS

Career pathing consists of helping employees plan their professional goals within an organizational context. It results in a road map an employee can use to achieve professional growth and advancement. At the same time, it provides the EDP organization with an orderly method of fulfilling its personnel needs. Career planning is most appropriately done at performance review time.

Two major career ladders should exist in any EDP organization: technical and managerial. There is, clearly, much overlap. Managers must have a strong technical background, and must be alert to technological developments. Technicians must be sensitive to management issues and must be prepared to occasionally compromise technical considerations in favor of political or organizational factors.

Nevertheless, some individuals prefer technical challenges, others prefer the give and take of working with people. Because EDP is so profoundly influenced by technology, the rewards and satisfactions of a technical career must not be slighted in favor of the managerial ladder. Unfortunately, too many organizations force brilliant technicians to become mediocre managers in order to justify increases in pay and status. This is not necessary. There is no reason why a highly skilled technician should not earn as much or more than a project leader, middle-level manager, or even head of the EDP department. The amount that appears on the pay stub is the sincerest way of saying, "you're valuable, we need you."

Figure 8–1 illustrates typical career paths through a medium- or large-sized EDP organization. It is not intended to cover the myriad possibilities that exist for talented, ambitious individuals. Rather,

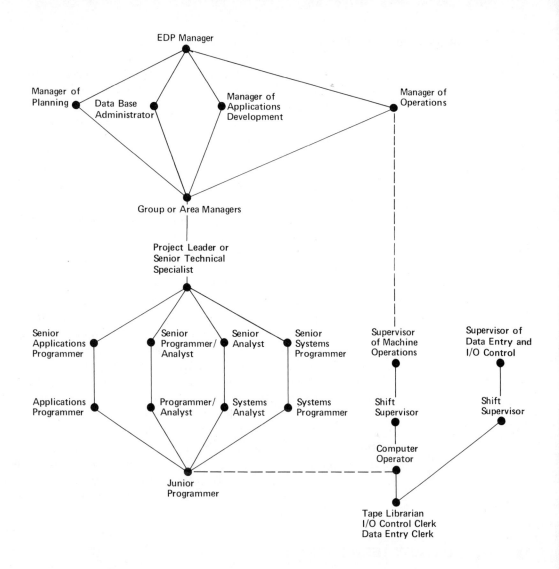

FIGURE 8–1. Typical EDP Career Paths, Medium or Large Installation

it portrays the options that can be reasonably expected in most installations. Salient features of Figure 8–1 are the following:

- Lateral movement is frequently possible, particularly at higher management levels. However, at middle and lower levels, a drop of one or two steps may be temporarily needed in order to acquire the necessary technical skills to move from one functional area to another (e.g., a senior systems analyst wishing to become a systems programmer).
- Supervisors of machine operations whose experience does not include programming are generally not qualified to serve as operations managers unless the operations function does not include software support.
- Programmers with several years' experience generally choose between continued application programming, exposure to systems programming, or entry into systems analysis. This choice normally determines the degree to which an individual becomes immersed in the business problem end of EDP versus the strictly technical end. Systems analysis is oriented toward the design and implementation of application systems. Application programming, although directed at the solution of business problems, is to a large extent independent of the business problem. Systems programming is almost entirely divorced from the business problem.
- Progression from computer operator to programming, although once popular, is no longer very common (hence the dashed line). Progression from data-entry clerk or input-output control clerk to programmer without an intervening stint as a computer operator is even less common.

INVOLUNTARY TERMINATIONS

Involuntary termination is the most drastic tool available to a manager. Firing, or being fired, is never a pleasant experience. However, it is an everyday reality in the working world and its mechanics and implications must be learned as surely as those relating to promotions, salary administration, and personnel evaluations. Adherence to the following three principles can reduce the problems associated with firing people.

- *Document.* Always maintain a complete record of memoranda, verbal warnings, and personnel evaluations leading to a termination. This serves to persuade that the termination was necessary and justified. Failure to carefully document key events will place an organization in a vulnerable position in case of grievance procedures or lawsuits by the employee.

- *Establish a termination procedure and follow it.* The existence of and compliance with a standard procedure in dealing with inadequate performance bespeaks a fair, even-handed approach to personnel management. It also reduces the incidence of involuntary termination by giving people a chance to upgrade their performance. Standard procedures generally include a series of reviews and improvement plans accompanied by verbal and written warnings when an employee's performance is inadequate.

- *Terminate people quickly.* Once a decision is reached to fire an employee, the termination proceeding should be fast, firm, and final. By this time there should be no turning back, no deals, no extended leaves of absence, or any other maneuvers to delay the inevitable. The employee should be given fair severance pay and should be encouraged to leave the premises as quickly as possible. A terminated employee can be a serious source of discontent and even sabotage if he or she lingers at a job.

There is one exception to the quick termination rule: if a firing takes place due to mutual incompatibility rather than professional inadequacy or malfeasance, the termination may include an agreement to find new employment within a specified time period. In the interim, the employee may remain in her or his current position and continue to perform normal functions. In this circumstance, the termination is generally confidential and is accompanied by a reasonable degree of mutual trust and amicability.

CHAPTER APPENDIX

Theory X

Theory X postulates an essentially pessimistic view of work behavior. It makes the following assumptions about people.[1]

- People are naturally lazy; they prefer to do nothing.
- People work mostly for money and status.
- The main force keeping people productive in their work is fear of being demoted or fired.
- People remain children grown larger; they are naturally dependent on leaders and need constant supervision.
- People expect and depend on direction from above; they do not want to think for themselves.
- People have little concern beyond their immediate, material interests.
- People need specific instructions on what to do and how to do it; larger policy issues are of no concern to them.
- People are naturally compartmentalized; work demands are entirely different from leisure activities.
- People naturally resist change; they prefer to always do things "the old way."
- People must always be selected, trained, and fitted to predefined jobs.
- People are formed by heredity, childhood, and youth; as adults they remain static, and do not change significantly.
- People need to be inspired, pushed, and driven.

Theory Y

Theory Y represents a more modern, optimistic view of peoples' attitudes toward work. It postulates the following:[2]

- People are naturally active; they set goals and enjoy striving.
- People seek many satisfactions in work: pride in achievement, enjoyment of the work itself, sense of contribution, pleasure in association, the stimulation of new challenges.

---

[1]Paraphrased from Douglas McGregor, *The Human Side of Enterprise,* McGraw-Hill Book Co., New York, 1961, and a lecture by Goodwin Watson in Reports of the National Training Laboratories Key Executive Conference, 1961.
[2]Ibid.

- The main force keeping people productive in their work is a desire to achieve their personal and social goals.
- People normally mature beyond childhood; they aspire to independence, self-fulfillment, and responsibility.
- People close to the work situation see and feel what is needed and are capable of self-direction.
- People who understand and care about what they are doing can devise and improve their own methods of doing work.
- People need a sense that they are respected as capable of assuming responsibility and self-correction.
- People seek to give meaning to their lives by identifying with nations, communities, churches, unions, companies, causes.
- People need ever-increasing understanding; they need to grasp the meaning of the activities in which they are engaged; they have cognitive hunger as extensive as the universe.
- People crave genuine respect from their fellowmen.
- People are naturally integrated; when work and play are too sharply separated both deteriorate. "The only reason a wise man can give for preferring leisure to work is the better quality of the work he can do during leisure."
- People naturally tire of monotonous routine and enjoy new experiences; in some degree everyone is creative and seeks self-realization.
- People are primary, not the job. Therefore, jobs must be designed, modified, and fitted to people.
- People constantly grow; it is never too late to learn; they enjoy learning and increasing their understanding and capability.
- People need to be encouraged and assisted.

Limitations of Theory X and Theory Y

No single theory is sufficient to explain the way an organization should be managed. Theory X and theory Y are useful as constructs, but they are not, in any consistent sense, replicated in real life.

In all organizations some jobs lend themselves to a theory X view and others are more suited to theory Y. Repetitive work that does not require a high skill level may not provide much satisfaction. Therefore, a harsher theory X approach to management may be required. But even in this case there are exceptions: a young ditch digger may require less supervision and may be more dedicated than a vice-president who is two years away from retirement. In addition, there is no compelling evidence to suggest that all (or most) people will behave in a predictable fashion in a given set of circumstances. People are too inconsistent and too different from each other to neatly fall into theoretical categories.

Maslow's Hierarchy of Needs

> "To the millions who have to go without two meals a day, the only acceptable form in which God dare appear is food."
>
> *Gandhi*

As the Gandhi quote implies, man's basic needs (hunger, thirst, etc.) demand satisfaction before psychological needs can be actuated. Although "man doth not live by bread alone," the bread is needed first.

Abraham H. Maslow, a noted psychologist, has described human motivation in terms of a pyramid of needs, as illustrated in Figure 8–2. He teaches that work incentives must be developed in accordance with the position of a worker in the pyramid. In data processing, the basic survival needs of employees are met, at least to the extent that a firm can satisfy those needs by paying salaries that provide the essential material goods needed to sustain life. However, the next higher level of needs (protection, comfort, predictability) are not always available, particularly to younger employees who have not yet achieved the degree of job security that professional competence and seniority provide.

Acceptance, affection, worth, and self-actualization are important to everyone after the basic survival and safety needs are met. However, as with safety, they are meaningful only when lower-level needs are satisfied.

Awareness of Maslow's pyramid may be useful in the day-to-day management of EDP personnel in the following ways:

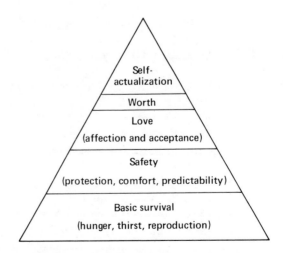

FIGURE 8–2 Maslow's Hierarchy of Needs

- Money, as a means of acquiring life's necessities, is rarely a motivator except for people who have overwhelming financial burdens.
- Salary *is* important as a symbol of worth, status, and success. However, if the work environment fails to genuinely provide these things, the money will soon pall, will fail to motivate people, and will not serve to keep them in the firm's employ. (Although people almost always state that salary is an important reason they are changing jobs, this is often a comfortable lie that removes the need to discuss the real reasons: lack of fulfillment, personality clashes, boredom).
- People in highly paid jobs are usually motivated more by challenge than by higher salaries. In some cases, salary may be almost totally irrelevant.
- The data-processing environment must provide a high degree of technical challenge, positive as well as negative feedback, and people-oriented management. The continuing shortage of qualified people makes this approach absolutely essential in the EDP profession.

The limitation of Maslow's theory is that people do not always evolve through the levels illustrated in his pyramid. They get stuck at one level and fail to move on, even when the move seems, by any objective criteria, appropriate. For example, a technician may sacrifice personal challenge and self-actualization to the comfort, protection, and predictability of a job he can perform in his sleep. Another person may be so financially undisciplined that he or she will sacrifice security, a challenging work environment, and personal job satisfaction to feed an insatiable appetite for money.

The problem with theory X, theory Y, Maslow's hierarchy of needs, and other motivation theories is that they are all ultimately foiled by the limitless individuality of human beings. There is no room for dogma in the repertoire of a good manager, and there is no substitute for action based on knowledge of and sensitivity to individual people.

Management by Objectives (MBO)

Management by objectives is a process whereby a professional employee[3] and his or her manager jointly identify common organizational goals in terms of the specific results expected of the subordi-

---

[3]MBO is generally practiced only among professional employees. People with repetitive jobs receive their goals by fiat from management or by agreement between management and their unions.

nate and then use these goals to measure the employee's performance. Thus, organizational goals are translated into specific goals for individuals for a specific time period. Individuals are then evaluated on their ability to meet these goals.

MBO is a six-step process:

1. Identification, in writing, of goals and objectives for each functional area of the organization.
2. Translation of these goals and objectives into concrete deliverables for individuals.
3. Setting priorities for deliverables and the development of work plans.
4. Achievement of mutual agreement between the employee and superior that the goals and deliverables are important and that the work schedules are reasonable.
5. Comparison of the goals identified for each period with the accomplishments for that period.
6. Isolation and analysis of discrepancies between goals and accomplishments.

Management by objectives is implemented through the use of a standard MBO form or report. The form contains sections outlining the period's accomplishments, the discrepancies between the period's accomplishments and the period's goals, and the goals for the next period.

Accomplishments for this period and *goals* for the next period should have the following key features:

- They should be "100 percent events." That is, they should represent discrete, concrete deliverables, not vague goals such as "improve programming productivity." Examples of 100 percent events are completion of program specifications for a specific program, the development of a general design document, a clean compile, completion of program testing, and user sign-offs on a report.
- A time period must be attached to each goal. Otherwise, the degree of success in achieving it cannot be measured. The time period is, of course, implied by the fact that it appears on the MBO for a specific period.
- Goals and schedules must be achievable. A lack of realism will erode respect for the MBO program and will fulfill the letter but not the substance of the MBO concept.
- Goal setting must be practiced from the top down. Every organiza-

tional level, from the president to the lowest-ranking professional employee, should be part of a formal chain of objectives and deliverables that support the goals of the organization.

The *problems and solutions* section indicates discrepancies between goals and accomplishments. To be effective, it should have the following characteristics:

- All discrepancies between goals and accomplishments should be covered, even when a goal was not achieved because it was canceled by management.
- Each problem must have a proposed solution. Even if a problem has no solution, a means for circumventing it or coexisting with it must be suggested.
- General problems that are not directly related to failures to achieve specific goals should be included if they affect overall productivity. For example, poor working conditions (noise, lack of supplies, etc.) may not be traceable to specific deliverables or schedules, but may, nonetheless, affect the department's overall productivity.
- Potential problems should be included. They serve as a warning to management that the goals set for the next period may be in danger. Action may then be taken to forestall problems.

A very important factor in successfully implementing an MBO program is consistency of format and terminology. Deadlines for the completion of MBO's must be strictly enforced and, unless people report goals and accomplishments using the same terminology and sequence from period to period, a manager will have difficulty evaluating MBO's and combining them for higher levels of management.

The advantages of a properly administered MBO program are threefold:

- It forces each organizational entity to seriously consider its role and its accomplishments. This increases the organization's ability to develop effective schedules and work plans.
- It provides a manager with objective criteria for judging performance and enables her or him to more effectively support promotions, salary increases, and termination decisions.
- It encourages mutual understanding and agreement between a manager and employees on what is expected in terms of job performance. The employee is not left in the dark about the expectations of management.

The disadvantages of MBO are that it is relatively time consuming and can sometimes hide incompetence. MBO becomes inordinately time consuming if its administration is inconsistent and undisciplined. Managers must spend time collecting late reports and must sift through piles of MBO reports that do not relate well in terms of internal sequence and language to previous reports.

MBO can mask incompetence by dogmatically overstressing the achievement of goals and understressing the nature of the goals. For example, a person who contrives relatively simple goals and then meets those goals may be mistakenly considered a better employee than a person who sets more difficult goals but does not meet them as frequently. The manager must learn to differentiate between poor planning and poor performance; they may not necessarily be the same.

Discussion Questions

1. Do you believe that EDP people are "different" from their counterparts in other professions? Why or why not?
2. Describe the seven steps taken in establishing personnel requirements.
3. What are the advantages and disadvantages of using personnel agencies to hire staff? What are other sources of personnel?
4. Describe the role of the personnel department in the hiring process.
5. Discuss the interviewing techniques described in the chapter.
6. What is the relative importance of personality, intelligence, education, and experience in choosing EDP personnel?
7. What is a skills survey? How is it used?
8. What are the advantages of using comprehensive internal education programs instead of outside courses?
9. What type of EDP education (if any) is needed for user personnel?
10. Describe some key elements that contribute to effective personnel reviews.
11. What is career pathing? Describe some typical career paths in an EDP organization.
12. Contrast Theories X and Y. Which do you agree with? Under what circumstances?
13. Describe Maslow's hierarchy of needs.
14. What is the purpose of management by objectives? Describe how it works.

9

CHOOSING HARDWARE AND SOFTWARE

INTRODUCTION

The following chapters address three very important aspects of EDP management:

- The selection of computer hardware and software.
- Sources of EDP services.
- Financial and contractual arrangements.

Chapter 9 presents guidelines for determining hardware and software requirements, developing a request for proposal (RFP), selecting system components, and evaluating potential vendors. Chapter 10 discusses sources of EDP services and how to use those sources effectively. Chapter 11 addresses the financial and legal issues involved in the acquisition of computer components and presents suggestions on how to deal successfully with vendors. Figure 9–1 illustrates the relationship between these topics.

IDENTIFYING FUNCTIONAL REQUIREMENTS

Functional requirements, in the present context, refer to the specific computing goals that hardware and primary software must satisfy. Hardware includes all input, storage, computing, output, and telecommunications equipment needed to support primary software and applications systems.

Primary software includes operating systems, utilities, language compilers, automated program development tools, and other software needed for the development and operation of application systems. The development of functional requirements for application systems is described in Chapter 6.

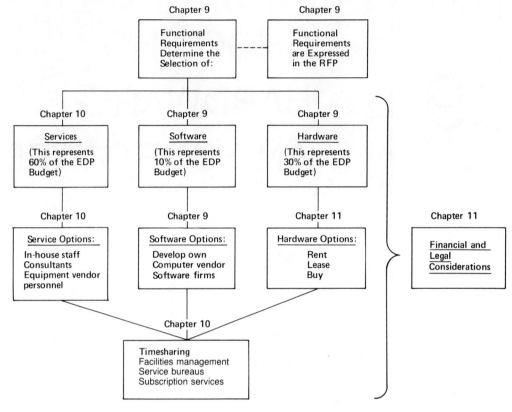

FIGURE 9–1.

Functional requirements do not dictate specific hardware or software solutions. Rather, they define specifications the EDP configuration must address in order to perform a satisfactory job for the end user. Requirements should be developed in a way that encourages consideration of alternatives offering a variety of specific answers. In addition, trade-offs between the use of hardware, software, and services to satisfy computing requirements should be analyzed. The following four examples illustrate computing requirements and potential, sometimes overlapping, solutions.

- *Problem:* Process batch application programs A, B, C, D, and E according to a fixed schedule and desired elapsed times.

  Potential Solutions

  —Serial processing on a very fast machine.

  —Multiprogramming on a slower machine.

—Program segmentation versus virtual storage paging.

—Use of high-level, less efficient programming languages.

—Use of low-level, more efficient programming languages.

• *Problem:* Support an on-line data base of 100 million characters.

Potential Solutions

—Fixed head mass storage device (drum).

—Nonremovable disk.

—Removable disk.

• *Problem:* Transmit a specified volume of transactions from remote terminals to the central computing facility.

Potential Solutions

—Type and number of lines (e.g., half-duplex, full duplex, private, leased).

—Use of front-end processor and/or store-and-forward devices.

—Extensive use of intelligence (e.g., microprocessors) at remote locations.

• *Problem:* Provide printing capability for 1.2 million print lines daily with a peak processing capacity of 96,000 lines per hour for a consecutive 4-hour period each day.

Potential Solutions

—Impact, laser or Xerox graphic printing technology.

—Microform output (e.g., microfiche or microfilm).

—2200 line per minute printer.

—Two 1200 line per minute printers.

—Off-line printing, on-line printing, off-loading to a smaller, dedicated computer.

As these examples show, there are different alternatives to almost any computing problem. In fact, a trade-off frequently exists between the use of hardware, software, and people. The first problem illustrates these complex trade-offs. Operational throughput can be enhanced by using a very fast serial processor combined with appropriate supporting peripheral devices, by the use of segmentation or virtual storage paging, by multiprogramming, and through the use of programming languages that lend themselves to faster program execution. Although these solutions are not necessarily mutually exclusive, they favor different factors of production. Hardware and software solutions represent a capital investment; solutions that require a higher order of programming skill represent an investment in labor.

After functional requirements have been identified a request for proposal (RFP) may be prepared. The RFP is of particular importance when acquiring complex, expensive components available from a wide variety of vendors. Preparation and use of the RFP is described in the next section.

REQUEST FOR PROPOSAL (RFP)

The request for proposal is a document given to selected vendors after functional specifications have been developed for hardware, software, or an application system. It contains the specifications, instructions on how the vendor is to reply to the RFP, and the criteria the organization will use in evaluating proposals. RFP's can be binary or value. The binary RFP results in a go or no-go decision. That is, a proposal either meets the criteria set forth in the RFP or it does not. The value RFP, which is generally more useful, results in the grading of responses. Each proposal is rated on a point system and the proposal with the highest value is selected.

RFP's are useful for four reasons:

- The analysis needed to prepare the RFP clarifies functional requirements and decision criteria by which alternatives should be judged. Questions asked by vendors also help in this process. Specifications and selection of criteria developed for internal consumption only tend to be less comprehensive and less rigorous than a document sent to vendors.
- The RFP injects a degree of objectivity into the selection process that is generally not present in a less formal approach. This translates into a stronger justification for the components that are ultimately selected.
- Because the RFP forces a consistent, organized game plan, it ultimately saves time in the selection process, even though time must be spent to develop the RFP.
- The RFP is the most effective way to organize competitive bidding. If competitive bidding is required by law, as for many government agencies, an RFP is a necessity.

The RFP process consists of preparing the RFP, identifying potential vendors, distributing the RFP, evaluating vendor proposals, and making the selection. Preparation consumes about 50 percent of the total time. Vendor meetings, telephone calls, and other supporting activities consume about 10 percent. The selection process usually takes 30–40 percent. The major steps needed to develop the RFP and select the desired product are described next.

Preparing the RFP

Preparation of the RFP requires the development of functional specifications, vendor instructions, and the procedures to be used in evaluating vendor proposals.

Functional specifications include the following:

- System requirements.
- Technical constraints (e.g., compatibility with specified hardware and software).
- Performance requirements.
- Development and installation schedules.
- A glossary if vendors are not likely to be familiar with the terminology used in the RFP.

The functional specifications section is the key element of the RFP. Unless the language and concepts are clear to vendors, an intelligent response will not be possible. It is particularly important to remember that the vendor may not be familiar with application or industry-specific terminology; therefore, its use should be avoided whenever possible.

Vendor instructions explain the mechanics of the bidding process and the contractual arrangements that will be required. The purchasing, contract administration, and legal departments should participate in their development. Vendor instructions include the following:

- Contract provisions that must be included by the vendor in order to be responsive to the RFP.
- Dates by which proposals are due.
- The required format for the proposal. This is important because, if each response is in a different format, comparisons are very time consuming.
- The names, business addresses, and/or business telephone numbers of people that can answer vendor questions.
- Expected proposal contents, that is, the information that must be included in the proposal in order for it to be considered responsive. This will probably include background information on the vendor, as well as a detailed account of the solutions the vendor proposes in response to the functional specifications.

The evaluation procedures section describes the methodology that will be used to evaluate vendor proposals. It specifies the minimum criteria vendor proposals will be expected to meet in order to be considered responsive, the schedule that will be followed in making evaluations, and planned agendas for meetings that will take place during the selection process.

Identifying Potential Vendors

Datapro, the ICP Software Directory, Auerbach, trade journals and many other sources of information exist on vendors of EDP products and services. These sources can suggest vendors that are likely to offer the kinds of components that will satisfy the RFP. The selected vendors, usually 10 to 12, can then be contacted and asked to provide information about their products. After a review of this information, the RFP should be delivered to the most likely candidates.

The selection of potential vendors should be done primarily through a review of the literature. Contact with salespeople should be avoided at this time. It is easy to be manipulated by persuasive salespeople into prematurely attending demonstrations and becoming involved in other sales activities that are best left to a later stage of the selection process. The stress at this stage should be to review information, not to mingle with vendors.

Shortly after receipt of the RFP, a preproposal conference may be held. This is a formal presentation to selected vendors followed by a question-and-answer period. The purpose of the preproposal conference is to familiarize vendors with the organization and to outline the contents of the RFP. A preproposal conference is particularly useful when complex specifications or contractual arrangements are contained in the RFP.

Evaluating Vendor Proposals

The evaluation process begins after potential vendors have been identified, the RFP has been distributed, and responses have been received. The selection criteria developed as part of the RFP are applied to the proposals and are supported by a variety of tools described in the Evaluation Tools section. A numerical value is usually assigned to the degree of success each vendor exhibits in satisfying the criteria. Invariably, however, formal responses do not tell the whole story. Therefore, a series of follow-up meetings, presentations, and site visits to the vendors' customers are needed.

A follow-up meeting is generally held after responses are received. This meeting is particularly important if vendors uniformly misunderstood a portion of the RFP or failed to comply with some of its provisions. In that case, the meeting may serve to clarify the misunderstood portion and to request an addendum to each proposal.

Provisions that are not realistic can, at this time, be officially removed from consideration.

The number of vendors that satisfy most provisions of the RFP, or have even responded to it, has, by this time, usually shrunk to five or six. A series of presentations clarifying vendors' capabilities and explaining, in greater detail, how they propose to meet the terms of the RFP are now held. These presentations usually consist of a formal audiovisual portion followed by workshops and working sessions with users of the system. For example, in an accounting application package, programmers may be shown how to design access requests for special information not provided on standard display screens, accounting personnel may be given a lesson in how to define a new entry to the chart of accounts, and managers may be instructed on the use of key system reports.

In addition to vendor presentations, site visits to customers who use the products being proposed are now held. Customer visits should be approached with caution and with a degree of skepticism. Since the vendor will recommend only happy customers, a list of *all* customers should, if possible, be obtained. Calls should be made to obtain a cross section of opinion about the product. Customers selected for site visits should be asked candid questions, preferably outside the presence of the vendor's representatives. However, care must be taken to filter out comments not relevant to the specific situation. For example, disgruntlement about spare parts delivery from an Idaho customer may not be relevant to a New Yorker.

Although the experience of specific customers cannot always be extrapolated to another situation, certain key elements should be carefully evaluated. Lack of vendor responsiveness, inadequate product documentation, an abnormally high incidence of system failures, inexperienced or unavailable vendor personnel, and difficult installation procedures may be common, pervasive problems. Vendor products and services may improve with time. This is why recent experience is the best guide. But sometimes problems are endemic, and a vendor's assurance that a particular problem no longer exists (or has never existed) should be carefully verified.

Making the Selection

After the field has been narrowed to two or three candidates, the final selection is made. Sometimes the decision clearly favors one vendor. More likely, the selection will be close: one vendor may have a more experienced, more available support force and the resources of a large organization; another vendor may be of questionable stability but may offer a superior product; yet another may have an excellent all-around reputation but may price products substantially higher than the competition.

To a large extent, close calls are settled instinctively, no matter what a point matrix tells us. Such decisions may be based on important factors that are difficult to quantify: the rapport established with the vendor, a perception of the vendor as responsive and eager, or the impression of competence.

The final step of the selection process is to settle the details of product acquisition. Major contractual and financial questions were discussed during the vendor evaluation process. However, a residue of unresolved issues may remain. Financial terms, delivery schedules, performance guarantees, and other considerations that do not directly affect the technical criteria established in the RFP may be finalized at this time.

One other important point should be noted: it is always a good policy to seriously pursue at least two alternatives to the very end of the selection process. Vendors are usually more experienced in the negotiation of terms and conditions than buyers. Therefore, it is not to the buyer's advantage to become locked in to a specific vendor before *all* negotiations have been completed. If the bridges have been burned, the vendor, rather than the buyer, will participate in final negotiations from a position of strength.

EVALUATION TOOLS

As indicated in the previous section, the first step in the evaluation process is to verify that each potential "solution" will, in fact, solve the problem. This is difficult to do and will frequently be the result of educated guesswork. The tools that are commonly used to support this process are simulation, hardware and software monitoring, benchmarking, the estimation of performance power, and structured walkthroughs.

Simulation

Simulation is the process of approximating run times for specific computer jobs. This is done by feeding simulation programs data on the characteristics of the application being simulated. Hardware characteristics include internal (CPU) speeds, the input-output channel configuration, the speed of the peripherals, and instruction execution speeds. Application characteristics include data volumes and program-specific data such as the number and types of instructions in the program.

Hardware and Software Monitoring

Hardware and software monitoring captures information that is useful in determining the extent to which the present system needs to be upgraded in order to accommodate a desired loading factor (e.g., the percentage of total computing power being used at a given time, usually during peak processing periods). The monitor is a software or hardware component that tracks the usage of system resources such as I/O channels, CPU cycles, core storage, and disk drives.

Benchmarks

A benchmark is a comparison test. It pits the current configuration against a proposed configuration. A series of actual production jobs are run on both machines, and run times are compared.

Performance Power

Performance power is an approximation of the time needed to execute a "typical" mix of instructions. It is based on execution times of individual instructions and a predetermined mix of these instructions. The mix is run on both the current configuration and on the proposed configuration.

Structured Walkthroughs

Structured walkthroughs are used to expose proposed configurations to careful scrutiny by various organizational units within EDP. Walkthroughs are described in Chapter 7.

The most accurate evaluation tool is the benchmark. The reason for this is that current production programs are actually run on the proposed configuration. However, even this seeming accuracy has pitfalls because production conditions cannot always be accurately imitated in a benchmark. This is especially true in a multiprogramming environment.

The tool that is least applicable to real-life conditions is performance power. No "typical" instruction set exists. Therefore, performance power is more useful in comparing the theoretical performance of two machines than in ascertaining the ability of a proposed system to meet application requirements.

Simulation is somewhat more applicable to real-life situations but is restricted by the quality and accuracy of the simulation programs as well as by the accuracy with which the characteristics of the application are predicted. For example, if incomplete or simplistic formulas are used to calculate disk access times, specific data volumes, and file organizations, the simulation will be inaccurate.

Hardware and software monitoring is most applicable to evaluating upgrade options. It can be used to alert operations management to a need for increasing computer power and can help estimate the nature of the needed upgrade.

Evaluation tools are not foolproof. Their use should always be tempered by considerations such as the reputation of the vendor, past experiences with similar products, and technical evaluations by objective parties.

COST CONSIDERATIONS

After potential alternatives for meeting functional specifications have been identified, the costs of each alternative are compared. Following are the major costs that must be taken into consideration.

Installation Costs

These are the costs that will be incurred in order to install the product. Installation costs are important when a specific alternative requires expensive environmental conditions not needed by its competitors. For example, special plumbing for a water-cooled computer may represent a significant installation cost.

Conversion Costs

These are the costs of ensuring the compatibility of a new hardware or software component with existing components and application systems. The most dramatic example of significant conversion costs is the conversion of an installation from the hardware and software of one computer manufacturer to that of another. Frequently, hundreds of computer programs must be rewritten or translated from the old machine to the new.

Application Development Costs

These are the additional system design and programming costs that may result from the use of the selected product. An example is the cost of increased systems development time experienced by many users of data-base management systems and other complex software. Another example is the presence (or absence) of productivity aids, such as interactive program development software, associated with each alternative. The existence of such tools may result in a cost advantage for one or more of the proposed alternatives.

Operating Costs

These are all the direct costs associated with the day-to-day operation of the product. They include rental or amortized purchase price, maintenance charges, environmental support costs such as air conditioning, and the personnel costs that may increase to successfully use the product.

Training Costs

These are costs of preparing the EDP staff to use the selected product. Both direct and indirect costs should be considered. Direct costs are incurred in training people to make the product work. Direct training costs for new hardware include training operators to operate the equipment and training system programmers to support the software. Indirect costs are the "use" costs incurred in making the product perform its ultimate function. Indirect costs of new hardware may include training user personnel to operate a different kind of terminal. Indirect costs of installing an applications package may include learning how to use a new set of display screens and reports. Training costs between alternatives may vary widely. Differences in product complexity, the range of features that are available, and the degree to which the product differs from familiar components are all important factors.

Evaluation Costs

These are the costs associated with evaluating alternatives. They include travel to installations that have similar equipment, the costs of using evaluation tools, consulting costs (if consultants are used to help evaluate competing products), and the internal cost of personnel who perform the evaluation. If the evaluation costs associated with a specific alternative are prohibitive, that alternative may be dropped from consideration. For example, if a trip from New York to Hawaii is required to evaluate a $1,000 software product that is similar to locally available products, that alternative should probably not be considered.

After the above costs have been totaled for each alternative, they are compared to the benefits that each alternative represents. If cost is important as a selection criterion, and it usually is, the product with the most favorable cost-benefit ratio is selected. A note of caution must, however, be interjected: frequently, the option selected is the one perceived as the best alternative at a reasonable cost. Although clear proof of cost-benefit optimization can often be determined when selecting hardware, such as mass storage devices, this proof is much more problematic in the evaluation of complex hardware-software configurations.

SELECTION GUIDELINES

Following are specific guidelines that should be followed when selecting hardware and software. Important vendor considerations are also included.

Hardware

The selection of hardware is probably the most critical and far-reaching product decision made by an EDP manager or user department. It should be preceded by the development of functional specifications and, preferably, an RFP. Cross-disciplinary expertise is needed to make an effective hardware selection. Therefore, the selection is performed with the help and cooperation of a number of individuals in the organization, some from EDP, others from other departments. A hardware selection team is assembled to evaluate each alternative. The team should consist of specialists from various areas, but, except in very large installations, individual team members may represent more than one skill. The following technical specialists are required:

- *Team leader.* This is the person who coordinates the selection process. He or she organizes presentations and customer visits, develops and monitors the schedule for hardware selection, and acts as the main contact for vendors. The team leader is generally a manager or project leader in the operations or software area. In smaller installations, the EDP manager may fill this role.
- *Hardware specialist.* This individual is familiar with the operating characteristics and specifications of the current hardware configuration. He or she is also, presumably, up to date on hardware developments in the computer industry.
- *Software specialist.* This person is intimately familiar with in-house software and is well versed in software developments in the industry. She or he helps optimize the hardware-software mix by a knowledge of how the selection of particular hardware components will affect software performance.

- *Measurement analyst.* This individual is knowledgeable in computer performance evaluation (CPE). She or he knows how to organize and use simulation, hardware monitoring, and other evaluation techniques.

- *Applications programmer-analyst.* The programmer who uses the hardware and software on a day-to-day basis is a valuable source of information. He or she is the person who directly experiences the annoyance and inconvenience of insufficient test time, inadequate space on program libraries, poor turnaround time for compilations and tests, and poor documentation for support utilities. The function of the programmer-analyst is to represent the needs of the applications staff.

- *Operations manager.* This individual is the single most important member of the team. She or he is most keenly aware of the operational impact of various alternatives and is generally the most knowledgeable hardware person in the installation. This person must juggle resources, rerun jobs, and answer the complaints of disgruntled users when production jobs are late. The operations manager is usually the most influential member of the selection team.

- *Purchasing and legal representatives.* Just as the data-processing specialists ensure a sound technical analysis, so the purchasing and legal representatives safeguard the contractual integrity of the acquisition. The purchasing and legal departments ensure that the procedural and contractual requirements of the firm are included in the RFP and that the most advantageous provisions are negotiated. Another reason to include purchasing and legal representatives, albeit one that is greeted with little enthusiasm on the part of the EDP manager, is that a non-technical view may inject a healthy objectivity into hardware selection. Contractual differences between proposals are sometimes great and may, in fact, rival the importance of technical considerations. This is particularly true when only minor technical differences between products exist.

- *Financial staff.* The financing alternatives available for each hardware option critically affect costs. As with legal and purchasing considerations, financing may tip the scales in favor of a specific alternative. The financing arrangements the firm wishes to consider should be clearly identified in the RFP, and financial people should participate in the final selection process.

What specific factors are particularly applicable in analyzing hardware alternatives? The hardware must, of course, satisfy functional requirements. However, this is only the first step. The following questions should also be asked for each alternative:

- *Compatibility.* How compatible is the alternative with hardware and software currently in place? Will reprogramming or other extensive alterations be required?
- *Upgradeability.* To what extent can this alternative be upgraded to accommodate growth? Will extensive changes be required in order to accomplish upgrades?
- *Costs.* What are the costs associated with this alternative? These costs include installation costs, conversion costs, increased (or decreased) application development costs, operating costs, training costs, and evaluation costs. For a more detailed description of relevant costs, see the Relevant Costs section of this chapter.
- *Vendor support.* How effective and extensive is vendor support? What is the response time to hardware problems? What is the availability of spare parts? How easily can home office talent be tapped in case of problems? How well trained are vendor personnel?
- *Hardware reliability.* Are reliability statistics available? How do they compare with the competition? Is backup readily available?
- *Applications and software skills needed.* Is this hardware popular? Are many applications programmers skilled in its use? Is software widely available from sources other than the vendor?

Software

The acquisition of software is a make or buy decision. In this context, "make" means the development of systems in-house. "Buy" means the acquisition of systems from outside vendors, either through rental, lease, or purchase arrangements. Most firms buy primary software, that is, operating systems, utilities, and programming aids, but make most of their applications systems, because application systems are very installation specific; there are almost as many different kinds of applications as there are business problems. Therefore, it is frequently not possible to develop applications with enough commonality to suit multiple users.

Primary software, on the other hand, addresses a far more limited range of needs. The functions it must perform are largely determined by hardware characteristics, EDP operational considerations, and development support requirements that are fairly similar from one installation to another and even between different families of computers. For example, the relative slowness of I/O in comparison to CPU speeds mandates I/O operations that overlap with internal processing; limited computing resources mandate the ability to run multiple production jobs at one time; and program development requires the use of tape compare routines, debugging aids, and core dumps. In addition, most organizations simply do not have the skills to develop and maintain complex primary software. It requires a knowledge of computer internals and a high level of assembler language skills because most primary software is written in assembler language. Neither is widely available at user installations.

Although application systems have traditionally been developed in-house, more and more firms today are turning to packages. Functions such as inventory control, general ledger, and payroll are so standardized throughout a particular industry that little justification exists *not* to acquire off-the-shelf products. The benefits of a buy versus make decision are cost and quality:

- *Cost.* The cost of developing a system is about ten times greater than the cost of buying it from a vendor. This does not mean that a vendor can develop a system for less money. Rather, the cost is shared by many customers. Thus, a vendor can sell a million dollar system to 20 customers for $60,000 and still get a 20 percent return on the investment.
- *Quality.* Individual software vendors specialize in a limited range of application systems (inventory control for retailers, for example). This specialization frequently translates into higher-quality systems than those developed by installation personnel.

There are, however, disadvantages associated with packaged application systems. Every new system must be fitted to its environment. This may require program changes to satisfy user needs, changes to hardware and primary software to enable the new system to run successfully, modifications to application systems that interface with the new package, the development of new user and operations procedures, and extensive retraining of user and operations personnel.

Of particular significance may be the cost of modifying the package to meet specific user needs. Frequently, such modifications can be done only by the vendor because the vendor retains control of the source code. Thus, modifications can escalate the cost of a package to the point where an in-house system can be developed more cheaply.

In addition to installation, conversion, and training costs, operating costs must be considered. These include maintenance charges, rental or amortized purchase cost over the expected life of the system, and the computer time needed to run the system. As in hardware selection, evaluation costs should also be considered.

How do the costs of an application package compare with the costs of developing and maintaining a system developed in-house? As stated previously, in-house development costs are almost always significantly higher than the cost of buying or renting the system from a vendor. However, in-house systems can be designed to minimize disruptions to the user and the operating environment. Therefore, installation and training costs may be higher for packaged systems. Day-to-day operating costs are a mixed bag: a well-written in-house system can run more efficiently than a package because all the code is specialized to the specific environment; however, in-house systems can also be very inefficient if they are poorly designed. The costs of system maintenance and enhancements are similar between in-house and packaged systems.

If a decision is made to buy rather than develop the application system in-house the following steps should be taken to evaluate the package:

- *Carefully review package documentation.* This helps determine if the features claimed in sales brochures exist in the software. It is also a good measure of how easy (or difficult) it will be to install and work with the system. Manuals that are confusing, badly written, or poorly organized can have a very negative impact on the usability of a system. A written promise not to divulge information may be required by a vendor before documentation is given to a prospect.

- *Check the amount of vendor support that is provided.* Find out the number of days of no-charge assistance the vendor will provide to help install the software. The amount of free support should depend on the difficulty involved in specializing the software to run in the customer's environment. The support offered by the vendor may be as little as three person-days or may be as much as is needed to make the system work according to specifications. The latter arrangement is rare and is usually limited to new products that are difficult to sell without such support.

- *Find out about training.* The vendor should provide, at no charge, training for a sufficient number of people to initially install and operate the system. The frequency and location of this training is important. Infrequently offered courses may not be convenient from a system installation timing standpoint. Location is important because the customer normally pays travel expenses when attending out-of-town training classes.

- *Get the literature first; see the salesman later.* It is to the advantage of the vendor to establish rapport with a prospect as quickly as possible. Unfortunately, this is not in the best interests of the prospect. Discussions with salespeople should be held only after a product's potential usefulness has been established, and this can only be done by reading about the product.

- *Read overviews first; save the details for last.* Don't get bogged down in the detailed technical specifications of a product before its potential merit has been established. Time spent in probing details prematurely is better spent on the analysis of major features and benefits.

- *Demand a complete list of customers.* You might not get it, but it doesn't hurt to try. Willingness to divulge the names of all customers, subject, of course, to a customer's desire to remain anonymous, indicates the confidence of a vendor in the product. After getting a customer list, at least three customers should be contacted. This is in addition to customers whose names were specifically provided by the vendor as references.

- *Verify the existence of claimed features.* Salespeople sometimes tend to confuse what is available *now* with what *will be* available 2, 4, or 12 months from now. Don't let the vendor sell ahead of the product. Talk to one or more customers that actually use the claimed feature if that feature is important to you.

- *Remember motive.* Computer manufacturers sell software as a sideline to selling hardware. It is not necessarily in their best interests to minimize resource usage. Therefore, software produced by hardware manufacturers may be relatively top-heavy with complicated features and relatively crude with respect to the efficient use of hardware. Although the change to charging separately for software has, to some extent, made manufacturer-produced software more resource efficient, companies whose existence depends on software sales are more likely to produce an efficient product.

Vendors

The effectiveness of computer hardware and software depends to a very large extent on the maintenance and enhancements provided after the system is acquired. Therefore, evaluation of the vendor may be as important as the evaluation of the products offered. This evaluation centers on the vendor's integrity, professionalism, financial strength, and support capabilities. A dozen critical issues in evaluating vendors are described next.

- *Experience.* How long has the vendor been in the computer business? How long has the vendor been developing and selling the type of product you are evaluating?

- *Size.* What are the vendor's annual gross sales? How large is the staff? How much corporate muscle can the vendor bring to bear on solving a problem or developing a new product?
- *Profitability.* Is the vendor profitable? If so, for how long? Have profits been erratic or steady?
- *Commitment.* Is software (or hardware) the vendor's only business? Is it the primary business? Does it only exist to support sales of other products (e.g., software that supports hardware sales)?
- *Staff.* Are the vendor's people well trained? Is turnover high? What is the average level of experience?
- *Customer base.* How many customers does the vendor have? How many customers use the specific product you are interested in? Are there many customers in your geographic area?
- *Financial condition.* How strong is the company financially? Is it overloaded with debt? Is it undercapitalized? Can it afford continued development of new products? This information is not always possible to receive because vendors prefer to discuss profits and size rather than debt. However, this type of financial information is very important in judging the viability of a long-term relationship with the vendor.
- *Education and training.* Does the vendor offer a comprehensive series of training courses in the use of his products? Are they taught frequently in a wide variety of locations? Or are they only taught at the vendor's headquarters or regional offices?
- *Emergency service.* What sort of hot-line provisions does the vendor offer? Are some vendor personnel on call at all times? How quickly and easily can the most knowledgeable home-office personnel be reached?
- *Contract terms.* Does the vendor always use a standard contract, or is the contract custom tailored to the client? What kinds of warrantees does the vendor offer? What financial liabilities is the vendor willing to assume in case of product malfunction?
- *References.* How is the vendor rated by customers? Are the vendor's sales and technical personnel professional and responsive?
- *Local service.* Is there adequate service coverage in your area? What is the ratio of service personnel to customers? Is there an adequate local stock of spare parts (if you are buying hardware)? What is the average response time to a service call? Is there a minimum guaranteed response time?

All of these factors should be seriously considered when deciding whose hardware or software should be acquired.

Discussion Questions

1. Define "functional requirements" as they relate to the selection of hardware and software. Give examples.

2. What is a "Request for Proposal" (RFP)? What information should it contain?

3. How can simulation, hardware/software monitoring, benchmarks, performance power analysis, and structured walkthroughs help in evaluating hardware or software components?

4. Identify the major types of costs that must be considered in evaluating system components. Give examples of each.

5. Describe the hardware selection team.

6. What are the advantages of acquiring packaged software instead of developing that software in house?

7. Describe some of the product and vendor factors that must be considered in evaluating software packages.

10

SOURCES OF EDP SERVICES

INTRODUCTION

The previous chapter described the process by which in-house hardware and software is acquired. This chapter discusses the temporary acquisition of services, that is, the temporary purchase of skills and computing power as opposed to the purchase of specific hardware and software components.

The skills of people may be acquired by hiring permanent in-house staff, by engaging consultants, or by contracting with an organization such as a service bureau. Management skills can be acquired through the use of facilities management services. Computing power can be in-house or it can be rented through time sharing, subscription services, or service bureaus. Chapter 8 discusses the hiring and management of in-house staff. This chapter describes outside consulting and computing services that are available to the EDP manager.

CONSULTING SERVICES

Types of Computer Consulting Firms

Computer consultants perform feasibility studies, EDP audits, programming, systems design, and related functions. They are normally used on a temporary basis for a specific project or projects. Consulting firms that represent the most important segment of the EDP consulting business are large accounting firms that offer consulting services through their management services staffs; programming firms or "body shops" that provide programmers and systems analysts; and specialized, high-technology firms that are hired to perform very specific technical tasks.

Accounting firms that offer management consulting services are normally thorough, expensive, generally interested only in high-revenue engagements, and develop conservative, well-documented systems that make fairly standard use of computer technology. Great leaps of technological imagination are rarely exhibited. Accounting firms are almost always hired at the behest of financial executives who feel comfortable working with firms run by accountants. Engagements are generally on a package basis. That is, the consultants have total responsibility for a project, be it a feasibility study, the general design of a system, or a complete implementation. Rarely will a large accounting firm provide individual consultants to work under the direction of an in-house manager or project leader. The most effective use of large accounting firms is for developing financial and accounting systems and for performing high-level requirements studies.

Programming firms provide systems analysts and programmers individually, in groups, or for a whole project based entirely on the client's needs. These firms are generally the least expensive source of consulting services, provide competent people, and are generally most useful in basic applications work. They are a good source of personnel in situations when a firm is temporarily short-handed.

High-technology firms are more expensive than programming firms, but often less expensive than large accounting firms. They provide high-caliber personnel skilled in developing custom software, system tuning, computer performance evaluation (CPE), the design of teleprocessing networks, and other highly technical activities.

Many consulting firms are a cross between programming and high-technology firms: they consist of a few highly skilled technicians and a large number of less experienced programmers and analysts.

Justification for Using Consultants

There are five major reasons a firm may wish to use consultants:

- *Unavailability of in-house staff.* Perhaps the most common reason for the widespread use of EDP consultants is that firms with extensive systems development plans frequently have great difficulty hiring capable individuals in sufficient numbers to staff projects. The competition for EDP personnel is fierce, and consulting firms, with their constant variety of challenging assignments, attract a lion's share of talented, ambitious individuals.

- *Limited engagement.* Large organizations are generally hesitant to incur the disruptions and morale problems caused by hiring in-house staff for a project and then terminating people after project completion. Consultants are, of course, temporary. They can be hired and fired at will.

- *Expertise.* Consultants are exposed to a wide variety of clients and data-processing systems. Frequently, they have in-depth experience in developing specific types of systems or dealing with specific kinds of clients. Thus, consultants offer a depth and range of expertise rarely available within a single company. In addition, the quality of consultant personnel is sometimes higher than that of the client. This is a result of the challenging assignments that attract capable people to consulting firms and the constant pressure to excel that is often absent in the client organization.

- *Concentration.* Because most capable individuals in an organization have a variety of responsibilities, it is often difficult for them to bring their undivided attention to bear on a project for an adequate period of time. Constant interruptions and problems demanding immediate attention may force the substitution of consultants for busy in-house staff.

- *Objectivity.* In theory, outside consultants are totally objective. They are not involved on a day-to-day basis in organizational politics and are not captive to any vested interests. Therefore, they should be capable of rendering objective, professional judgments. Objectivity is, in fact, exercised in many instances. Unfortunately, the economics of the consulting business dictates a high degree of deference to the person or organizational entity that hires the consultant. A consultant will, for example, rarely admit the folly of a project she or he is paid to conduct, even if convinced that the project is a waste of money. Objectivity may therefore, be the weakest "legitimate" reason to hire a consultant.

Misuse of Consultants

Consultants are hired at least as often for the wrong reasons as for the right reasons. They are sometimes cast into one of the following dubious roles:

- *The consultant as surrogate manager.* The studies and reports a consultant produces can support but can never be a substitute for the tough decisions a manager must always make. Ultimately, it is the manager, not the consultant, who is responsible for the successful operation of his area. Unfortunately, weak managers sometimes use consultants to evade or postpone responsibilities.

- *The consultant as scapegoat.* Projects that are doomed to failure are sometimes assigned to consultants. This may be done purely for self-preservation or because of unwillingness to undertake difficult, thankless projects. In either case, the consultant must be prepared to accept blame for a failure for which he or she was not responsible.

- *The consultant as possessor of secret knowledge.* Consultants frequently possess skills absent in the client organization. However, they are not demigods. Unfortunately, people sometimes assume that consultants, *because they are consultants,* have all the right answers. Nothing could be farther from the truth. It is a sad irrationality of organizational life that the conclusions and recommendations reached through expensive studies frequently enjoy greater cachet than the same conclusions reached by people within the organization.

- *The consultant as budgetary chimera.* A common practice, particularly in government agencies, is to use consultants on a permanent or semipermanent basis because the peculiarities of budget allocation discourage hiring additions to in-house staff. A large staff creates the impression of a bloated, ever-expanding bureaucracy. In spite of the fact that the long-term use of consultants is far more expensive than hiring additional people, the cost of consultants is sometimes easier to camouflage.

- *The consultant as yes-man.* Consultants are sometimes hired to lend their name and prestige to decisions reached by management. Since people tend to value that which is expensive, the opinion of the consultant is used to justify decisions that have already been made. This practice dilutes the effectiveness of the consultant by making him or her an echo instead of an objective voice.

In addition to the misuse of consultants by clients, a number of dubious practices are abetted or encouraged by consulting firms. The most widespread and serious of these is the creation of spurious requirements that are intended to provide the consultant with add-on business. This can take the form of recommending proprietary software products developed by the consultant; recommending the development, by the consultant, of course, of a custom system when a cheaper off-the-shelf component is more appropriate; or the development of standards only the consultant, because of intimate knowledge of the subject, can implement. The latter is particularly insidious when a consulting firm is hired by a government agency to develop industry reporting requirements and then sells its extensive knowledge of those requirements to companies responsible for compliance.

The use of consulting firms by ex-members of that firm who are now employed by the client may also be a questionable practice. Although it may sometimes be justified because of the certainties of dealing with a known quantity, in many cases it is simply professional nepotism. The effect is insidious if otherwise qualified firms, or, for that matter, internal personnel, are summarily disqualified from projects. This practice is particularly tempting when an individual has been placed in an influential job with a client through the influence of her or his old firm. A way of saying "thank you" is to make extensive use of the old firm's consulting services.

The use of people from the management services (consulting) side of an accounting firm to develop systems their peers on the audit staff will certify is, in the opinion of many, a conflict of interest. Accounting firms hotly deny pushing management services to preclude system certification problems. They claim that the auditing function is independent from management services and that high standards of professional ethics exist. However, the fact is that one side of the firm helps the other. Individuals who have been involved in selecting vendors to develop large accounting systems know that innuendos are occasionally made by an auditor that his firm "understands" the EDP requirements better than the competition. This is code for "if we develop the system you can be sure your auditor will find no problems with it".

Finally, consultants are sometimes too self-serving to offer their true professional opinions when those opinions may be unpopular with the client. A good consultant should be capable of presenting even the most unpalatable facts and recommendations to the client without offense. Once the client has been informed, the responsibility of the consultant to the unvarnished truth ends. It is up to the client to choose whether or not to accept the consultant's views.

Effective Use of Consultants

The use of consultants can be a valuable strategy in the development of data-processing systems. However, it is important to understand the circumstances and conditions under which maximum benefits are achieved. Following are guidelines that should prove useful in making the most out of consulting services.

Have a clear understanding of what you want done. Remember, it is to the consultant's advantage to have an open-ended arrangement. The more nebulous the goals of the project, the higher the consultant's fees will be. Why? Because most consultants, given a choice between a broad and a narrow interpretation of an assignment, will choose the most profitable interpretation. They will invariably settle on the most elaborate and expensive approach. In addition to the scope of the project, the nature of the deliverables must be defined. If oranges are needed, you don't expect to pay someone $50,000 to give you bananas. Therefore, you must specify oranges; you cannot expect the consultant to be a mind reader.

Develop high-quality formal specifications. This is a cousin to the "clear understanding" guideline. If the consultant is hired to code programs, the specifications should be very clear and very precise. Internally, people can sometimes be less rigorous in their specifications because verbal clarification can take place later. However, a consultant who writes a series of programs is here today and gone tomorrow. By the time a misunderstanding is discovered, the individual who coded the program has left.

Insist on good documentation. Good documentation is a two-way street: the consultant should be given good specifications and, in turn, should return thoroughly documented programs and systems to the client. Internal staff will frequently not have the luxury of calling the consultant in case of future problems. The documentation that is left behind is the only source of reference client personnel will have when the project is over.

For very large projects, separate the feasibility study from the system implementation. Make it clear that the consulting firm that does the feasibility study will probably not receive a contract to implement the system. Unless such a proviso is made, the conclusion of the feasibility study is foreordained: develop the system! Frequently, such separation is difficult to achieve. If a consulting firm does a good job on the study, it is highly tempting to take advantage of their newly gained knowledge by hiring them for follow-on work. Resist the temptation whenever possible.

Don't have your mind made up before a consultant does the job. If you are asking for a feasibility study, a general systems design, or enhancement recommendations to an existing system, allow the consultant to perform his or her analysis before second-guessing the consultant. Unfortunately, consultants are sometimes hired to justify long held opinions that lack credibility because they are not backed by an "objective" outside source.

Develop a continuing relationship with the consultant, but don't use her or him on an on-going, permanent basis. Inordinate reliance on consultants is a reflection of poor management. If people with a specific set of skills are needed for long periods of time, hire them; it is cheaper than using consultants.

Insist on a work plan and carefully monitor the consultant's activities. Many people are under the delusion that consultants need little or no direction. Consultants are, by and large, self-starters; they must be in order to work successfully in a client environment. However, consultants can be sidetracked, can miss deadlines, and can misinterpret instructions. They cannot be left to their own devices for long periods any more than can internal staff. Therefore, project planning and status reporting must be carried out as rigorously with consultants as with the firm's own employees.

COMPUTING SERVICES

Computing service organizations are firms that offer a permanent or temporary alternative to the acquisition or use of in-house data-processing facilities. The following sections describe these services and when they are used.

Justification for the Use of Computing Services

The use of outside computing services is prompted by considerations of cost, availability of resources, and specialization. Cost represents the dollars-and-cents trade-off between renting computing services from outside and performing those services in-house. The implicit assumption is that there is a reasonable choice. Availability of resources is a factor when there is little hope of being able to perform certain services in-house, at least not for the types of applications, the data volumes, and the frequency of use that is required. Specialization is a less tangible factor. It focuses not on considerations of hard cash, but rather on the concentration of the firm's talents and energies on a support activity (EDP) that is unrelated to the firm's main business.

Cost. Despite dramatic improvements in the price performance of computer hardware, the development of user-oriented computer languages and simplified systems development methodologies, in-house data processing is still a big consumer of resources. Therefore, organizations that sell comprehensive EDP services and high-quality, turnkey systems have continued to thrive, despite the wildfire spread of minicomputers into even the smallest firms. It should be noted that hardware cost savings enjoyed by small firms are also enjoyed by organizations selling EDP services. Therefore, service bureaus, time-sharing firms, and subscription services have been able to lower rates to remain competitive with cheap in-house systems.

Resource availability. The use of outside computing services may be required when an application is very infrequently run or when hardware requirements substantially outstrip in-house computing power. An example of an infrequently run application is budget modeling. Since budgets are developed annually, budget personnel spend only several weeks a year to develop budget alternatives. Although the software used for budget modeling may be purchased and run on the firm's in-house computer, this may be grossly impractical. It is far more convenient, and probably less expensive, to subscribe to a time-sharing service on a use-only basis than to maintain such a capability in-house. An example of an application that cannot be processed on an in-house computer is a complex engineering calculation that requires a very large, powerful main frame. Firms that need such calculations performed may not have the extensive processing capabilities needed to do the job.

Specialization. Specialization, as used in this context, refers to a make-or-buy alternative that poses the question, "Do we want to concentrate our energy on producing a service that does not represent our main business, even if that is the least-cost alternative, or should we channel all available resources into our main line of work?" Only providers of EDP equipment and services are in the data-processing business. Everyone else uses EDP as a tool that supports the manufacture of nuts and bolts, the sale of insurance policies, the dispensation of government services, or some other end product.

Many firms have chosen not to be involved with EDP. They prefer to pay someone else to worry about it. This is sometimes a sensible approach, particularly when most of the company's applications are in support areas such as accounting. However, the weakness of this solution is that data processing, if used effectively, *is* an integral part of running the business. It is not simply a necessary activity, such as sweeping the halls, that can be entrusted to the lowest bidder. Modern data-processing applications should do more than process payroll checks and prepare bills; they should produce timely information on which tactical and strategic business decisions can be based. In addition, the advent of word processing, electronic mail, and the "paperless office" makes the in-house computer an integral part of the total environment. It is extremely difficult for organizations using these office aids to divorce themselves from everyday control of data processing.

Following is a description of the major options open to firms that do not wish to perform data-processing services in-house.

Time Sharing

Time sharing is the "simultaneous" use of a powerful computer by unrelated users. "Simultaneous" is in quotation marks because, from a technical standpoint, there is no real simultaneity of processing unless multiple CPU's are used; however, processing appears simultaneous to the end user.

Time sharing, as used in this context, does not include the sharing of a company's computer by different individuals or departments from remote terminals using software such as IBM's Time Sharing Option (TSO). Rather, time sharing is a computer sharing service commercially available to the general public. It enables even the smallest firm to enjoy the benefits of very powerful computers. Time sharing is widely used for scientific and modeling applications involving intense processing of small volumes of data, that is, many iterations of complex formulas.

Time sharing has grown in sophistication and flexibility since its early days. Although scientific and modeling applications still predominate, many more features are or may soon become available:

- Intelligent terminals enable users to perform some editing and other processing functions on site. Therefore, the time sharing computer can be used to better advantage.
- Many time-sharing services now focus on specific applications areas such as financial management. Arcane scientific applications no longer monopolize the time-sharing market.
- Packet data networks enable the user to route messages to different host computers. This results in greater efficiency and reliability.
- Proposed computer utilities such as American Telephone and Telegraph's Advanced Communication System (ACS) will automatically assign and route job requests to different locations and computers. The routing is based on the lines, locations, and computers that are capable of fulfilling the request most efficiently.
- Computer utilities will perform the jobs time-sharing services traditionally provided. In addition, they will make the processing of many batch and mixed batch/on-line applications cost effective in a time-sharing environment. The result is that capabilities once offered independently by time-sharing services and service bureaus can be provided by computer utilities.

Terminals with dial-up facilities are generally used as the medium for transmitting data to the computer and calling the desired programs. Output may be received on the terminal or it may be routed to a printer at the customer's site.

The central processor used by the time-sharing service may be a conventional business computer or a large computer especially designed or configured for time-sharing applications. In addition, some time-sharing networks offer computer-to-computer interconnections that enable customers to combine substantial in-house processing with the power of a large, time-sharing computer. Time-sharing services are billed on a straight usage basis, but may involve connect charges and a minimum monthly fee.

Service Bureaus

Service bureaus provide two kinds of services: process only, that is, the renting of computer time to test or run application systems developed elsewhere; and full service, the provision of application systems as well as operations services.

Service bureaus of the process only variety are often used in the following circumstances:

- When it is more convenient or less expensive for an organization to rent computer time than it is to acquire in-house capacity.
- When a firm has exhausted in-house capacity and is awaiting the delivery of additional hardware.
- During periods of unusually high activity (e.g., month end, period-end, or year-end processing).
- During system development when testing cannot take place in-house due to capacity problems or because appropriate hardware and software components are not yet in place.
- When performing parallel testing of production systems that are being migrated to a new computer or operating system. Production is run on site and at a service bureau with the appropriate new configuration. Results are then compared.
- When converting mass volumes of data for use in a new system. Such conversions may overburden in-house capacity.
- When a reliable source of backup is needed but its provision is not possible, secure, or convenient on site.
- In emergency situations when in-house computing power has been destroyed by fire, flood, or other disaster.

Full-service arrangements are useful when a firm does not wish to acquire in-house computing capabilities or staff. This decision may be based on cost factors, on a reluctance to divert attention away from the company's main line of business or on the expectation that the service bureau can provide a better quality product.

Cost is the most persuasive argument for a full-service arrangement. Despite dramatically lower hardware costs that have greatly increased the number of firms with in-house computing capabilities, the expense of maintaining an EDP staff continues to make service bureaus attractive. The desire to limit the time and energy company personnel spend on activities such as data processing may also be a good argument. This is particularly true if the applications do not require extensive interaction with company personnel during processing. Expertise in providing a good product is a good justification when using highly standardized applications such as payroll and billing systems. Packaged application systems offered by service bureaus can be a good alternative, especially when the service bureau is a subsidiary of a bank or other institution with whom the firm does business.

Fees charged by service bureaus are usually based on transaction volumes and/or computing time needed to run the jobs. The costs of developing or leasing the application systems may also be borne by the customer.

Subscription Services

A subscription service enables clients to share an application system as well as computing facilities. Processing is done serially. That is, data for all customers are passed through each program. Tables and reports are specialized, but the programs are generally the same for all clients.

An example of a shared application is Honeywell's Hospital Computer Sharing System (HCSS), an accounting and billing system for small hospitals. Room rates, charges for various services, and other hospital-specific data are maintained on separate files for each hospital. Data are transmitted from the hospital to the subscription service via telecommunication lines or by messenger. The data are then processed by the system. Report delivery occurs by mail, messenger, or routing reports to a remote printer located in a hospital's business office.

Subscription services are almost always limited to the provision of very specialized applications to a very specific market (e.g., small hospitals).

They offer two principal advantages:

- *Low cost*. Because application software, as well as hardware, is shared by many clients, the costs of developing or specializing the software and the costs of processing the data may be substantially lower than doing the same job in-house.
- *Specialization*. Subscription services normally sell only one product to one industry. Thus, their staff has a level of expertise that is not usually available in-house.

Facilities Management

Facilities management is not, strictly speaking, a computing service. Rather, it is an agreement to manage and operate a company's EDP installation. A facilities management group takes over an existing installation, including staff, hardware, software, and application programs. The facilities management arrangement is frequently on a fixed-fee basis. It can, however, be organized in any fashion suitable to the client and the facilities management firm.

What is the justification for facilities management? Normally, this rather drastic step is carried out when a firm has lost all hope of being able to effectively manage its own data-processing activities. Facilities management represents the total abdication of responsibility for the data-processing function. It is sometimes precipitated by impending unionization, which under certain circumstances can be avoided by disposing of the EDP department through facilities management; the facilities manager fires all data-processing personnel and rehires only those who are nonunion. Although this step is of dubious legality, it has been done successfully in a number of cases.

A facilities management arrangement may result in the following benefits:

- Reduced costs through better management. Facilities management firms have experience in upgrading the performance of poorly managed EDP departments. Managers possessing these skills may be difficult for the firm itself to hire on the outside.
- Reduced management attention to the operational details of EDP. If a data-processing installation is poorly run, managers at all levels and in all functional areas of the organization end up paying inordinate attention to EDP problems.
- Reduced cost through buying power. The facilities management company can sometimes exercise more influence than a single user in getting price discounts from EDP vendors.
- The elimination of problem personnel. People who may be difficult to fire for reasons of seniority or internal politics are much more vulnerable under facilities management.

Unfortunately, there are also significant disadvantages to the facilities management arrangement. The principal disadvantage is loss of control. When responsibility for the EDP function is removed from company management, the day-to-day responsiveness and flexibility of the department may be seriously reduced. After all, the facilities management contract usually runs for a fixed period, and facilities management personnel report only to their own management, not to the client.

Another disadvantage is the lack of understanding that an outsider may have of the company and the industry of which it is a part. This may be a serious handicap in developing responsive systems and in achieving consensus and cooperation with EDP users.

Finally, the use of management imported on a temporary basis from outside may result in morale problems. Data-processing people may resent reporting to outsiders who have little understanding of the installation and who have little stake in dealing fairly with existing staff. Managers in other departments may feel threatened by the removal of an entire company function from normal organizational politics and control.

If facilities management is contemplated, and it is proving to be a less popular option than in past years, the following facts should be carefully considered:

- The desire to contract with a facilities management firm frequently indicates management failure to provide adequate direction and leadership to EDP. Facilities management does not resolve this problem.
- There is a very high failure rate among facilities management firms. Therefore, a careful evaluation of the firm's financial condition is always necessary.
- Contract arrangements must be precise. Fees and other charges should be clearly described. Sufficient flexibility in hardware, software, and policies must be allowed to accommodate changing conditions.

Discussion Questions

1. Name the five major reasons why EDP consultants may be useful to a firm.
2. Discuss the guidelines given in the chapter for effectively using consultants.
3. What are the reasons why a firm may wish to use outside computing services?
4. Describe the concept of time sharing.
5. What are the differences between service bureaus, subscription services, and facilities management?

11

FINANCIAL AND LEGAL CONSIDERATIONS

The preceding chapters addressed the selection of hardware, software, and sources of EDP services. This chapter deals with the financial alternatives available to an organization in acquiring those resources. In addition, contractual arrangements are discussed and appropriate relationships between vendors and customers are suggested.

ACQUISITION ALTERNATIVES: RENT, LEASE, BUY

Three options exist in acquiring hardware and software components: buying the component outright, renting it, or leasing it. Components that are not purchased can be rented from the vendor or can be leased from a third party, that is, from a firm which buys from the vendor and then leases the component to its customers. (The difference between renting and leasing is described later.)

The choice of financing alternatives is largely determined by the degree of permanence the organization desires in the components it acquires, the availability of funds, and the competing uses to which money may be put. The purchase of a component is normally the least expensive alternative. However, it is also the most permanent: the buyer is at the mercy of the marketplace and, therefore, may not be able to make substitutions without suffering material financial loss. Rental is the most expensive but also the most flexible arrangement. Normally, only 30 to 90 days' notice is required to exchange or remove a component. A third-party lease is less expensive than renting equipment from a vendor, but, in the long run, it is generally more expensive than an outright purchase. Third-party lease arrangements are more flexible than purchases, but less flexible than a straight rental, mainly because the lease is of a longer duration and less flexibility is allowed for exchanging or removing components. The advantages of rental or lease versus outright purchase are summarized next.

- *Capital is not tied up.* Investment in EDP resources is not (generally) an integral part of the company's main business.
- *Reduced risk of "paying too much" for a component.* The price of EDP hardware continues to decline. Therefore, it may be wiser to be in a position to exchange components frequently than to buy hardware at higher prices.
- *Reduced risk of technological obsolescense.* Because rented or leased equipment can be quickly disposed of, a firm can constantly upgrade its configuration with state-of-the-art hardware components. Purchased hardware leaves the buyer vulnerable to market conditions that may prevent sale at reasonable prices.
- *Reduced risk of poor performance.* Once a component is purchased, you are stuck with it. Rented or leased components can be jettisoned if performance is inadequate.
- *Purchase option credits.* These can actually make rental followed by purchase as inexpensive over the long run (5 to 10 years) as outright purchase, but without the disadvantages. Purchase option credits are points awarded for each month a component is rented. After a certain period of time, usually 3 to 5 years, enough points are accumulated so that the component can be purchased for a fraction of its original cost. Typically, purchase option credits enable a hardware component to be purchased for 10 percent of its cost when new.

Despite the advantages of renting or leasing, the purchase of hardware components may also be advantageous. Following are positive reasons for buying.

- *Cheap.* Purchase is the least expensive alternative.
- *Tax advantages.* Depending on tax regulations in effect at the time of purchase, a firm may be eligible for an investment tax credit, which will further reduce the cost of purchase versus rent or lease. Investment tax credits represent a reduced tax liability as a reward for buying capital equipment.
- *Extensive usage.* If a hardware component will be used two to three shifts per day, 7 days a week, rental charges may be very high because usage exceeds the normal amount stipulated in the rental agreement. This may be an additional incentive to buy.

A rental arrangement takes place when a customer rents a hardware (or software) component from the original manufacturer. A lease arrangement occurs when a component is rented from a third party, that is, from a firm that has purchased the equipment from the manufacturer and is leasing it to the end user.

A lease can be an operating lease, in which case the terms of the lease do not cover the total cost of buying the equipment, or a financial (full payout) lease in which the end user commits to a payment period of sufficient duration to cover the cost of equipment, expenses, and profits to the lessee. The former arrangement is usually carried out with a leasing firm that has hardware in stock and leases it to a series of customers. The latter is more of a custom arrangement that is closer in spirit to a purchase on the installment plan than it is to an operating lease.

Leasing arrangements are often complicated and creative. They are limited only by the imagination of the lessor, lessee, and the source of financing. Leasing can offer a multitude of mutually beneficial tax advantages and may provide an attractive alternative for companies that cannot afford, or do not wish, to buy, but who desire a cheaper way of acquiring hardware than through a standard rental arrangement. Leasing also offers a viable alternative in cases where 100 percent short-term financing is impractical or unavailable; thus, leasing may be a poor man's substitute for outright purchase.

How can a leasing company buy and then lease hardware cheaper than the original manufacturer? The answer lies in market forces, tax laws, and the specific terms under which equipment is rented or leased by the end user.

A manufacturer discourages rentals and encourages outright purchases because he is able to recover development investment more quickly through sales than rentals. After all, rental results in the inflow of money in dribs and drabs rather than in large chunks. Therefore, it is more advantageous for a manufacturer to sell to a leasing company than to rent to the end user. This dampens the incentive for a manufacturer to offer attractive rental rates.

Tax laws influence the situation because the purchaser (lessor) can take advantage of investment tax credits and a faster depreciation schedule, whereas the original manufacturer, the "producer," cannot. And, due to high development costs, the manufacturer's depreciation schedule is longer.

The specific terms under which leasing takes place also affect the situation. Since a leasing company offers less service, requires more stringent cancellation provisions, and is less flexible with regard to exchange privileges, the lessee is not subject to the same expenses as the vendor. Therefore, the monthly cost to the lessor is not as great.

The disadvantages to leasing are that maintenance and service are normally inferior to that provided by a vendor, software support is generally not available, contracts are more difficult to abrogate and are longer term (5 to 7 years), and hardware components are more difficult to exchange or remove.

Many large- and medium-sized computer installations follow a three-tier acquisition strategy: hardware components that are least likely to become obsolete, such as memory banks and the central processing unit, are purchased. Peripheral equipment that supports the bulk of the installation's processing and is of a semipermanent nature is leased. And components that are of questionable longevity or whose technology is volatile, such as mass storage devices and display terminals, are rented directly from the manufacturer. This mix of options enables the firm to maximize the benefits of each acquisition alternative.

VENDOR RELATIONS

Reasonable ground rules can prevent embarrassing, wasteful, and sometimes harmful relations from developing between vendors and customers. It is the vendor's job to sell a product. It is the data processing manager's job to make sure that the salesmanship exercised toward that end does not harm the EDP department and is not inimical to the personal and professional interests of the staff.

The following can serve as useful guidelines for developing healthy customer-vendor relations.

- Require the salesperson to become familiar with your needs and your hardware-software environment. Salespeople who fail to familiarize themselves with your situation will end up wasting your time. If necessary, ask for a different salesperson; most firms will oblige if the alternative is a lost sale.
- Be sure that all vendor visits have a specific purpose. Shun drop-ins who arrive unannounced to cultivate your subordinates or to ingratiate themselves with your management. Salespeople should have a reason for each visit, should schedule the visit in advance at your convenience, and should be prepared to state their purpose and the time needed to achieve that purpose.
- Once you have agreed to a sales call, be sure to provide your salesperson with the appropriate audience. Invite people to attend the meeting who can ask relevant questions and who are likely to un-

derstand the features and implications of the salesperson's product. For example, a knowledgeable systems programmer or the operations manager should be invited when a sort or teleprocessing monitor is being described by a software vendor.

- Don't accept gifts or entertainment; sooner or later you will pay for them. An occasional lunch or dinner is appropriate. So is a free trip to company headquarters to see the product demonstrated. However, anything more than this can be potentially embarrassing and can reduce your objectivity. A particularly insidious give-away is the "study," an allegedly objective analysis performed by the vendor to ascertain your need for his product. (Guess what the study will recommend?)

- Don't allow your subordinates to talk to salespeople without your explicit permission. Most programmers and systems analysts are putty in the hands of an experienced salesperson. They are easily conned into providing them with the most intimate details of your organization. Any vendor representative caught visiting your people after being told not to should be sent packing.

- Maintain rapport with your management. A good salesperson will begin a sales campaign at the highest level of the organization. The theory is that a downward referral almost always results in an audience with the person to whom the salesperson was referred. Therefore, expect the salesperson to call on your boss before calling on you. If your rapport is not good with management, the salesperson may be able to sell over your head, even if the product is not appropriate for your installation.

EDP CONTRACTS

Contract law is a complex subject about which few unqualified statements can be made. Every generalization is invariably plagued by a dozen exceptions. The resolution of contract disputes depends on the circumstances surrounding each case, the state in which the dispute takes place, and other specifics. Rather than delving into the theory of contracts, the following practical suggestions and guidelines are offered.

Don't Be Your Own Lawyer

A skillfully prepared contract can make a significant difference in the support an installation receives from its vendors. Therefore, sound legal advice is essential. Your company's legal counsel should be involved when the contractual provisions of the RFP are developed and when vendor responses are being evaluated. Above all, don't guess at the law and don't leave the preparation of contract provisions to the eleventh hour.

Get It in Writing

A written contract which addresses the obligations of each party in a comprehensive fashion is the best guarantee of compliance. It is dangerous to rely on memos, letters, oral agreements, or anything else outside the written contract as proof of obligations between the vendor and the buyer. In fact, most standard EDP contracts contain an "entire contract" or "integration" clause that explicity states that the written agreement constitutes the entire agreement between the parties and that it supercedes all prior agreements, understandings, and negotiations. The importance of including all understandings in the contract is further emphasized by the parol evidence rule which postulates that a court should not admit evidence of oral understandings that negate a written contract.

Prudence, good business sense, and the provisions of the law suggest that, if an issue is important enough to cause serious concern, it is important enough to be included in the contract. After all, it is cheaper and easier to write a comprehensive contract than it is to litigate after promises have been broken.

Get an Explicit Warrantee

The vendor should be willing to warranty the performance of his hardware and software in writing. Without this, the hapless buyer must rely on the vagaries of "implied warrantee," the concept that the consumer has a right to expect a product to work the way it was designed. Such reliance is extremely risky, particularly in the case of services. The sale of services is not as extensively covered in the body of the law dealing with commercial transactions as is the sale of goods (e.g., hardware).

Be Sure Your Understanding of the Product Is Adequate

Information on which the contract was based must be sufficient and accurate. Wrong or insufficient data can cause serious misunderstandings and can result in a contract that does not reflect the needs of the customer. Three depressingly common scenarios are often played out when hardware and software acquisitions take place.

- *A configuration that does not do the job.* Competitive pressure may tempt a vendor to undercut the competition. That is, hardware and software components are proposed with the knowledge that these components may not be adequate to fulfill the needs of the buyer. However, the cost is less than that of the competition and the strategy is to get in the door and then convince the buyer to upgrade. The best way to avoid this situation is to insist on specificity in the contract with respect to volumes and other application characteristics the configuration must accommodate.

- *Promised system enhancements that never materialize.* Vendors are always publicly optimistic about the speed with which product enhancements will take place. This is partly wishful thinking and partly simple misrepresentation. Sometimes, a vendor has neither the intention nor the capability to develop promised enhancements within stated time periods. The best way to avoid this situation is to shun any product that does not meet key user needs *right now.* The next best way is to include a penalty clause in the contract that forces payment of an appropriate sum of money, or termination of product rental charges, if promised features are not implemented by a specified date.

- *Failure to mention hidden product disadvantages.* Information about the consequences of system failure or incorrect or unusual usage may be intentionally suppressed by the vendor. The result may be detrimental reliance on the product by the customer. For example, many first-time computer users too eagerly dismantle their manual operations, and then discover, to their great surprise, that the automated system they purchased requires expensive back-up facilities. Or a user may discover that procedures assumed to be simple to perform are, in fact, laborious and time consuming. File purges and system changes are common examples. The best way to avoid these situations is to carefully identify the uses to which the product will be put and to analyze the possible consequences of system failure. Appropriate up-time and other provisions may need to be included in the contract.

All these scenarios can be avoided if a thorough analysis of each product is undertaken and if appropriate provisions are included in the contract. The following section describes the typical contents of a thoroughly prepared EDP contract.

CONTRACT PROVISIONS

The success of a computer system can be greatly influenced by the provisions written into the procurement and maintenance contracts under which it is acquired. The accuracy with which the system meets the needs of the user and the responsiveness with which the system is maintained by the vendor is influenced by the force of the legal agreement. This requires a comprehensive contract that describes, in detail, the obligations and understandings surrounding the acquisition of the system.

The first step toward an effective contract is a thorough understanding of the functional requirements the system must satisfy. This, in turn, requires a thoughtful, well-written request for proposal (RFP). See Chapter 9 for information on how to prepare an RFP.

The second step is to identify the responsibilities of each party involved in the acquisition. Parties to a contract may include the following:

- End user
- Consultants
- Site preparation personnel
- Software and application package suppliers
- Insurance agents
- Hardware vendors for both the central processing unit and for each peripheral device
- Leasing company
- Communications companies (including the phone company) that supply teleprocessing equipment
- Forms and supplies companies
- Furniture and equipment movers
- Owner of the computer room site

In most situations, all these parties will not be involved. It is, however, advisable to review every aspect of the acquisition and installation in order to identify the parties that do have responsibilities. Specific responsibility for providing and installing the following items is of particular importance:

- Operations manuals
- Communications and peripheral equipment
- Utility routines and diagnostics
- Language translators, compilers, assemblers, and other program development software
- Application systems
- Systems and programming documentation

The major areas that must be considered when writing the contract are described next.

System Requirements

Functional specifications that the hardware and software must accommodate should be explicitly stated. These should include system accuracy standards (if appropriate), processing volumes, and performance requirements for each hardware and software component.

Site Preparation and Operations Requirements

These are the environmental requirements needed to make the vendor's system work. They include space, air conditioning, humidity, electrical, and other physical factors (also see the Site Preparation section, Chapter 12).

Personnel

How much training is the vendor obligated to provide? At which locations? With what frequency? For how many students? At what cost? The answers to these questions should be included in the contract.

In addition to personnel training requirements, it is necessary to reach an agreement on the number of people at various skill levels that are required to operate and maintain the system. This is of particular importance in cases where there is a suspicion that the vendor is deliberately underestimating the ease with which the system can be used and maintained.

Delivery and Acceptance Criteria

This section of the contract stipulates delivery dates for various system components and outlines criteria on which system acceptance, and, therefore, commencement of payment to the vendor, will be based. Acceptance criteria are usually stated in terms of uninterrupted, problem-free service lasting a stipulated number of hours or days. Remedies may include forfeiture of rental charge until acceptance criteria are met or outright payment by the vendor when serious economic consequences result from system malfunction or from the inability of the system to meet acceptance criteria on schedule.

Financial Arrangements

This part of the contract deals with the financial arrangements of the acquisition. It should include the following information:

- Rental charges (including shift or usage differentials).
- Tax payments and credits (including tax obligations of each party and expected tax benefits, such as depreciation and investment tax credits).
- Shipping and site preparation charges.
- Insurance charges.
- Penalties (if any) for nonperformance.
- Use and distribution rights (e.g., can software components be used at multiple locations or will such use result in additional rental charges?)

In the case of hardware acquisitions, the vendor may include the operating system and supporting utilities in the cost of the hardware or he may charge separately for these components. This determination should be made prior to the final hardware selection, and the terms under which hardware is offered should be described in the contract.

Hardware Maintenance

Who will perform hardware maintenance and at what cost? During what hours will routine maintenance occur? What work is performed as part of routine maintenance? What are the skill levels of maintenance personnel? Is maintenance available 24 hours per day, 7 days per week? What is the guaranteed average and maximum response times in case of hardware failure? These questions must be answered in the contract. If no explicit answers are forthcoming, the buyer can be sure that the most pessimistic prediction of service levels is justified.

In addition to the impact hardware maintenance provisions have on system performance, the user should always endeavor to acquaint himself with the procedures the vendor follows in resolving a problem. For example, how much time is a field engineer required to spend on a problem before that problem is referred to the regional field service office? The head office? What kinds of spare parts are stored within easy distance of the installation? What kind of access is the user allowed to the company's development personnel? (This is a particularly important question when acquiring a relatively untested product.)

Software Maintenance

When acquiring applications software, the vendor normally provides free maintenance for the first 1 or 2 years of a system's life in the installation. After that period of time, the user must pay a monthly maintenance fee that covers modifications and enhancements to the software and the resolution of problems.

Care must be taken to ensure continued maintenance even if portions of the system were modified. User-modified application packages will rarely quality for free maintenance, but vendor modifications should be covered.

Primary software, such as operating system and compilers, is normally maintained free of charge by the hardware manufacturer. Free maintenance includes software, enhancements, and problem resolutions. It does not include modifications for a specific user. Primary software acquired from a software company is generally maintained on the same basis as application packages.

The growth of distributed processing has, however, reduced the enthusiasm of vendors for providing free maintenance because of the extensive mixing of hardware, software, and teleprocessing components from different vendors. This added dimension of complexity has made software maintenance more difficult and more expensive.

Cancellation Provisions

Even the best relationships sometimes sour. Therefore, no matter how much you trust your salesperson or respect the quality of the product you are buying, it is always wise to consider escape clauses. Of particular importance are provisions that specify time periods within which hardware and software components can be cancelled, the financial penalties for making such cancellations and the circumstances under which the vendor has a right to terminate services. The latter is a very important issue to consider if the vendor's product must be modified in order to satisfy your processing requirements or if you plan to mix components from competing vendors. Hardware vendors in particular are often reluctant to support hybrid systems.

Conversion Terms

Almost every major change from one hardware-software configuration to another entails incompatibilities. A new operating system may require application program or job control language modifications. Conversion to hardware supplied by a manufacturer foreign to the installation can cause very serious operational disruptions.

Therefore, in situations where considerable effort may be expended in making the new system work, at least some help can reasonably be expected from the beneficiary of the change, the vendor who supplies the new equipment. Unless such support is explicitly mentioned in the contract, an amazing scarcity of vendor personnel invariably develops during conversion time.

Patent Indemnification

There is always a danger that the system components you are acquiring are of questionable parentage. Therefore, the vendor should always include a clause in the contract that states, in effect, that the vendor will absorb all litigation costs resulting from disputes about the technological ownership of the product.

Warrants and Assignments

The providers of EDP system components dislike making warrantees because they claim, with some justification, that the user must bear primary responsibility for the effective use of the system. However, this argument does not remove the vendor's responsibility for the basic viability of the products. For example, a printer rated at 2400 lines per minute should come close to that performance figure in actual use, and the vendor should be prepared to warranty this level of performance.

Assignments refers to the potential disposition of a vendor's outstanding contracts and commitments in case of bankruptcy or the sale of the vendor's assets to another company. End users should have some control over who they are obligated to in such situations. At the very least, customers should insist on the right to terminate or renegotiate contracts if the original parties are no longer involved. Assignments can also work the other way: EDP vendors attempt to secure provisions to protect themselves against potential customer insolvency or purchase by another company. The latter is sometimes used to abrogate the contract.

Attachments

All attachments to the contract should be explicity mentioned. In addition, references to memos, correspondence, reports, and other written material should be included if these items materially affect contract provisions.

Discussion Questions

1. What are the advantages of purchasing hardware instead of leasing or renting it?
2. What is the difference between a lease arrangement and a rental arrangement?
3. Discuss the guidelines offered in the chapter for maintaining healthy customer/vendor relations.
4. Why is it important to "get it in writing" when negotiating contracts with vendors?
5. Identify the parties often involved in the acquisition of a computer system and the components they are potentially responsible for providing.
6. Identify four areas an EDP contract should cover, and explain their importance.

12 OPERATIONS MANAGEMENT

INTRODUCTION

Computer operations is the production arm of EDP. It is to programming and systems analysis what the production line is to the engineer, perhaps not very glamorous but necessary to produce the final product. The function of operations is to operate computer hardware and to perform activities directly related to the production environment (job scheduling, data entry, input-output control, operating system tuning, etc.).

In many respects, computer operations is the stepchild of data processing. It has traditionally been ignored in favor of programming and systems analysis, its more exciting cousins. The management of EDP operations is not considered as prestigious as the management of other EDP functions. Career opportunities in operations, with the exception of systems programming, are, likewise, not viewed as very promising.

There are a number of reasons for this rather negative reputation. As with production functions in other fields, computer operations is perceived as a predominantly mechanized rather than creative activity. The factory environment that seems to be an integral part of operations (e.g., a sea of data-entry clerks, whirring tapes and disks, clattering printers, stacks of listings) is not as comfortable to white-collar workers as the office environment most EDP professionals work in. The discipline and tough management style required to successfully execute the operations function is anathema to many EDP people who are used to keeping their own hours and working at a pace geared to mental rather than physical activity. Finally, a larger percentage of jobs in operations require lower skill levels than jobs in programming and systems analysis.

Some of these reasons are accurate. Lower skill level jobs such as data-entry clerk and computer operator do indeed comprise the bulk of operations personnel. The need to run production systems on time requires the kind of clock-punching usually associated with a manufacturing production line. And the management of people who perform essentially boring jobs tends, of necessity, to be less liberal and enlightened than the management of skilled programmers and analysts.

However, what should not be ignored is the fact that operations is one of the most important functions in EDP. In today's complex environment, the skill with which production programs are scheduled and run, operating systems tuned and computer resources allocated has a tremendous impact on the overall effectiveness of EDP. Operations management is a tough, challenging job that ambitious data processors would be well advised to accept with enthusiasm.

The operations function has changed significantly over the past 20 years, and the proliferation of mini- and microcomputers promises to usher in even greater changes. As main-frame computer systems have become more powerful and more sophisticated, the following changes have occurred in EDP operations.

- *Increased skill levels.* The complexities of dealing with powerful operating systems and widespread teleprocessing networks has made the computer operator's job more challenging than in the days of one-job-at-a-time processing. Even the data-entry clerk may need to be more skilled than in the days of keypunching; for example, the validation options available when entering data into a CRT screen can require a wider variety of thoughtful responses than the very limited set of responses needed to be a successful keypunch operator.

- *Increased machine intensity.* Fewer, more highly skilled operators are needed to run increasingly complex hardware-software configurations. This is a result of the substitution of machine intelligence (i.e., the operating system) for the human labor that was once required to prepare and run individual production jobs. In addition, labor-intensive unit record equipment (card readers, sorters, card punches, and other electromechanical devices) has now been largely replaced by CRT consoles and mass storage devices. Therefore, less physical activity is required to operate a computer system.

- *Increased need for formal documentation and control.* In the days before the advent of complex operating systems, the need for high-quality operations documentation was not as great as in today's environment. A mistake in serially processing individual jobs was less likely to result in dire consequences than a mistake in a multiprogramming environment. Therefore, the controls that are exercised to effectively manage the operations function are likely to be more formal and more highly structured today than in the early days of computing. Again, this is a result of the vastly increased power of the hardware and software.

- *Increased complexity of error relationships.* In a simple operating environment, a computer system malfunction was likely to be caused by bad data, an applications program bug, or by a hardware failure. Complex operating systems, data-base management software and the extensive use of teleprocessing has added two more categories of possible errors: software problems and TP network malfunctions. In addition, the increased layers of software sometimes mask serious errors until substantial damage has already been done. The old three-dimensional error universe (program-data-hardware) required only two participants to resolve: the programmer and the operations staff. The five-dimensional error universe may now require the services of the software vendor (for possible software problems), the telephone company (for TP line problems), and the communications equipment manufacturer (for TP hardware failure). Therefore, problem resolution is more technically and organizationally complex than in years past.
- *More pleasant operations environment.* Improved noise-reduction techniques, the substitution of electronic for electromechanical hardware components, and the widespread use of display terminals for data entry has contributed to a more pleasant, less factorylike operations environment.

The changes noted have occurred in computer installations using large, main-frame, general-purpose computers. Mini- and microprocessors are sometimes exempt from these trends. To wit: a large degree of operational simplicity has been restored; the skill level needed to operate minis is frequently minimal; and if communication is not occurring between minis or between the mini and the main frame, documentation and control requirements are reduced. For more information on the impact of minicomputers and distributed processing see Chapters 3 and 15.

Functional Overview

Following are descriptions of the major functions performed by an EDP operations department. They are primarily applicable to installations containing one or more general-purpose computers that process a variety of applications. Installations with special-purpose mini-computers or systems dedicated to one application do not necessarily require the performance of all the tasks described.

Some functions, such as machine operations, are performed in all installations, even if the installation is so small that one individual performs multiple jobs. Other functions may not be relevant to all installations or may be performed by other organizational units within EDP. An example is software support (systems programming), which may be done by the applications development area. A discussion of where each function belongs within EDP is found in the organization section.

Operations functions can be categorized into three general groups: functions that constitute the day-to-day production activities of the department; support and administrative functions that are needed to maintain the production environment, to successfully interact with other parts of the data-processing organization, and to support the needs of end users; and planning functions needed to ensure the successful long-term continuation of operations activities. Each of these categories is described next.

Production Functions

Production is the heart of EDP operations. Its function is to successfully operate the computers. The tasks that comprise production are described next.

Machine Operations

Machine operations consists of the actual operation of computer hardware in the installation. In a batch processing environment, machine operations is a relatively physical activity: it requires mounting and dismounting tapes and disk packs, loading computer paper into the printer, operating unit record equipment, and manning the CPU console. In very large installations, hardware may be widely dispersed; therefore, these activities may be performed by different people at different physical locations.

Machine operations for small, dedicated minicomputers may be performed on a part-time basis by data entry or other clerical personnel. However, a general-purpose computer normally requires full-time machine operators.

Input-Output (I/O) Control

The function of I/O control is to monitor the integrity of data between the user and EDP operations. Specifically, three types of data controls are performed:

- Reconciliation between data sent by the end user and data received for processing by EDP operations. Reconciliation between data sent and data received can take place in one of the following ways: if machine readable data are produced by the user, a tally of volumes is made during the first computer processing step and the results are compared to the user's records of transactions keyed in; if operations performs data entry, an additional comparison is made between the number of source documents received from the user for keying and the source documents recorded as keyed in.
- Run-to-run batch controls between computer processing steps. Run-to-run controls generally consist of comparing the number of records processed in one program to the number of records processed in the next program. If the numbers don't match, a problem exists.
- Quality assurance of output reports. Quality assurance of output reports consists of verifying processing totals and checking report figures and volumes for reasonableness. I/O control cannot normally ensure the validity of data that are dependent on application-specific knowledge. However, some comparisons of data coming in with data going out can be made. In addition, operations documentation normally contains volume estimates and other report characteristics that enable I/O control personnel to check the reasonableness of printed output.

Data Preparation

This may include keying data into the computer system, or , if data entry is done by the end user, it may be limited to receiving data and checking its completeness. Data preparation may also include the input reconciliation activities described previously. Thus, data preparation can include source document receipt, batching, control, and entry.

Library Control

In most computer installations the volume of files containing data, program source code, and program object code is enormous. Libraries that contain thousands of reels of magnetic tape and hundreds of disk packs are not unusual. The only way this sea of data can be controlled is through very strict enforcement of storage, labeling, and classification procedures. These procedures are generally supported by a program library utility system such as Panvalet or Librarian. Library software provides a convenient, rational way of monitoring, controlling, and updating test and production program libraries. Although hardware vendors provide some program library manipulation capabilities as part of their primary software, these capabilities have only recently become competitive with the comprehensive library packages provided by software vendors. Personnel charged with library control responsibilities perform the functions necessary for ensuring that data and program libraries are maintained in an orderly fashion.

Job Scheduling

The process of scheduling jobs to be run on the computer is a critical but thankless task in today's complex multiprogramming environment. It is critical because the success with which the mix of jobs to be run is defined will, to a large extent, determine the efficiency with which EDP resources are used. It is thankless because the scheduling process involves judging the relative importance of various EDP jobs; naturally, users whose applications are not in the front of the queue are not happy about being second-class citizens.

Job scheduling is based on an analysis of the following factors:

- *Run times.* The average length of time a specific job takes to run.
- *Priorities.* Some jobs are more important than others; for example, payroll is more important than personnel skills inventory reports.
- *Frequencies.* The frequency with which a job must be run: daily, weekly, monthly, quarterly, yearly, or on request.
- *Output schedules.* When are the results of the job due?
- *Critical path.* What are the dependencies between jobs?
- *Resources.* What computing and data resources are needed to run this job? Computing resources include CPU memory, tape drives, printers, disk drives, and card readers. Data resources include transaction files, code tables, and master files.

The way in which these factors are combined to produce an operations schedule is part magic and part rational analysis. The magic part is based largely on the past experience of the scheduler; the rational analysis part is based on deadline scheduling and job network algorithms that perform critical path analysis for scheduling activities, and on job accounting data gathered through the use of software monitors such as IBM's System Management Facility (SMF) and Resource Management Facility (RMF). For more information on job accounting, see the productivity aids section of Chapter 7.

Work Rules

Operations personnel must adhere to the following rules:

- No eating or smoking in the computer room.
- Proper labeling of all machine-readable media such as tapes, disks, and card decks. Standard conventions for this should exist in every installation.
- Proper storage of all data and program files.
- Careful attention to lunch and coffee break timing. Operations is a production line; it cannot function without strict time discipline.
- Proper logging and recording of all processing results and unusual events. An alert operator can save thousands of dollars in rerun costs by spotting an operations problem while it can still be fixed through a rerun.
- Meticulous cleaning and maintenance of hardware. Certain maintenance tasks, such as the cleaning of tape drive read-write heads, are the responsibility of computer operators, not vendor personnel. Neglect of peripheral devices and other components can result in poor hardware performance.
- Strict adherence to all operations standards. This is very important because failure to properly label, store, and manipulate data and production program files can result in serious operations failures.

ADMINISTRATIVE AND SUPPORT FUNCTIONS

The activities described next are necessary to effectively support production and system development activities.

Documentation Control

A very important operations function is to monitor the accuracy, completeness, and clarity of operations turnover documentation prepared by systems development personnel. No application system should be put to use without the seal of approval from operations that the documentation is adequate. The documentation approval function also includes quality assurance testing of job control language (JCL) to ensure that the JCL conforms to the operations specifications documentated in the run books. Most installations contain separate test and production libraries with movement from test to production controlled by operations.

Training

Many large installations maintain a training department that develops and teaches courses in programming, systems analysis, and other EDP topics. Nevertheless, a need exists for in-the-field training that can only be provided by people most closely associated with the subject matter. Therefore, operations is sometimes called upon to train users and systems development personnel in the use of remote terminals, system software utility programs, and other operations-oriented components.

Standards Development

Operations documentation, restart procedures, message formats, the routing of output, and the use of technical features that affect computing resources are proper concerns of the operations department. Therefore, operations should take a leading role in the development of standards that address these topics. Unfortunately, operations is often too busy with day-to-day production problems to participate in standards development. This is very short sighted because standards have a profound impact on the operations environment.

Software Support

The software support function addresses the maintenance of primary software, that is, the operating system, utilities, compilers, and other program products that support application systems. Software support activities include generating, testing, and fine-tuning the operating system; implementing and, in some cases, developing utility programs; consulting with systems development personnel on efficient coding, file organization, and utilities usage techniques; and, in some organizations, helping install and use data-base management systems.

Communications Support

Installations with an extensive teleprocessing network generally require people to advise teleprocessing users on the proper use of the network and to assist in resolving TP problems. These problems may be caused by line failures, terminal malfunctions, TP software bugs, and other telecommunications difficulties. Communications support requires a special combination of hardware and software knowledge that is most likely to be available in the operations department. In fact, software and communications support activities are often performed by the same group of people.

Billing and Request Processing

Both of these functions are essentially clerical in nature. They consist of periodically providing users with job accounting data and logging and monitoring requests for EDP services. However, the design of the job accounting system needed to calculate charges for the use of computing resources and the development of effective request procedures will have a substantial impact on the cost and responsiveness of EDP services. It is a complex and politically sensitive task. Job billing systems are discussed in Chapter 13. Request processing is in Chapter 7.

Physical Security

EDP operations is the most capital intensive EDP function. It has responsibility for the safekeeping of a vast amount of hardware, software, and data that is extremely expensive, and sometimes impossible, to replace or re-create. Because the resources of the operations department consist mainly of physical objects stored within close proximity to each other, they are vulnerable to rapid, total destruction.

The development and enforcement of effective security procedures should, therefore, be an important operations functions. They include physical site access security, media (data) security, fire protection, and other types of security discussed in Chapter 14 and in the Site Planning Considerations section of this chapter.

Technical Review

Operations should participate in application system development walkthroughs and design reviews. Specifically, software support personnel should actively participate in coding walkthroughs and, when appropriate, system design walkthroughs. The function of operations personnel is to ensure that the coding and design techniques used to develop application systems are viable, will not have an adverse impact on computing resources, and will not disturb other application systems.

Operations management should always be given copies of design documents. Since the development and installation of any computer system affects the operations environment, operations should carefully evaluate all design documents in light of proposed systems' impact on computing resources. For more information see Chapter 7.

PLANNING FUNCTIONS

Operations planning is needed to ensure the continued availability of computing resources. Its major functions are capacity planning and the evaluation of hardware and primary software.

Capacity and Resource Usage Planning

Operations is charged with delivering computing resources that are adequate for production and system development needs. Therefore, operations must constantly monitor loading factors on current hardware and must translate projected future use into hardware and software requirements. Capacity planning is a sophisticated and complex activity. It requires extensive knowledge of hardware and software, as well as familiarity with computer performance evaluation (CPE) tools.

Hardware and Software Evaluation

Operations plays a key role in the selection of new hardware and software. Operations personnel have the requisite "bits and bytes" knowledge to help applications development personnel translate functional specifications into hardware and software requirements. In addition, operations personnel are in the best position to estimate the impact of proposed components on the current environment. The selection of any computing resource, including application packages, should, therefore, include participation by operations personnel.

ORGANIZATION

The organization of most operations departments closely parallels the operations functions described in the previous sections. Two typical structures are illustrated in Figures 12–1 and 12–2.

Note that in both examples the operations manager reports to the EDP manager. An exception may occur when computing resources are decentralized, but the systems development staff is centralized. In that case, the operations manager in a specific installation may report to a line officer at that location or subsidiary. The corporate EDP manager controls the development staff but has no computing resources.

Technical support activities are generally performed by operations. However, in smaller installations, this may be done outside operations. Data entry may be performed by operations or by the end user.

The major organizational difference between small and large installations is in the degree of personnel specialization. In a large organization, each function is performed by a different person or group of people. In a small installation one or two people may be responsible for all operations activities.

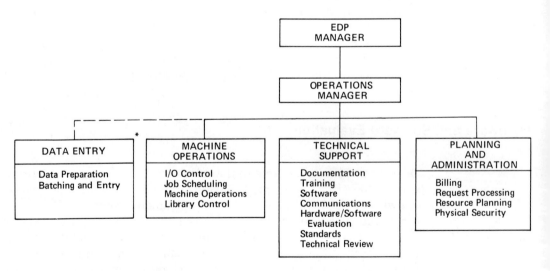

* Data Entry may be performed by system users

FIGURE 12–1. Operations Organization of a Typical Medium to Large Installation

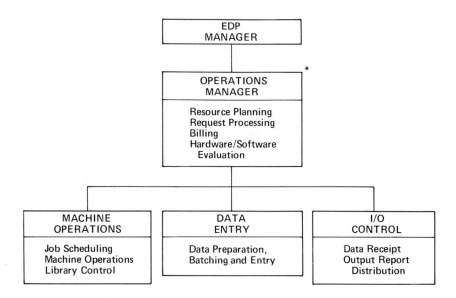

*In very small installations, there may not be an Operations Manager. Machine Operations, Data Entry, and I/O Control may report directly to the EDP Manager.

FIGURE 12–2. Operations Organization of a Typical Small to Medium Installation

SITE PLANNING CONSIDERATIONS

Site selection, the design and construction of the computer room, and the scheduling of component deliveries, though seemingly mundane, are, in fact, activities that can crucially affect the long-term success of the EDP function. Therefore, top EDP management should be involved in major site-planning decisions and activities.

A major site move should generally be coordinated by an installation committee composed of operations and systems development people. The function of the committee is to plan the move and to oversee its successful execution. Important factors that must be considered are described next.

Location

The physical location of the computer room should meet the following requirements:

- It should accommodate the flow of data and supplies. That is, the machine room should be located near the tape library, the supplies storeroom, the data-entry area, and other sections of the installation on which the running of jobs relies.

- Installation hardware should not be on prominent public display or located in areas of heavy public traffic. The tendency of companies to show off their computer facilities in the 1960s was substantially dampened by bombings and other sabotage that took place during that decade. "Out of sight, out of mind" is not a bad maxim in dealing with the public's awareness of your computer site.

- The installation should be located where it can expand to accommodate growth. Therefore, the surrounding space should be potentially available for annexation. It is normally not wise, for example, to locate in a dead end surrounded by space belonging to other companies.

- The installation should not be placed near an area that is used for storage of combustibles or across from a powerful radio antenna. The former poses a fire hazard; the latter can result in radio frequency radiation, a condition that can distort or destroy bit settings on magnetic storage media, such as tapes, and in the CPU itself.

- Computer hardware should be placed on a strong floor. Therefore, some office buildings should be avoided because they were not constructed with the loading stress factors that computers require.

- The condition of areas directly above and below the computer room should be known. Plumbing malfunctions on floors above the installation can cause flooding. The presence of combustibles on lower floors can cause fire damage.

Floor Requirements

Floors that have a load bearing factor of less than 75 to 80 pounds per square foot are inadequate to support a large, main-frame computer. If the floor in the proposed site is not strong enough, it must be strengthened, or preferably a different site should be selected. However, the increasingly lighter weight of newer computers, resulting from the miniaturization of many components, may somewhat reduce floor load-bearing requirements.

Safety and convenience considerations dictate the use of raised floors. This accommodates cabling and the required air supply for air conditioning and ventilation, and enables operators to walk from one end of the computer room to the other without tripping. If carpeting is used in the computer room, it should be of the antistatic variety. Otherwise, damage can result to files stored on magnetic media.

Space and Layout

Three considerations are of paramount importance in space planning for a computer room:

- Adequate service clearance for all components. Thirty inches is normally required to enable field service personnel to perform maintenance on tape drives, disk drives, CPUs, and other hardware.
- Ergonomically efficient placement. Computer operators must be able to mount and dismount tapes and disk packs, feed paper into the printer, operate unit record equipment, and perform other physical activities without losing track of various events that occur in the system.
- Allocation of space for supporting activities. The computer room must have conveniently located space for the temporary storage of computer tapes and other items of immediate importance to computer operations. Therefore, the placement of hardware components must consider support activities.

Power Requirements

If frequent brownouts occur, a standby power source should be considered. Despite their cost, power-conditioning systems such as Uninterruptible Power Systems (UPS) may be essential for applications with difficult-to-reconstruct data. Less expensive and in some cases more effective motor-generator-based systems can also be used. In addition, the power connection used by the computer system should not be shared. Otherwise, computer hardware becomes vulnerable to power failures caused by other areas.

Safety and Fire Requirements

Computer room planners should follow the applicable state or federal fire and safety regulations, whichever are stricter. These regulations deal with the placement of emergency exit doors, the proximity of combustible materials, and other safety factors. Four additional fire and safety requirements are important when designing a computer installation:

- An effective early warning system that sounds an audible alarm.
- An adequate fire extinguishing system. This can be an expensive Halon or carbon dioxide flooding system, more modest hand-held fire extinguishers, or a combination of systems.

- Air conditioning and other ducts designed to minimize the spread of fire.
- Clearly marked, unobstructed power-off systems.

For more information, see the Security section of Chapter 14.

Acoustics and Lighting

The most significant acoustics and lighting considerations are the adequate dispersal of noisy hardware components, the use of sound-absorbing materials in the computer room, the avoidance of direct sunlight, and a provision for emergency lighting. Noise isolation is becoming less relevant as vendors develop increasingly noisefree components.

Environment

Environmental considerations address air quality, temperature, and humidity control. The following environmental factors are important:

- The computer room air conditioning system should be under the exclusive control of the computer room. Sharing with other areas such as data entry can lead to problems caused by uncomfortable personnel changing air conditioning settings or shutting the system off entirely.
- The computer room air conditioning system should not be connected to the computer room power console. Air conditioning will be lost if the console is accidently disabled or shut down.
- Air conditioning units with appropriate Btu ratings should be selected. Btu ratings are influenced by projected machine loading (i.e., intensity of use), the number of people normally present in the computer room, the presence of glass walls and door openings, and the degree to which fresh air is inducted into the computer room.
- The optimal computer room environment consists of temperatures of 69° to 75°F and humidity of 45 to 55 percent. These figures are based on the requirements of general-purpose main frames. The air conditioning and humidity needs of some mini- and microcomputers are less stringent because they are specifically designed for use in adverse environmental conditions.
- Equipment that monitors temperature and humidity should be used. It should be connected to buzzers and visual warning systems that alert computer room personnel when environmental limits are exceeded.

- Effective air filtration and circulation must take place at all times. This necessitates frequent air conditioning filter changes and proper underfloor ducting.
- Optimal environmental conditions for the storage of tapes and disks are somewhat more liberal than conditions for hardware components. Tapes can be safely stored at temperatures of 40° to 90°F and at 20 to 80 percent humidity. Disks can be kept at 60° to 90°F with humidity ranging between 10 and 80 percent.

Furniture and Decor

Computer room furniture should be simple, clean, and functional. Clutter should not be allowed. Chairs should be covered with non-static material, and at least one telephone is mandatory.

Site Preparation Schedule

The sequence of events leading to the installation of hardware components begins approximately 1 year prior to installation. The following must be accomplished at that time:

- Determine machine components required and review hardware and software orders. One year is the average lead time required to receive some expensive items such as CPUs. Therefore, the ordering process should not begin later than 1 year prior to the planned installation date.
- Determine site location and prepare a preliminary machine room layout. Depending on the site and on the desired configuration, construction of a computer room can take up to a year. Therefore, the process should begin early in the installation cycle.
- Review all major aspects of the planned installation with the vendor's installation planning representatives and your own organization's construction staff. Major difficulties in the installation plan should be identified early enough to enable changes in the plan if problems are encountered.
- Identify security provisions and extraordinary restrictions. Unusual requirements that can cause site preparation problems should be identified early so that their resolution can be factored into site planning activities.
- Develop preliminary delivery schedules for air conditioning systems, power, and other major components. This will enable the timely ordering of these critical items.

Delivery and installation schedules of all major components should be reviewed 6 months prior to installation. If changes are needed, they should be made at this time. The computer room layout should be finalized and approved no later than 4 months prior to installation. This provides enough time for cables and other supporting components to be ordered.

The site preparation scenario for the last month prior to installation should be as follows:

- *One month.* Equipment-moving logistics are now developed. Details on who delivers what to which dock should be worked out and appropriate provisions made to store and install the equipment.
- *Two weeks.* Cables should be delivered and installed.
- *One week.* All air conditioning, power, and other support systems should now be in working order in anticipation of component deliveries.

The installation is now prepared for delivery day. Although problems can still develop, careful adherence to preparation schedules will reduce the probability of major crises.

Discussion Questions

1. What major changes in the operations environment have occurred over the past 20 years?
2. Describe each of the five major production functions performed by operations.
3. What is the role of operations in software support, standards development, and documentation control?
4. Why is the participation of operations important in the development of application systems? What activities should this participation include?
5. What are the major planning responsibilities of operations?
6. Describe a typical operations department organization structure for a medium-to-large computer installation. How may this organization differ when computing resources are decentralized?

7. Describe three important site planning considerations.
8. Identify the major site planning activities and decisions that must take place one year, six months, and one month prior to hardware installation.

13

AUDITING THE EDP FUNCTION

This chapter discusses the principles of EDP auditing and the methods by which EDP costs can be allocated. Two facets of EDP are subject to audit: the management of the EDP function and the quality of application systems.

The management audit attempts to answer the questions, "Are we doing the right work?" and "How well are we doing the work?" It is a wide-ranging evaluation of EDP management that is almost invariably performed by outside consultants who enjoy the confidence of top management. The systems audit examines the quality of individual systems and the controls that influence them. It may be performed independently or it may be part of a management audit, or of a financial audit performed by a firm of certified public accountants. The descriptions of management and systems audits are followed by a discussion of how audits are actually conducted.

Cost allocation, though it is not a topic that may be immediately connected in the reader's mind with EDP auditing, is also included in this chapter because cost allocation, a pivotal aspect of EDP management control, is a major consideration of the management audit.

EDP MANAGEMENT AUDIT

A management audit of the EDP department addresses management control, resource allocation, operations and technology management, and project management. Each of these areas is critical to the overall success of the EDP function and represents the most important aspects of an EDP manager's job. Each of these audit areas is described next.

Management Control

Proper management control of the EDP function requires two mechanisms: a financial reporting system and a link between the providers of EDP services (i.e., the EDP department) and the users of those services (i.e., the user community). The purpose of the financial reporting system is to compare actual EDP costs and expenditures against budget. It enables corporate management to monitor the EDP manager's success at staying within budget. The skill with which budgetary constraints are followed may not necessarily be a sign of how well EDP is managed. However, it indicates the effectiveness with which the EDP manager is able to predict his or her needs and accomplishments, an important management skill. A continuing inability to deliver promised products within budget destroys the credibility of EDP. Virtually all organizations have financial reporting systems. Therefore, the EDP management audit is more likely to focus on the effectiveness with which budgets are met than simply on the existence of a financial reporting mechanism.

The second aspect of management control is the establishment of a link between EDP and the user community that attempts to approximate the value of EDP services to the user. It consists of a method for allocating EDP costs. This can be done in a direct fashion by charging individual users for EDP services, or it can be done indirectly by defining EDP as an overhead activity.

The most common unit of measure for estimating the value of EDP is the dollar amount users are willing to pay for EDP services. Although this is normally in budget dollars rather than real dollars, it should reflect expenditures users would make if they were to purchase EDP services from outside sources. However, unless the EDP department is a profit center, the amount charged for services should cover costs but should not include profit. The linkage between EDP and the user is very tenuous if EDP is viewed as an overhead function. The relationship becomes subjective and is based on satisfaction rather than on a user's willingness to spend part of a budget on EDP services. Cost allocation is discussed in detail later in the chapter.

Resource Allocation

The allocation of EDP resources is a key management function and is a reflection of the priorities established for the EDP department in the long-range plan. The factors influencing the setting of priorities are extensively discussed in Chapter 2. The management audit should focus on how closely resource allocation follows the EDP plan and how well it accommodates the changing needs of the host organization. The ability to adhere to a plan can be positive or it can be negative. On the positive side it can indicate effective planning that successfully predicts future needs and effectively reflects EDP's ability to follow a long-range strategy. On the negative side, slavishly following a plan can be a sign of inflexible attitudes toward the changing needs of the organization. After all, the objective is not necessarily to follow a plan but to perform the EDP function in the best interests of the organization.

If the organization has a long-range EDP plan, it is relatively easy to compare the resource allocation projected in the plan to actual allocation. It is much more difficult to gauge the sensitivity of EDP to changing user needs. Answers to the following questions provide an indication of how effectively the EDP department allocates resources:

- Is resource allocation sensitive to the organization's changing financial position? For example, in periods of belt-tightening, does EDP cooperate in postponing or canceling marginal projects?
- Is resource allocation congruent with commitments already made? That is, does resource allocation reflect the intention to honor current commitments or is there a large degree of juggling in order to keep everyone happy?
- Does the commitment of resources to various projects appear reasonable in amount and in quality?
- Do the major EDP applications to which resources are allocated represent cost-effective solutions to important business problems?
- Is resource allocation congruent with organization goals?
- Is the EDP project development "portfolio" balanced between high-risk and low-risk applications? (Also see the Project Risk section of Chapter 2.)
- Are all appropriate levels of personnel involved in the resource allocation process, or is allocation done simply by management fiat? Unless project-level personnel, as well as managers, are consulted, a serious gap can result between expectations and reality.
- Has EDP been successful in developing systems within promised resource constraints? This can be determined by examining project history data.
- How do users feel about the ability of EDP to meet its commitments? Although this is a highly subjective topic, overwhelmingly positive or overwhelmingly negative comments are probably an accurate indication of EDP's success in this area.
- Does management interface on a day-to-day basis in resource allocation? If projects are mandated, changed, or abandoned with little

attention to continuity, EDP is clearly not in a position to control its commitments or its allocation of resources. Therefore, ineffective resource allocation may be a management rather than an EDP problem.

These questions can be answered by interviewing top management, users, and EDP staff, as well as by reviewing appropriate documentation.

Project Management

The project management dimension of the management audit attempts to determine the effectiveness with which EDP projects are managed. The most important prerequisite for high marks in project management is the presence of and adherence to formal procedures for planning and monitoring project activities. These must include the following:

- The use of project-control techniques such as critical path (CP) analysis and Gantt charts.
- A clear definition of project responsibilities.
- Regular status meetings and reports.
- Schedules and work plans, complete with milestones and resource requirements.
- A uniform method for measuring progress and adherence to plan.
- A mechanism for correcting schedule slippages and undesirable changes in project direction.
- Procedures for performing a postimplementation audit.

After the presence (or absence) of these procedures is established, the degree of effectiveness with which they are used must be determined. It is altogether too easy to follow the *letter* but not the *spirit* of project-control techniques. The best way to probe the spirit aspect is to check project-control documentation for accuracy, timeliness, and reasonableness. Sloppy estimates, carelessly set (and unmet) deadlines, unrealistic milestones, and an overly mechanical (i.e., thoughtless) approach indicate poor project management, regardless of how formal and structured the process appears to be.

Project leaders and team members should be extensively interviewed to gauge their commitment to good project management. Do people take deadlines seriously? Is anyone ever fired for not meeting deadlines? Are salary increases at least partly influenced by on-schedule performance? Are project managers trained in modern project management techniques? Are postimplementation audits carried out? Is good project management rewarded?

For specific information on project management principles and methodology, see Chapter 4.

Technology and Operations Management

The purpose of this aspect of the management audit is twofold: to determine the effectiveness with which data-processing technology is used by the EDP department in the solution of business problems, and to determine the degree to which the day-to-day functioning of EDP operations is satisfactory to the user community.

Technology. The technology part of the audit can only be performed by specialists. Generalists are quite useless here; they can only cause misleading conclusions and inaccurate judgments. Before an auditor is selected for this part of the management audit, a careful assessment of both his or her practical and theoretical experience must be made. Without practical experience, the auditor cannot assess the real-life limitations of the technology and the constraints frequently imposed by circumstance. For example, the unimaginative use of sophisticated technology may be the result of poor performance of the technology or restrictive organizational constraints rather than underutilization by the EDP department. Theoretical knowledge is also important. Without a firm understanding of the potentials of the technology, the degree to which it has been exploited in a specific situation is difficult to determine.

The first step in the technology audit is to verify the accuracy of the installation's hardware-software inventory. Although such an inventory is an indispensable part of operations documentation, it is lacking or inaccurate in many installations. This can (and usually does) result in the proliferation of purchased and in-house software whose functions overlap. It also leads to the underutilization of existing hardware.

The next step is to become sufficiently familiar with the business problems addressed by current and planned application systems to identify alternate technologies (if any) that can be used. The problems of primary software in supporting business applications must also be examined and alternate approaches identified.

Finally, installation technical personnel must be interviewed. This helps determine the extent to which technical staff is aware of the problems and potentials of current technology. The interviews should cover both the technology currently used at that specific site and people's knowledge of other technology available in the marketplace.

Operations Management. An audit of computer operations centers on three essential areas: performance, personnel, and procedures. Operation performance is measured by the following:

- Turnaround time for the production of on-request reports (if those reports have already been programmed).
- The amount of rerun time as a percentage of total run time (to the extent that reruns are due to operator error).
- The utilization of hardware and software components (e.g., how effectively does job scheduling utilize computing resources?).
- User satisfaction with system timeliness, accuracy, and data delivery (to the extent that these factors are operational rather than inherent in the design of the application system).

The effectiveness of personnel management in the operations section is analyzed by traditional productivity measures such as the amount of time lost due to absenteeism. In addition, the success of the operations manager in securing attractive career paths, quality training, and good salaries for his or her people is an important measure of the manager's effectiveness.

Operations procedures are analyzed for their effectiveness in providing backup, recovery, and security. They are described in greater detail in the Systems Audit section and Chapter 12.

SYSTEMS AUDIT

The focus of the systems audit is on eight key types of control that affect the quality, security, and auditability of application systems:

- System controls
- Program library controls
- Program controls
- Remote job entry (RJE) controls
- Batch controls
- Program execution controls
- User security controls
- Programmer security controls

Following is a description of each.

System Controls

System controls address the quality, integrity, and auditability of the system. They are not program or function specific. System controls include features that prevent undesirable events from occurring and alert system users to potential problems. Major system controls include the following:

- Complete, accurate, high-quality documentation.
- Performance of the system according to its stated specifications.
- Sufficient independence of individual components to ensure that failure of a single component does not endanger the entire system.
- Clear, logical, modular data flow, including:
  —Modularity of function.
  —Independent controls imbedded in each system.
  —Protection of individual components from contamination by errors occurring in other components.
- Feedback of all important events, particularly variances between actual and expected performance (e.g., error conditions and unauthorized accesses).
- Independent processes to check behavior, particularly computation of data for control purposes (e.g., record counts and hash totals).
- Passage to users of only those resources required to do the user's assigned function (the rule of least possible privilege).
- Logging of all system resource usage with adequate reference to the external environment (e.g., who does what, where, when, and under what conditions).
- Audit trails that enable program and file changes to be traced back to their point of origin.

Program Library Controls

Library controls support the integrity of application and software libraries. These controls include the following:

- Only one person should control and monitor changes to a program library.
- All changes to the library should be authorized by management.
- All changes to the library should be journalized as to event, content, and authority.
- Contents of the library should be known to at least two people (e.g., developer and user, operations and user).

- Actual contents of the library should be reconciled to expected contents on a regular basis.
- An audit trail should enable a load module to be unambiguously related to its associated source module.
- Procedures should exist to maintain a tie between different versions of a program, its documentation, and its test results.
- Libraries of specifications, procedures, and documentation should be recorded on structured and responsive media (e.g., magnetic) with appropriate update capabilities.

Programming Controls

Programming controls are standards and guidelines that encourage the effective, efficient development of application programs. They include the following:

- A program should be limited in size and scope or be composed of modules that are limited in size and scope (e.g., 50 verbs, 5 pages of source code, 52K bytes of object code).
- A program should be limited in complexity. It should employ limited control structures (e.g., SEQUENCE, IF-THEN-ELSE, DO-WHILE).
- A program should be predictable in result, use, or effect. That is, it must be rigorously specified and obvious in its intent.
- Volatile data (e.g., code tables) should not be "hard coded" into a program. The reasons for this are threefold: so that such data do not obscure the program's intent; so that the program can avoid contamination by its own data; and so that the program does not require recompilation when the data change.
- Program specifications should be complete. Of particular importance is the inclusion of:
  —Anticipated output.
  —Anticipated response to errors.
  —Test data.
  —Descriptions of all interfaces between a program and its environment.
- A program must pass to other programs only those resources (data or processes) that are consistent with its specifications. To the extent that the resource to be delivered is variable, mechanisms must be included to permit a very limited number of people to control the resources that are passed.
- A program must log all communications (event and content, stim-

ulus and response) between it and other processes in its environment (users, the operating system, access software, the data-base management system).

- All communications between a process and its environment should contain enough redundancy (e.g., parity bits, longitudinal redundancy checks, hash totals, acknowledgments, and confirmations) to enable the receiving process to recognize that data have been lost, added, or modified; to fix accountability; and to facilitate corrective action.
- A program or procedure must record the event of its own use, with reference to the user, unless another process in its environment, such as the operating system, does so for it.

Remote Job Entry (RJE) Controls

RJE controls are needed to maintain the security and integrity of the entry process for jobs submitted from a remote terminal. The following rules should be followed:

- All jobs should be properly identified with the submitter.
- Output should be returned only to the individual indicated as the output recipient.
- All resources used or consumed should be journaled and properly accounted for.

Batch Controls

Batch controls are designed to ensure proper control over the batch-processing environment. Major batch controls that should be examined during a system audit are the following:

- Identification of all jobs with both the end user and the person actually submitting the job (this may be accomplished by some combination of naming conventions, job ID, installation accounting routines, and administrative procedures).
- Restriction of jobs to data required to perform its function (this restriction can be implemented via data-set passwords or appropriate installation or application code).
- Automated journaling using job accounting software to track resources used by a job, including CPU time, I/O capacity, and data. These journal records should be reconciled to expectation.

Program Execution Controls

These are controls applied at program execution time:

- A production program should never be executed by its author. Exceptions to this rule should be limited to cases where the data are local and exclusive to the user, as in personal computing or testing. In either case, access control must be adequate to ensure that the conditions for the exception are met.
- Both the author and the user of a program should be notified of its failure or abnormal termination.
- Core dumps and other data associated with the failure of a production program should not be indiscriminately circulated to programmers for problem resolution because such material may contain confidential information from data files.

User Security Controls

User security addresses the security requirements that should normally be imposed on the interaction between users and their application systems. The following rules should be followed:

- A separation of responsibility should exist. Specifically, one person in the user department should not have the power to both authorize and implement, originate and authorize, or initiate and approve changes to sensitive files.
- Users should have access to a system at a limited, documented number of points. That is, unrestricted entry into a system at any point in the processing cycle should not be allowed.
- The most sensitive 1 to 10 percent of accounts and transactions should be periodically audited for accuracy.
- A random 0.1 percent of accounts, transactions, and activity should be periodically audited.
- The user should not have access to a resource and the records for controlling that resource. For example, stock clerks should not be allowed to modify inventory programs.
- Access by individuals in the user area should be restricted to resources and functions minimally required to perform the job (the rule of least possible privilege).

Programmer Security Controls

Programmer security rules have a direct impact on the integrity of application systems. They consist of the following:

- Procedure should exist for enforcing adherence to rules, standards, and conventions. Such procedures should be sufficiently rigorous to make variances obvious to management.
- Procedures should exist for requiring and recording acceptances and authorizations by users and by systems development management.
- Procedures should exist for maintaining the integrity of module and version names.
- Procedures should exist for maintaining a record of the creation and maintenance of all programs.
- Procedures should exist for reconciling programs to specifications. These should include program testing, independent reviews, and structured walkthroughs.
- Procedures should exist for reconciling resources consumed (e.g., programmer time, computer time) with expectations.

PERFORMING THE AUDIT

This section describes the organizational aspects and methodology of EDP auditing. In addition, it identifies the documentation needed to successfully conduct the audit.

Organizational Aspects

EDP management audits are almost always conducted by outside consultants. Systems audits may be performed by an internal audit staff or by outside consultants. The internal audit staff can do an adequate job performing a systems audit because systems audits have a relatively high technical content and a relatively low political content. The overall quality of EDP management is not judged, although, of course, the findings of the audit reflect the success with which EDP is managed.

A successful EDP management audit on the other hand, is difficult to conduct by internal auditors. Unlike the systems audit, the EDP management audit is almost always mandated by the highest levels of management. Therefore, the politics of the situation are extremely sensitive and repercussions of the audit may reverberate throughout the organization. Another reason outside consultants are better suited to conduct a management audit is that internal auditors generally have less contact with other companies. This reduces their perspective in making the rather subjective judgments management audits inevitably require.

To establish the proper framework within which a management or a systems audit can take place, the following three prerequisites must be met:

- Appropriate terms of reference between the auditor, the audited, and the individuals who hired the auditor must be established. These terms of reference include:
  —Agreement on the scope, work plan, limitations, and deliverables of the audit.
  —Honest explanations to the organization being audited of what is being audited, how, and for what purpose.
  —Official introductions to all key individuals who must participate in the audit.
- Sufficient notice must be given to the groups and individuals who are expected to provide documentation and who will be interviewed by the auditors, because the task of organizing the materials needed by auditors is frequently time consuming and laborious. Therefore, vacation and work schedules must be considered in planning interviews.
- Background material on the company, including organization charts, annual reports, and other general information, must be provided (and studied) prior to detailed analysis. This is particularly important for EDP management audits.

Audit Methodology

All audits are conducted through the use of interviews, surveys, observations, and reviews of documentation. Each of these techniques is described next.

Interviews. Interviews are essential for both management and system audits. The truest measure of how well the EDP function or a specific system is working is derived by speaking with people who pay for EDP, who use it, and who participate in its development and operation. Naturally, interviews must be conducted with skill, discretion, and a degree of skepticism: people's attitudes, likes, and dislikes will color their perceptions of how well systems perform and how effectively these systems address business problems. Interviews should be conducted with the following:

- Top management (management audits only). This provides an indication of how well EDP has been tuned in to corporate goals and how successful it has been in selling itself to top management.

- User management, particularly if users are directly charged for EDP services. The person who pays the bills is, in the final analysis, the best arbiter of system effectiveness.
- System users. People who work with the system on a day-to-day basis are in the best position to evaluate ease of use, data integrity, and the degree to which a system provides useful information.
- EDP staff. Information gleaned from these interviews permits an evaluation of how closely project management techniques are followed, how data processors feel about their management and their company, and how alert the department is to new technological developments. Interviews with EDP people are also important because:
—Documentation can rarely be trusted or fully understood without discussions with people charged with maintaining the system or performing the function being evaluated.
—An integral part of evaluating a system or a series of procedures is an understanding of the context within which development and growth took place. Oral history is sometimes the most effective way to gain this knowledge.

Surveys. Surveys supplement interviews. They are helpful in the following ways:

- Surveys help the auditors focus on important issues. A strong response by many people to a particular question or issue indicates that interviews with survey participants should cover those areas.
- Surveys provide anonymity to respondents. Therefore, a greater degree of candor can be expected from surveys than from face-to-face interviews.
- Surveys statistically "prove" the strength or unanimity of concern for various issues. This makes it easier to sell management on the need to focus attention on those issues.

Despite the usefulness of surveys, particularly when performing EDP management audits, care must be taken to ensure that questions are phrased objectively, that specific types of responses are not encouraged, and that survey results are properly interpreted. Questions that are vague, confusing, or loaded can make survey results misleading and counterproductive. Objective interpretation of survey results is likewise important.

Observation. This can be one of the most reliable tools of a skilled auditor. Documentation and interviews frequently tell us only how a function is supposed to be performed. Attending a program walkthrough or observing I/O control procedures is often more revealing than reading the standards manual or interviewing people. The major drawback of observation is that the act of observing sometimes changes the nature of the phenomenon being observed. This is particularly true when the observed are aware of what the observer is looking for. Observation is performed to best advantage when it is done subtly and when the desired response is not obvious to the people being observed.

Review of documentation. No audit can be performed without an extensive review of documentation. This not only enables us to learn about the systems being audited but provides an indication of the skill and thoroughness with which documentation activities are performed. Despite its importance, documentation should never be accepted at face value without verifying its accuracy. In many installations, documentation is out-of-date, inadequate, and inconsistent. Therefore, it rarely presents an accurate picture of how a system actually works or how a function is performed.

The following are specific types of documentation that may be reviewed as part of an audit:

- Systems documentation. This includes functional specifications, overviews, and the basic architecture of the system.
- Organizational memos and status reports. These reflect the interactions that took place between system users and system developers and impart an understanding of the quality of that interaction.
- Program documentation. Documentation for specific programs should be selectively reviewed for completeness and for an understanding of how programs are constructed. Of specific interest is consistency of format and consistency of technique (e.g., consistent use of structured programming).
- Operations documentation. This enables us to understand the production environment within which the system operates. As with other types of documentation, it also provides clues to the quality of work being performed and the quality of the interaction among operations personnel, users, and development staff.

Following is a checklist of documentation that may be required to conduct a successful system or management audit. The material may be found in systems, programming, operations, and user documentation, as well as in memo files and policy manuals.

- Organization structure and description.
- Job titles and descriptions.
- User instructions.

- Control and access restrictions.
- Operations logs and manuals.
- Retention, protection, and backup policies and procedures.
- Equipment maintenance records.
- I/O control instructions.
- Program maintenance controls.
- Request procedures and history.
- The long-range plan.
- Budget statistics and descriptions.
- A list of users and applications.
- Hardware-software inventory.
- Standards manuals.
- Billing algorithms.
- Meter logs.
- Job run schedules.
- SYSGEN listings.
- Run logs.
- Past audit reports and reviews.
- Correspondence and memos.
- Status reports.

EDP COST ALLOCATION

Allocation Philosophies

The allocation of EDP costs represents the link between the buyer of EDP services (i.e., the user) and the provider of those services (i.e., the EDP department). The type of link that is chosen and the mechanism used to implement it will have an important bearing on the relationships between the user and EDP.

The two basic cost allocation philosophies are overhead and chargeout. If EDP expenses are defined as overhead, they are absorbed by the company as a whole. EDP joins heat, electricity, building maintenance, and other items that are absorbed by each department in equal or proportional measure. This implies a cost-center philosophy, because no revenues are received from users. Chargeout, on the other hand, is a system whereby users are billed according to their use of EDP resources. Subsets of the chargeout philosophy are partial chargeout, under which all EDP costs are billed to users and other costs are absorbed as overhead; and full chargeout, under which all EDP costs are billed to users.

With the chargeout philosophy, a direct tie is established between specific EDP users and the cost of services provided to these users. Even though EDP is not normally expected to earn a profit, the chargeout basis of cost allocation implies that EDP is a profit center. That is, it incurs expenses and receives revenues on the basis of the services offered.

Chargeout can provide more direct incentives for the accountability of both the user and the provider of EDP services. The user is accountable because she or he must spend part of the budget on EDP and must, therefore, monitor expenses carefully. Departments that pay for EDP services are unlikely to be profligate in their use of EDP. The EDP department is accountable because users tend to be more demanding when they must pay for EDP out of their own budgets. This forces the EDP department to operate more efficiently. The difficulty is that EDP expenditures are buried in departmental budgets under chargeout and are less visible to upper management. Therefore, abuses at the department level are more difficult to monitor.

The choice of EDP cost allocation philosophies is determined by the maturity of the EDP department and its users, by organizational issues, and by the types of applications the organization wishes to develop. These factors may change over time. Therefore, a cost allocation philosophy that is appropriate at one stage of a company's development may not be appropriate in another stage.

In general, overhead is appropriate for a company with little experience in EDP and chargeout is appropriate for companies with extensive experience with EDP. The following key questions should be asked when selecting a cost allocation philosophy. To the extent that these questions can be answered in the affirmative, a chargeout philosophy should be used.

- *Management Awareness.*
  —Are major opportunities for computer applications known and understood by users and management?
  —Are users knowledgeable about the costs and limitations of computers?

  These questions deal with the user's ability to rationally select computer services. To the extent that users are inexperienced, they should rely on EDP and upper management, rather than departmental budget considerations, to play the leading role in the selection of application development priorities.
- *Organizational Issues.*
  —What is the operating philosophy of the company; are decision-making and control highly decentralized?
  —Are the development and operation of major EDP systems usu-

ally justified strictly on the basis of departmental advantage rather than overall company benefit?

Organizational issues are important. A centralized decision-making style and considerations of long-term corporate benefit versus short-term departmental payoffs tend to encourage an overhead approach to cost allocation.

- *Management control*

  —Does user involvement in EDP provide sufficient checks and balances over the management of the EDP function? (Conversely, is close attention by top management required?)

  —Are outside services readily available and can their prices be compared with internal EDP costs?

Management issues address accountability and comparability. Overhead cost allocation tends to make EDP less accountable to users but more accountable to upper management. It also complicates the task of comparing the cost of in-house services against the price of those same services purchased externally.

Following is a summary of advantages of each cost-allocation philosophy.

Advantages of Overhead

- The cost-allocation mechanism is simple and cheap because, in fact, there is no cost-allocation mechanism. EDP costs are absorbed without regard to resource consumption by specific departments.

- EDP costs are readily obvious because they are not hidden in departmental budgets. This may make EDP more accountable to upper management.

- The striving for efficiency in EDP is not affected by the rationale that if users are willing to pay for the service (no matter how bad it is) that's all that matters.

- Barriers of expense and short-term profitability are not as likely to prevent the development of useful applications.

- EDP is insulated from budget cuts imposed on user departments. This is important because it allows major development projects to proceed in spite of temporary budget fluctuations.

Advantages of Chargeout

- It enables users to apply a meaningful cost-benefit analysis to their EDP systems.

- It provides a useful map which identifies how much users pay for EDP services.
- Comparisons between in-house and outside EDP services can be made.
- Gives users a powerful stake in their systems because they are paying the bills.
- It provides an economic basis for resource allocation by the user, including the cancellation of marginal systems.

In actual practice, the benefits of each philosophy are ultimately dependent on the circumstances surrounding the specific situation. EDP accountability may be enhanced by attention by upper management, or, conversely, it may be enhanced more through attention by users; efficiency is not necessarily increased, or decreased, through the existence of a pseudomarket mechanism; and the insulation of EDP from budget cuts may not be an unalloyed benefit—after all, EDP must be subjected to the same fiscal discipline as other company functions.

Allocation Mechanisms

Once a decision has been made on which cost-allocation philosophy is most suitable for the company, a workable mechanism must be developed to perform the cost allocation. This mechanism is used for billing only under a chargeout philosophy. However, it may also be used internally by EDP for control purposes, even when EDP is considered an overhead expense.

Either full or partial chargeout can be used. Under full chargeout, all EDP costs are allocated to users. Partial chargeout implies that some costs are allocated and others are absorbed by the EDP organization. Partial chargeout is commonly used when computer operations costs are allocated to users but system development costs are absorbed. Expenses to be charged can be based on resource utilization estimates, transaction processing volumes, or on actual resource usage.

Utilization estimates, once established, are the easiest to use: a fixed cost is charged to the user each month regardless of the actual expenditures of machine and people resources for the system. This is the most insensitive allocation method because it does not reflect usage fluctuations, which are a part of every EDP operation. It also does nothing to influence the efficiency with which the user interfaces with the system because there is little incentive to provide good data that minimize reruns. The only virtue of fixed utilization estimates, other than simplicity, is the predictability of costs to the user.

Another method of cost allocation is based on volume usage. That is, costs are allocated to users in proportion to monthly transaction volumes. This is a more accurate reflection of actual resource consumption than utilization estimates. However, it too is simplistic because low volumes do not always reflect low resource usage and high volumes do not always reflect high usage (e.g., a low transaction volume update may consume immense resources if extensive master file searches take place). Despite these shortcomings, the volume method has the advantage of simplicity. Volumes are easy to track and represent a very argument-proof billing formula.

The most comprehensive method of cost allocation is actual resource usage. All hardware and software components are included in usage formulas and billings vary from month to month depending on the volumes and on the operations environment extant at the time jobs are run. Each hardware component is assigned its own billing rate and the use of each component is monitored by using job accounting software. The advantage of actual usage is comprehensiveness and accuracy. The disadvantages are its great complexity and variability. It is difficult to implement and maintain and is even more difficult to explain to users.

Determining Billing Rates

When using the actual usage allocation method, billing rates for various components are established by capitalizing their costs over their useful life. For example, a $50,000 fixed-head direct-access device that is amortized over 5 years must be charged out at $10,000 per year. If the storage capacity of such a device is 100 million bytes, the "rental" is one hundredth of one cent ($0.0001) per byte per year.[1] Therefore, a user whose master file occupies 50M bytes is charged $5,000 per year. Temporary use of work space is billed out according to the length of time it is used.

Overhead EDP expenses such as air conditioning, power, support personnel, and management can be factored into the rates assigned hardware components. Thus, indirect as well as direct costs can be covered. The costs of designing, programming, and maintaining systems, if billed to users, are usually covered by charging separately for those services on an hourly basis.

In summary, the name of the game is to decide how much of the

---

[1] Cost per byte is used here for simplicity; cost per track is a more common yardstick.

EDP budget is to be charged to users and to then develop billing algorithms and hourly personnel rates, if appropriate, that result in a payback of the desired expenses.

Characteristics of an Effective Chargeout Policy

The following features are part of any effective chargeout policy:

- *Accuracy:* The policy should be a realistic reflection of resource usage.
- *Repeatability:* Billings should not differ widely for similar amounts of processing.
- *Understandability:* The method of collecting job accounting data and assigning rates and costs should be explainable to users in straightforward English.
- *Comparability:* The rates and costs of internal EDP should be stated in or at least be translatable into terms that can be compared to those available from outside vendors.

If an actual usage system is used the following are also important:

- A data-collection mechanism must exist to capture job accounting data while jobs are being processed.
- A formula for allocating the cost of resources used to process a job must be devised.
- Rates for each hardware resource must be established.

Discussion Questions

1. What is an EDP management audit? How does it differ from an EDP system audit?
2. Identify the four areas an EDP management audit should cover.
3. What questions should be posed to evaluate the effectiveness of EDP resource allocation? Project management?
4. Describe the purpose of the technology and operations management portion of the audit.
5. Identify the eight key types of controls a systems audit should review. Describe three of these controls, and discuss their importance.

6. Why are consultants frequently used to perform audits?
7. Describe the techniques employed in performing audits, and identify documentation that must be reviewed.
8. What is the difference between chargeout and overhead cost allocation philosophies? Under what circumstances is each used?
9. Discuss the advantages and disadvantages of billing schemes based on estimates, processing volumes, and actual resource usage. Which is the most comprehensive?
10. How are billing rates commonly established?

14

PRIVACY AND SECURITY

This chapter discusses the issues of privacy and security as they relate to data processing. It defines privacy concepts, describes the current and potential impact of privacy laws on EDP systems, identifies major considerations of computer security, and suggests an approach to the development of effective privacy and security programs.

Privacy and security are related but not synonymous. Privacy addresses the use of data about individuals. Security is about the accidental or intentional theft, modification, or destruction of data. Although breaches of security may, in fact, compromise privacy, they may also be unrelated to privacy. For example, the theft of a mailing list stored on magnetic tape is a result of poor security and may compromise the privacy of individuals on that list. But the destruction of the tape, also a breach of security, does not necessarily have privacy ramifications.

PRIVACY: CONCEPTS AND LAWS

Privacy addresses the right of individuals to control the use of personal information contained in computer systems. It is not relevant to data aggregations or the "anonymous" use of personal data. That is, privacy concepts do not apply to the use of statistical information, regardless of how personal or sensitive that information may be on an individual level. The key issue is whether an individual can be linked to specific data.

Privacy laws that affect computer systems include the Federal Privacy Act of 1974, the Federal Financial Privacy Act, the Fair Credit Reporting Act, and a flurry of state legislation passed in the last several years. Generally, these laws cover credit data, financial information, and data in government data banks. However, as privacy concerns gain momentum, legislation will cover an increasingly broad range of data centers. Insurance companies, banks, hospitals, and mailing list providers, if they are not already affected, will become increasingly vulnerable to privacy legislation.

Regardless of which data banks fall within the purview of privacy laws, seven basic principles govern the concept of privacy in an EDP context. All seven must be present if EDP privacy is to be treated in a comprehensive fashion. These principles are described next.

Notification

The individual must be notified of the existence of a data bank or file containing information about him or her. Notification need not take place if the presence of the information is obvious, for example, an individual with a bank checking account should realize that information about him is carried in that bank's computer systems. However, the individual must be notified if the data are used in a nonroutine fashion. In the bank example, the person should be notified if the data are used for any purposes not related to processing checking transactions or other bank business.

Access

The access concept gives individuals the right to inspect the contents of records containing information about them, know the sources of this information, and know the identity of nonroutine data recipients. An example of nonroutine data recipients may be government agencies that subpoena bank records for individuals.

Correction

The right of correction gives the individual the opportunity to correct wrong information and, in case of conflict, to include a statement of disagreement in the file. The statement of disagreement serves as a record of the individual's side of the conflict.

Control

The right of control enables the individual to accomplish the following objectives:

- Consent to the collection and use of data.
- Consent to the disclosure of data, particularly to nonroutine

sources and across national borders (the latter is of particular importance with reference to government data banks containing information on aliens).

- Limit the collection of political and religious information. This may be an important privacy safeguard for people who believe they are the subject of unjustified surveillance by government agencies such as the FBI or the CIA.

Relevancy

Relevancy ensures that data are collected and used only for the purposes for which the data bank or system was designed. Data that are not relevant cannot be collected, and data that are collected cannot be used for purposes irrelevant to the original intent.

Data Management

The data-management principle mandates effective organizational and technical mechanisms for complying with privacy laws. It addresses the classification of data into appropriate categories reflecting privacy considerations, the accuracy of data, and the protection of data from unauthorized access and physical destruction.

Redress

Privacy protection is meaningless without the existence of legal remedies. These generally include the following:

- The right to get an injunction prohibiting use or dissemination of disputed data until the privacy issue under contention has been resolved.
- Penalties that discourage the abuse of privacy.
- The right to bring civil suit against parties alleged to have violated privacy statutes.

Examples in the Law

Following are specific examples of how one privacy law addresses the privacy concepts just described. The quotations are taken from Chapter 479, Section 4 of the Minnesota Privacy Act, which regulates the use of data about individuals by state agencies.

- *Notification:* "Agencies . . . must publish an annual notice of the existence and nature of each record system covered by the Act and make reasonable efforts to advise individuals of the fact that their records had been disclosed to others pursuant to compulsory legal process."

- *Access:* "An individual . . . shall be informed of the content and meaning of the data recorded about him or shown the data without any charge to him."
- *Correction:* "An individual shall have the right to contest the accuracy and completeness of data about him . . . . Data in dispute shall not be disclosed except under conditions of demonstrated need and then only if the individual's statement of disagreement is included with the disclosed data."
- *Control and relevancy:* "Agencies must limit the collection and retention of information about people to that which is relevant to agency purposes and functions."
- *Data Management:* "Agencies must . . . establish rules of conduct for those involved in the design, development, operation or maintenance of a record-keeping system and must establish safeguards to ensure security and confidentiality."

The concept of redress is illustrated by the Federal Privacy Act of 1974, which provides for fines and injunctions against parties in violation of the law.

IMPACT OF PRIVACY LEGISLATION

Current privacy legislation mostly affects government agencies, holders of credit information, and financial institutions. The Federal Privacy Act of 1974, as well as some state laws, regulates the use of data on individuals by government agencies. The Federal Financial Privacy Act requires notification when government agencies seek records on individuals from financial institutions. The Fair Credit Reporting Act, and various state laws affect the way credit information is used.

All indications are that privacy concerns will increase rather than diminish. The next logical step is the broadening of legislation to cover heretofore excluded areas of the private sector. In addition, increased control can be expected over institutions that have already been affected. The following organizations will experience the greatest impact over the next several years:

- Government agencies.

- Sellers of mailing lists.
- Financial institutions.
- Credit agencies.
- Insurance companies.
- Universities.
- Health care organizations.
- Retail establishments that issue credit cards.
- Other organizations that use or sell sensitive personal data.

System design and operation will have to change to accommodate privacy considerations. Following are the factors that require the most attention.

Notification

Procedures may need to be developed in the future for notifying each individual on file, and each new individual thereafter, of the existence of data. This may involve very substantial mailing costs.

Access and Change Requests

After the passage of legislation, large private and public data banks containing sensitive data on individuals could be deluged with requests to examine and change records. This will require the following:

- Effective clerical and mailing procedures to process requests.
- File design that facilitates the access and updating of records with a greater frequency than would be necessary in the absence of privacy legislation.
- Efficient access and update software.
- Comprehensive logging facilities for data usage and access.
- Provisions for lengthy statements of disagreement linked to the records of individuals.

Security

In the absence of privacy legislation, damages resulting from the theft or loss of data are borne almost entirely by the organization losing the data. Although the loss of computer data through poor security has resulted in some litigation, this has not been a common phenomenon. However, when legislation enables the subjects of data to seek damages if their data have been destroyed or stolen, security becomes important not only for protecting the data center but for avoiding lawsuits. Therefore, security takes on added importance.

Use of Identifiers

The use of social security numbers as personal identifiers in some computer systems may be questionable. People are becoming increasingly sensitive about providing social security numbers and are being supported by court decisions. The Massachusetts Supreme Court recently ruled, for example, that a qualified driver cannot be denied a driver's license for refusing to divulge his social security number to the state.

Although the use of social security numbers appears to be reasonable for systems such as payroll, it is questionable in cases where people outside the firm are expected to volunteer this information.

Privacy Impact Statements

Governments may, in future, demand analyses of how systems that manipulate large data banks with personal information could potentially affect privacy. These analyses may become analogous to environmental impact statements currently required before certain types of land development can take place.

Costs

Following are some of the potential costs private and public organizations may need to incur in order to comply with privacy legislation:

- Design costs associated with developing access, change, and notification procedures.
- Analysis costs for developing privacy impact statements.
- Costs of additional hardware and software needed to implement access, change, and notification procedures.
- Clerical, mailing, and telephone costs.
- Site security devices, such as badge readers.
- Salaries and extra personnel that may be needed to resolve privacy disputes and process requests from the public.

Approximations of total costs for complying with privacy legislation cannot be developed with any degree of accuracy at this time. The details of forthcoming laws will determine the costs of compliance. Figures as high as $1.5 billion have appeared in data-processing journals, but these estimates are largely self-serving because they were developed by traditional opponents of privacy legislation (e.g., credit agencies, financial institutions, and mailing list sellers).

IMPLEMENTING A PRIVACY PROGRAM

The development of EDP privacy programs for organizations potentially affected by privacy legislation should begin before such legislation goes into effect. Legislatures will not necessarily provide sufficient lead time for firms to develop adequate privacy programs; after all, politicians are not always sensitive to the difficulties regulated organizations face in complying with new laws.

The following steps can be taken even before detailed information is available on pending legislation:

- Write a policy statement that explains privacy concepts and alerts all departments, particularly EDP, to the possibility of forthcoming legislation. Regardless of the firm's opinion of privacy legislation, a strong commitment must be made at this time to comply voluntarily. Otherwise, employees will have the impression that management is only paying lip service to privacy concerns.
- Identify the manual and computer systems that may be affected by privacy legislation. The most likely candidates are systems that carry information about individuals outside the organization. However, payroll, personnel, and other systems containing information about employees may also be affected, particularly if data contained in them is sent to banks and other outside organizations.
- Insist on an assessment of each new computer system's potential vulnerability to privacy legislation. Although no vulnerability will be found in most cases, attention to this subject by computer people will increase their awareness of privacy issues. The privacy assessment should be incorporated into the EDP department's standards.
- Conduct an advertising campaign through internal newsletters and memos to make employees aware of privacy issues.

If these actions are taken, compliance with privacy legislation, when it arrives, will be less traumatic.

SECURITY

Security in an EDP context concerns the protection of EDP resources from unauthorized access, modification, or destruction. Both intentional and accidental breaches of security should be addressed in an effective security program.

Security is important because of the central (and expensive) role EDP systems now play in the life of major organizations. In some firms, notably insurance companies and banks, EDP systems do not merely reflect or support major business activities; they *are* the systems themselves. A case in point: check processing in banks using magnetic information character recognition (MICR) readers represents the actual business process as well as the computer system.

What are the biggest areas of concern? Recent studies have shown that over 50 percent of estimated dollar losses result from data-entry errors, computer program malfunctions, and operations failures. Other important causes of loss are, in order of importance, embezzlement, fire, disgruntled employees, water damage, and, lastly, the 1960s phenomena—bombings and other sabotage.

If these estimates are accurate, the biggest emphasis in computer security should be placed on developing effective controls and procedures, particularly with respect to backup, recovery, and fraud protection. The importance of site access security and protection against acts of God should rank a close second.

Controls and Procedures

Controls and procedures are described in detail in Chapter 13. System design features that support effective controls and procedures are described in Chapter 7. The following guidelines are of particular importance in affording security protection:

- Separation of responsibilities:
  - —Between operations and maintenance functions.
  - —Between critical applications.
- Program version control including:
  - —Attention to program hash totals.
  - —Existence of only one production version of any program.
- Backup and recovery through the use of:
  - —Appropriate software.
  - —Duplication and off-site physical storage of critical files and library tapes.
  - —Record and file level protection against unauthorized updating of data.
- An auditable record of:
  - —Production program changes.
  - —Data file changes.

- Identification and authorization procedures including:
  —ID and password checking routines.
  —Logging facilities that record both successful and unsuccessful accesses into important computer systems.
- Data control of:
  —Input (source document-transaction record reconciliation).
  —Processing (run-to-run totals and other internal system controls).
  —Output (appropriate statistics reflecting file update activities).

Site Access Security

Site access security consists of protection against unauthorized access to a computer site, hardware components, and storage media such as tapes and disks. Access security is commonly achieved through the use of the following techniques:

- *Surveillance.* This consists of using guards or receptionists, usually equipped with television monitors, to check the identity of persons entering the computer room. Surveillance has the advantages of enabling instant response to security breaches but also has a major drawback: the ease with which clever intruders invariably bluff guards by posing as telephone repairmen, janitors, employees, and other "authorized" personnel.

- *Closed-Circuit Television.* Television cameras may be placed at strategic locations to enable surveillance from a guard station. This is an extremely common security device and is effective if camera coverage is comprehensive and if the people that monitor the action are alert (which is not always the case). A photo-ID system is a sophisticated adjunct to closed-circuit television. It provides a split-screen projection of an ID card photograph on a TV screen alongside the actual image of the card bearer's face. This considerably reduces the recognition problems inherent in using either technique by itself.

- *Security Cards.* These are wallet-sized cards with machine-readable identification numbers encoded on a magnetic strip. Upon insertion into a badge reader, the numbers on the card are transmitted to a computer that checks a file of authorized ID's. This is a relatively inexpensive way of protecting the installation. However, security cards can be easily stolen and are sometimes loaned to unauthorized persons.

- *Locks.* A wide variety of door-locking mechanisms are available. They run the gamut from ordinary, and rather ineffective, tumbler locks that are key operated, to sophisticated push-button and combination locks. The latter may be equipped with a timer, a small "memory," and may be connected to alarm systems. This discourages fiddling with the combination for inordinately long periods of time and can record the number of times entry was attempted.

- *Light Beams.* Ultraviolet, infrared, or laser beams can be used in conjunction with alarms to alert guards to the presence of intruders. This technique is normally used only during shut-down periods when no one is allowed entry into the computer room without first deactivating the alarm system.

- *Hand Geometry.* This method works by digitizing fingerprint patterns and/or hand sizes and shapes of persons authorized to enter the installation. The decoding device "reads" the hands or fingerprints of a person requesting entry and compares his characteristics against those on file. Hand geometry, or handprint analysis as the technique is sometimes called, is presently very expensive.

- *Secure Storage.* The use of safes, vaults, and limited-access storage rooms helps protect data files and program libraries from theft and physical destruction. Safes and vaults are rated by the government according to the degree of fire protection they afford. Therefore, an appropriate choice can be made for safekeeping master files, encryption formulas and other sensitive data. Limited-access storage rooms are generally used for storing less sensitive data.

Eavesdropping and tapping into a computer network's telecommunication lines is also a potentially important access issue, although the latter is not as relevant to most installations as is physical site access. Eavesdropping can be done by retrieving core and file dumps that were carelessly disposed of, observing terminal sign-on procedures and then using a valid ID to break into the system. Photographing the contents of terminal screens and computer reports, either on site or from a distance using a powerful telescopic lens has also been used. Such photography can successfully capture printed material as far as 200 feet away without the use of super-expensive professional equipment.

The best protection against eavesdropping is to shred sensitive printed matter, keep terminals with access to sensitive information away from windows or areas of high public traffic, and be security conscious when designing access to application systems.

Tapping into telecommunication lines can be active or passive. Active tapping results in sending one's own data across the lines or modifying the sender's data. Passive tapping, which is more common, consists of recording and translating messages coming across lines. It is generally accomplished by using a tape recorder to record the phone signals and then translating those signals into readable form by connecting with an appropriate modem and terminal. Tapping generally results in the capture of large amounts of useless information within which a few nuggets may be buried. Therefore, simpler, more direct, ways of stealing data are preferred. Where there is a danger of tapping, it can be made more difficult through the use of scramblers, cryptography, authenticity checking, and telephone line junction box security.

Scramblers are used to scramble analog signals. Cryptography encodes digital data on the sending end and decodes it on the receiving end. It is a complex, expensive process that is rarely used for commercial applications but is extensively practiced by the military and by the intelligence community. Authenticity checking consists of appending a different two- or three-digit code to each message. The code is based on data in previous messages, a combination of clock readout and the sender's ID, or some other algorithm. Authenticity checking is also expensive, but is useful only in preventing active tapping. Since tampering with phone junction boxes is a common tapping method, their placement in unobvious places, as well as the use of locks and alarms, may be a simple yet effective way of reducing the risk of taps.

Acts of God

Fire and flooding pose the greatest physical danger to a computer room. As indicated in the Site Planning section of Chapter 12, protection against acts of God begins with good site planning. The judicious placement and design of the computer installation, including appropriate fire detection and extinguishing systems, is crucial. Carefully developed procedures, thorough training, and strict enforcement is also important. Specifically:

- Smoking or the storage of flammable materials in the computer room must be prohibited.
- Hand-operated fire extinguishers must be immediately available and regularly tested. Operations personnel must be trained in their use.
- Emergency procedures and safety measures must be clearly posted and must be learned by all personnel.

Finally, precautions must be taken to enable recovery if a fire or flood does occur. These include off-site storage of key files and program libraries, the use of fireproof safes and vaults to store important files and documents, and a contingency plan for re-creating master files and using emergency backup facilities.

Developing an Effective Security Program

The purpose of any security program is to reduce the probability and cost of loss to an acceptable level and to ensure adequate recovery potential. This means that the costs of security must be weighed against the potential costs of loss. Elaborate cost-benefit analyses are performed by large, security-conscious organizations such as banks, insurance companies, military installations, and government agencies. However, the concepts of analyzing loss potential and determining cost-effective prevention can be used by smaller installations as well. These concepts include the following:

- Identification of critical components such as source documents, master files, application systems, hardware, and manual procedures.
- Analysis of the types of security problems that can damage, destroy, or otherwise affect those components. Some files, for example, may be vulnerable to unauthorized access. Others may be vulnerable to inadvertent destruction because of frequent updating or complex operations procedures.
- The assignment of risk potentials to each security threat. "High," "low," and "medium" are usually sufficient categories and can be represented by ratios. For example, a high risk may be "one in a hundred"; medium risk may be "one in a thousand"; low risk may be "one in ten thousand."
- An approximation of the cost to the organization of each security failure. This can be fairly accurately done for the destruction of hardware components. It is very difficult to make similar determinations for the loss of data needed to operate the business.
- Identification of security measures that can have a positive effect on reducing the threat to critical system components.
- An approximation of costs for each security measure. This should include operating and maintenance costs, as well as initial or start-up costs.
- Comparison of cost of prevention with the cost and probability of loss. This is, of necessity, an inexact process. However, it must be attempted if reasonable trade-offs are to be determined.

Summary

The most effective security program is one that implements the most obvious, and usually least expensive, solutions. These are the following:

- Adequate computer site operational and program maintenance controls.
- Reasonable fire and water protection.
- Serious enforcement by management.

The latter is critical. Regardless of how elaborate and expensive a security program is, it requires commitment from management in order to work on a day-to-day basis. Without enforcement, the program exists only in theory and will ultimately fail to achieve its objectives.

Discussion Questions

1. What is the difference between privacy and security? How are they related?
2. What institutions are presently affected by EDP privacy legislation or may be affected in the near future?
3. Identify and describe the seven basic principles that define the concept of privacy in an EDP context.
4. Discuss the potential impact of privacy legislation on system design and operation.
5. What controls and procedures are particularly important in affording security for computer systems?
6. Describe some common techniques of computer installation access security.
7. How is a cost-effective security program developed?

15

THE FUTURE OF EDP MANAGEMENT

What do the 1980s hold in store for the data-processing manager? How will her or his job change? How can the EDP manager prepare to deal effectively with the future? Following is a discussion of major trends in EDP and their impact on the EDP manager's job.

INCREASING USER AND PUBLIC SOPHISTICATION

Computers have been widely used in business, government, and the academic community for well over 20 years. The number of computer science courses taught in colleges, universities, trade schools, high schools, and even grade schools, has proliferated. General public awareness of computer technology has greatly increased through newspaper and magazine articles, the use of personal computing, and through direct contact people have with computer systems in their daily lives.

This has resulted in a dramatic increase of public awareness and knowledge of computers. It has spawned a generation of young, college-educated managers that are not awed by the mystique and "black magic" of computer technology. More and more, the computer is considered a tool that is subject to the same controls and limitations as any other tool. It is used and respected not in its own right but only to the extent that it is capable of solving real-world business problems. In addition, the public at large is concerned about the potential abuses and the accuracy of computer-stored data on which so many important decisions are based. People are worried about the effect computers will have on their right to privacy and the degree to which public and private organizations are capable of storing personal data in an accurate fashion. This concern has manifested itself in the passage of federal and state legislation directed at curbing po-

310

tential abuses. The liability that system developers must shoulder is also becoming an increasingly important issue.

What impact does this have on the data-processing manager's job? He or she must become more candid with users and must become a better professional manager. Users are much less likely to tolerate cost overruns, schedules that are not met, and misinterpreted user requirements than they were in the past. Therefore, the EDP manager must learn to better control resources. He or she must also develop increased sensitivity to business problem solutions vis-a-vis the technical aspects of computer technology that are "transparent" to end users. Application programmers and systems analysts must be taught to be more concerned with user needs than with showing off their technical skills. In addition, privacy issues must be considered when developing new systems. The EDP manager must develop a greater sense of responsibility to the public, as well as to the immediate users.

DISTRIBUTION OF COMPUTING POWER, RESOURCES, AND CONTROL

Spectacular progress has been made in telecommunications, minicomputers, and microprocessor technology. This progress has been reflected in a reduction of hardware costs and, coupled with the development of user-oriented computer languages and design techniques, has served to push computing resources into every nook and cranny of the organization. Individual users have more opportunity to own and control computing power than ever before.

Distributed processing is having a profound effect on the management of the EDP function. The power of the EDP manager to control all corporate EDP resources has been diluted and there appears to be a movement back to a decentralized environment. However, there is a countertrend that further complicates the EDP manager's role: the increasing need to maintain corporate data with a minimum of redundancy and inconsistency across systems. This calls for greater central control. How can these conflicting demands be satisfied? The top EDP executive must retain control of systems and data of corporate-wide importance, but must be willing to surrender day-to-day operational responsibility for applications and computing resources that are most effectively placed in the user's jurisdiction. Most large organizations will evolve into a network of minicomputers and microprocessors connected to a large, central supercomputer. The main frame will be the major repository of large data bases to which terminals, minis, and micros will have access. Sometimes this access will be direct, for example, between a terminal and the central computer. But sometimes it will be indirect, that is, through a mini that carries a subset of the main-frame data.

Systems development work will be split between the central facility and the user's own EDP personnel. The user may develop reports and display screens and may design files and processing systems that have little or no impact on the rest of the organization. The central staff will develop large data bases that affect the entire organization and will offer assistance to users that have their own hardware but lack technical expertise.

Although this environment offers great opportunities to develop flexible, useful, systems, loss of central control is also fraught with problems. Hardware and software components can become incompatible. Standards development and enforcement becomes extremely difficult. Effective networking is hard to accomplish. The danger of data redundancy and inconsistency increases because of the data's wide distribution. And duplication of hardware, software, and personnel reappears, just as it did during the earlier decentralization phase experienced by many organizations.

The challenge to the EDP manager of the future is to function effectively within the distributed environment. She or he must assume a greater role as a compromiser and political arbiter between the sometimes conflicting data, hardware, and software needs of various departments. The manager must learn to function in a consultative capacity, because a high degree of network synchronization and compatibility between various systems must be achieved through persuasion rather than by management fiat. The EDP manager's responsibility will probably not decline. But formal authority to determine and satisfy the organization's EDP needs may well become diluted.

Proliferation of Automated Development Tools

The increasing availability of automated productivity aids is altering the role of system development personnel. Programming machines, interactive program development tools, diagnostic aids, data dictionaries, and design tools are continuing to have a profound impact. Their use serves to standardize the development process but, by the same token, it removes programmers from the "bits and bytes" of systems development. Although interactive programming tools and diagnostic aids increase a programmer's knowledge by exposing the assembler language effects of high-level language instructions, most development tools tend to isolate the programmer from the machine.

This isolation has been continuing steadily since the early days of EDP. The programmer was once responsible for laboriously coding all the instructions needed to make a program work. He or she had to develop routines to multiply and divide because these instructions were unavailable on many machines. The programmer had to program-atically select a read-write channel through which to access a periph-eral device, perform read-write error tests, and buffer read-write op-erations to increase efficiency.

All of these and many other functions are now performed by mac-ros, subroutines, or by the hardware itself. In addition, large por-tions of application code can be generated for common functions by feeding a program generator the required parameters. File design optimization, which was once accomplished by reference to storage capacity tables, and the solution of tedious algorithms is now, in many cases, automated. Data dictionaries are used to store system attributes and generate data-base definitions.

The evolution of automated development techniques will accel-erate. The very large storage capacities and machine speeds needed to make some of the more complex tools attractive to users become less of a problem as computing power increases and costs decline. In addition, the use of development tools tends to stabilize the skill lev-els needed for systems development, which reduces personnel pres-sure on the EDP manager.

The proliferation of automated development tools means that the EDP manager must educate his or her staff to be receptive to in-creasing standardization and the use of new development methodol-ogies. He or she must also accept the fact that automation potentially increases the efficiency of the development process; therefore, users will demand shorter development cycles. At the same time, the EDP manager must fight the danger of users underestimating the impor-tance of accurate system definition "the first time" because of the in-creasing ease of making system changes after a system is implemented.

CONTINUED EXPLOSION OF TECHNOLOGY

The dramatic technological progress in EDP will continue, albeit without the disruptive generation-gap incompatibilities experienced in the 1960s and early 1970s. Progress in the coming decade will manifest itself in reduced hardware costs and increased hardware performance; the incorporation of more operating system, utility, and support functions in firmware; the continued sophistication of data-base management systems; an increasing ability of disparate compo-nents of a distributed network to talk to each other; the continued spread of minis, micros, teleprocessing capabilities, and personal computing; and the continued proliferation of the automated development tools and "user-friendly" software discussed previously.

The most obvious effect of the new technology on EDP management will be the need to stay technologically current. The EDP manager cannot be expected to master all the nuances of new technology. However, she or he must be alert to major shifts and must be aware of the impact of technology changes on the solution of business problems. This is particularly important with respect to changes in price-performance patterns: a technical approach that was infeasible from a cost standpoint yesterday may, in fact, be the least-cost alternative today.

Relations with vendors will become more complex. A distributed network of minicomputers, micros, communications terminals, and remote printers loosely connected to each other and to a central computer will usually necessitate working relationships with a variety of hardware, software, and communications vendors. This is in contrast to an environment that consists of large main-frame computers connected to a series of display terminals. The single-source EDP installation is largely a thing of the past.

Changes in technology will result in greater people versus hardware costs. Therefore, trade-offs between capital and labor will increasingly be settled in favor of greater capital investment. For example, more hardware and more productivity software will be acquired at the expense of hiring more programmers if such a substitution can be made. In addition, fixed, long-term personnel costs that result in the hiring of permanent in-house staff will be avoided in many instances by hiring consultants on a temporary basis.

Finally, because the supply of qualified technical people does not seem to be catching up to demand, EDP installations must continue to be very personnel conscious in their attitudes and policies. This will keep personnel turnover to a minimum and will enable the EDP manager to attract capable people.

CONCLUSION

Many changes will occur in EDP over the next decade. However, as in other human endeavors, "everything changes, everything remains the same." Behind the glitter and excitement of the technology one overwhelming fact will remain constant: systems development is an inexact affair filled with all the uncertainties, quirks, and contradictions people bring to their activities. The success or failure of systems will, in large measure, continue to be determined by the chemistry that exists between the user and the developer. The rapport, sensitivity, respect, and professionalism brought to bear on the task will far outweigh the technical details of how a system is constructed and how it works. Systems that are developed with the user in mind will succeed, even if they have significant technical limitations. Systems that are not designed with the user in mind will *not* succeed. It is the data-processing manager's job to ensure, by good example and by skill in managing the EDP function, that systems are designed, maintained, and operated with this principle in mind.

Discussion Questions

1. Discuss the impact of increasing public knowledge of computers on data processing management.
2. How will the distribution of computing power affect the data processing manager's control of the EDP function? How will his role change?
3. What must the EDP manager do to effectively use automated productivity tools?
4. What impact will recent technological trends have on EDP management?

Glossary

INTRODUCTION

The purpose of the glossary is to convey an understanding of how key terms are used in this book. Although some basic EDP terminology is included, the reader is assumed to be familiar with basic concepts. Terms that are used interchangeably are grouped together and given common definitions. They are also listed separately for reference purposes. A cross reference between acronyms and definitions is included following the definitions.

DEFINITIONS

Application, Application Software, Application System. Computer programs that directly address a business process such as preparing the payroll, managing inventory, processing customer orders, or paying suppliers.

Application Data. Data used in application systems.

Application Package. See *Package*.

Application Programming. The process of writing computer programs for an application system.

Application Software. See *Application*.

Application System. See *Application*.

Batch, Batch Processing, Batch Application. Refers to an application system that has one or more of the following characteristics:

- Makes little or no use of teleprocessing facilities to examine or directly update application data.
- Sorts transactions into a convenient sequence prior to processing.
- Processes one group of transactions through the entire system before processing the next group.
- Does not update applications master files on line.

- Is primarily used to generate large quantities of data in report or micro-form format.

Batch systems frequently have on-line subsystems or components.

Batch Application. See *Batch*.

Batch Processing. See *Batch*.

Blocking, Blocking Factor. The number of logical records in each physical record.

Blocking Factor. See *Blocking*.

Bursting. The process of separating a continuous form computer report into individual pages. This is done on a device called a burster.

Business Problem. The business requirements that an application system must address. For example, an automated order entry system may require the entry and validation of customer orders within 24 hours of receipt.

Central Processing Unit (CPU). The arithmetic, control unit, and working (main) memory of a computer system.

Client. The end user of computer services. It is used most often in reference to a customer of a consulting firm.

Company, Corporation, Firm, Host Organization. The organization within which or on whose behalf data processing activities take place. This can be a private company, a university, a government agency, or any other user of computing resources.

Computing Requirements. The computer hardware and software needed to run and maintain a set of application systems.

Core, Core Memory, Core Storage. Refers to computer memory. Although commonly used, these terms are outdated. They imply the use of magnetic core memory technology, which is obsolete.

Corporation. See *Company*.

CPU Cycle Time. The time required for a CPU to perform a specific, low-level function—usually the time required to read one main memory storage location.

CPU Cycles. The unit of measure representing the time required to execute a single program instruction. See also *CPU Cycle Time*.

Critical Path (CP). See *Critical Path Analysis*.

Critical Path Analysis, Critical Path (CP), Critical Path Method (CPM), Critical Path Network. A planning and management technique that uses a graphical format to depict the relationship between tasks and schedules. Its key result is the identification of the optimum sequence in which a series of tasks must be performed. Critical Path Analysis is performed by analyzing the time, resources, and dependencies required to complete each task in a project. This information is then analyzed manually or, more likely, by CPM software. It establishes the minimum time that the project can take by identifying the task sequence that is the longest (i.e., the critical path).

The Critical Path methodology is particularly useful for large, complex EDP system development projects. It is also commonly used to manage the construction of airplanes, buildings, and other structures requiring the performance of many dependent tasks.

CRT (Cathode Ray Tube). A visual display terminal which utilizes cathode ray technology. CRT and VDT are often used interchangeably. See also *VDT*.

Cycles. See *CPU Cycle Time.*

Data Base (DB). A collection of data that is logically organized to reflect the functional requirements and data interdependencies of one or more application systems. A data base is usually accessed and updated through the use of a Data Base Management System (DBMS).

Data Base Management System (DBMS). Software that provides the mechanism for loading, storing, updating, and accessing application data on a data base. It provides an interface between application programs and the data. A high-level user language is often provided by the DBMS for the end user. DBMS technology differs from conventional file storage and access techniques in that it provides data base descriptions and identifies relationships between fields, records, and files independently of the programs in the application systems.

Data Entry. The process of converting application data into machine readable form. An example is the entry of inventory withdrawals that are recorded on source documents into a terminal such as a CRT. In the early days of data processing, data entry was done by keypunching.

DBMS Application. An application system that utilizes a data base management system.

DBMS Software. All program products associated with data base management systems. This includes the DBMS itself, data dictionaries, data base design aids, data base query languages, and other supporting software.

Decision Support System. An application system designed primarily to produce information to support decision making. This is in contrast to transaction processing systems, which are designed primarily to produce tangible products such as payroll checks. An example of a decision support system is sales forecasting, which provides data for market planning.

Decollating. The process of separating multiple-copy computer printouts through the use of a decollator. This device accepts a printout and, by using a series of rollers and pinfeed mechanisms, automatically separates the carbon paper (if present) from the report and places each copy of the report in a separate stack.

Default Value. The value assumed by a field in a computer record if no specific value is entered. For example, if a data entry clerk enters nothing into a numeric field, the data entry system may assume a default of zero and zero fill the field prior to the next computer processing step.

Deliverable. The tangible product that results from the performance of EDP activities. This term is commonly used in project control to refer to the expected output from a specific set of tasks. Examples of EDP deliverables are a feasibility study, a completed system design, and fully tested computer programs.

Direct Access Device (DASD). A peripheral device used for the storage of data. It is characterized by a capacity to store large volumes of data and by its ability to access records directly without the need to read a file from the beginning. This contrasts with peripherals such as tape drives and card readers that can read and write records only sequentially. The most commonly used DASD are disc drives.

Distributed Data Processing (DDP), Distributed Processing. The distribution of logically related information processing functions over multiple, geographically separated computer systems. For example, an inventory management application with a centralized Inventory Master file may provide minicomputers located at individual warehouses with subsets of the main file for inquiry, updating, and local reporting purposes. DDP is also used to refer to the distribution of computing resources (machines, people, primary software, applications) to diverse organizational units. However, this usually implies some hardware, software, and/or managerial interconnection or coordination between systems. This feature differentiates distributed processing from decentralized environments common in the 1960s.

EAM Equipment, Electronic Accounting Machines. Electromechanical devices that preceded and overlapped the extensive use of first- and second-generation computers. EAMs performed mathematical calculations on data contained on punched cards, reformatted and repunched these cards where appropriate for further processing, performed card sorting, and printed accounting reports. The steps needed to do this were "programmed" by physically changing the wiring configuration on removable control panels.

EDP Manager. The highest ranking data processing executive in the organization. He or she has responsibility for most of its computing resources, including people, hardware, software, and application systems.

End User. The individual or organizational unit that is the primary recipient of the output of an application system. This term is synonymous with "user" unless the distinction between the ultimate, or end user, and an intermediate user is being made. (An intermediate user may be a programmer using interactive programming software.) See also *User*.

Execution Time. The CPU time required to process a program, job step, or job stream. It may also refer to the time required to execute an assembler language instruction.

Firm. See *Company*.

Firmware. Refers to any computer hardware component that incorporates program instructions traditionally associated with software. An example of firmware is a CPU or direct access device with built-in file accessing capabilities previously invoked only through the use of file access software such as IBM's Index Sequential Access Method (ISAM).

Functional Requirements. The needs a system must fulfill for its users. Functional requirements are stated in terms of system features, responsiveness, and capacity. For example, an order entry system may be required to perform a series of input data validations, may need a less-than-five-second response time on interactive data entry terminals, and may be required to process 20,000 orders per day from 10 locations. Although functional requirements are generally associated with application systems, they are also relevant to the establishment of specifications for hardware and primary software.

Gantt Chart. A horizontal bar chart depicting a plan for and progress toward the completion of a project. The left portion of the chart lists each project task and the right portion is subdivided into time periods. A bar is drawn across the chart for each project task from start date to completion date. It is then filled in or otherwise marked over time to track progress. Gantt charts are the most commonly used pictorial representations for the management of EDP projects. Unlike PERT or CPM, Gantt charts do not explicity depict the relationships between project tasks.

Hardware. The equipment used in the operation of computer systems. This includes, but is not restricted to, the CPU, tape drives, direct access devices, card readers, printers, terminals, modems, and control devices that enable the equipment to work together. Hardware also includes data entry devices that are not directly attached to a computer system, such as keypunch machines and card sorters.

Host Organization. See *Company*.

Host Program. The program that calls a subroutine.

Input/Output (I/O) Control. The part of the EDP organization that is responsible for ensuring the completeness of data input, if it is received in batch form, and the completeness of output, if it is produced in printed or microform format.

Integration Testing. See *System Testing*.

Intelligent Terminal. A computer terminal or peripheral device that contains logic and memory enabling it to perform processing tasks, such as data editing, without reference to a CPU. This intelligence may be invoked by programming the device or it can be an integral part of the hardware.

Internals. The program code in primary software. This term is frequently used to describe the skills a systems programmer needs to work with a specific software system, as in "knowledge of OS/MVT internals."

Job. A logical unit of work performed by the computer in the process of running an application system. A job usually consists of multiple programs or job steps.

Job Accounting, Job Accounting Software. Software that captures information on the use of computer system hardware components. This is done by monitoring CPU cycles, disk storage, tape mounts, print lines, and other data that reflect computing resources used by an application system each time it is run. Charges can be assigned to each unit of use and applied to the accounting data. Computer users can then be billed accordingly.

Job Control Language (JCL). A shorthand computer language that provides information to the operating system describing the jobs to be executed.

JCL includes the names of programs to be run, their sequence, the peripheral devices that are needed, files that are used by programs in the job, and variable data, such as dates needed for processing.

Job Step. A logical subunit of work performed by the computer in the process of running an application system. This can consist of one or more programs and, along with other related job steps, constitutes a job.

Justification. The positioning of data in a field, in a record, or in core storage such that significant digits (i.e., data that are not blank and not zero) are moved against either the right or left boundaries of the field. This can be done programmatically or by the data entry clerk. Alphabetic data are frequently left justified, and numeric data are almost always right justified.

Keying. The process of entering data on a keypunch or into a terminal. Usually refers to data entry of application data.

Large Scale Integration (LSI), Very Large Scale Integration (VLSI). The memory and circuit technology used in the most advanced modern computers. It is characterized by a very high degree of component miniaturization and very fast internal processing speeds. An LSI integrated circuit contains from 100 to 5,000 logic gates or 1,000 to 16,000 memory bits. A VLSI circuit contains at least 5,000 logic gates.

Machine Language Programming. The earliest and most primitive method of coding programs. It required the preparation of machine-readable instructions directly by the programmer instead of by translation through a compiler or assembler. Machine language is a first-level language, compared to assembly and compiler languages, which are, respectively, second and third level.

Machine Readable. Describes information that can be read directly by a computer or peripheral device. This commonly includes data on magnetic tapes, disk packs, and punched cards.

Macro. A series of program instructions imbedded in an application to perform input/output, housekeeping, and other commonly used functions. Macros, which are written in a special macro language, are generally used in assembly language programs. Macros differ from subroutines in that they are usually shorter and are assembled with the host program instead of being called from the program library at execution time.

Magnetic Information Character Recognition (MICR). The ability of a device to read standard-sized characters encoded with magnetic ink and to translate this information for computer processing. MICR readers are commonly used by banks to interpret account number, check number, and check amount.

Mainframe. A medium- or large-scale general-purpose computer that is normally used to run a variety of application systems. This term appears when a distinction is being made between minicomputers and the primary computer to which the minis are connected or on which they have some reliance.

Management Information System (MIS). Any fully or partially automated system that provides management with business information. In the context of this book, MIS refers to a large application system that usually has the following characteristics:

- Data collection, maintenance, and distribution take place across organizational boundaries. That is, system impact and use is not restricted to one department.

- The information generated by the system is used primarily for decision making rather than for transaction processing (see *Transaction Processing System* and *Decision Support System*).

- The system is used mainly by middle and top management to support strategic planning and policy making. Control of day-to-day business operations by supervisory personnel may be facilitated but is not the major purpose of an MIS.

- Data can be quickly and conveniently accessed by management. This can be done on line or through the expeditious production of reports.

Mass Storage. See *Direct Access Device*.

Mass Storage Device. See *Direct Access Device*.

Master File. A machine-readable file containing relatively permanent, slow changing reference data for an application system. An example is a customer file containing name, address, and financial information about each customer. The file changes only when customer information is changed, when new customers are added, or when inactive customers are deleted.

Memory, Main Memory, Core Memory, Core Storage. Storage for digital information inside a CPU. Memory contains programs that are executing and the primary software needed to control those programs. Application data that are currently being manipulated are also in memory at that time. *Note:* Although the terms *core storage* and *core memory* are commonly used, they describe a type of memory technology that is now obsolete.

Microcomputer. A computer consisting of a CPU and memory contained on a single silicon chip. At present, most microcomputers are used for a specific, limited set of functions. This is in contrast to general purpose computers with a full range of peripheral devices, large amounts of memory, and the capability to process a wide variety of applications.

Microform. Printed material stored in reduced size on a roll of film (microfilm) or on film strips (microfiche). Microform documents can be viewed on a special desktop device with a lighted screen on which a blow-up of the desired page is projected. Microform technology enables translation of machine-readable output, such as magnetic tapes, into microfilm or microfiche. This provides a convenient, space-saving, long-lasting alternative to paper reports.

Microprocessor. The CPU in a microcomputer.

Migration. Refers to the movement of application systems or software from the control of one operating system to another. Can also refer to a movement to new hardware. Migration frequently requires JCL changes, program modifications, and changes to run procedures.

Minicomputer. A general purpose electronic computer, usually third or fourth generation, which differs from a mainframe in one or more of the following respects:

- Physically smaller in size and considerably less expensive.

- Shorter word length (8 to 16 bits versus 32 to 36 bits for a mainframe).

- Higher tolerance of poor environmental conditions such as heat and cold.

- Dedicated to a single or limited number of applications.

- Accommodates a smaller range of languages, utilities, and application packages.

- Slower CPU cycle time and smaller memory capacity.

- More limited in the number and variety of peripherals and terminals that can be used with it.

The difference between minicomputers and mainframes is blurred and is becoming even more so with the advent of increasingly powerful minis. However, the operative difference is that minis are affordable by smaller businesses and by departments within an organization.

Modem (Modulator/Demodulator). A device that provides an interface between a communications terminal and a computer system. It converts analog telephone signals into digital signals, and vice versa.

Multiprocessing. The ability of modern computers to execute more than one program at one time. This can be done by a computer with multiple CPUs, in which case the process is simultaneous, or it can be done on a single CPU computer. In that case, processing appears simultaneous but is really done by executing small portions of each program serially. Multiprocessing is frequently referred to as multiprogramming.

Office Automation (OA). The application of computer technology to clerical, secretarial, and data delivery functions. The primary current thrust of OA is word processing. However, electronic mail, calendar management, image facsimile, voice store-and-forward and context searching are also becoming viable OA technologies. Electronic mail is the storage and transmission of messages and memos to each individual with a terminal; calendar management functions include tickler systems that actuate personnel schedules; image facsimile is the production of quality copy at a remote location by electronic communication; voice store-and-forward is the use of recorded voice messages to transmit variable information such as meeting schedules; context searching is the capability to search large narrative data files based on a variety of key words.

On-Line, On-Line Processing. Most commonly used to describe computer programs or systems that provide a user with immediate access to files through the use of teleprocessing facilities. On-line can also refer to the availability of a file or peripheral device for a batch system as in "two disk drives must be on-line to process the payroll application."

On-Line Application. An application system that utilizes on-line processing.

On-Line Processing. See *On-Line*.

On-Line Program. A computer program that has on-line processing capabilities.

Operating System. The software used to control execution of programs on the computer and to allocate resources to these programs.

Operations. The organizational unit within EDP that is responsible for operating computer systems. This includes keying applications data (if this is not a user function), providing users with system outputs, and performing appropriate control functions in support of these activities. Operations also frequently performs systems programming, teleprocessing support, and hardware/software resource planning.

Organization Method. The technique used to store records on a direct access storage device. Three basic techniques are used:

- *Sequential.* The storage of records in key sequence (e.g., by customer number).

- *Random.* The scattering of records throughout the file based on an algorithm applied to the record key (e.g., customer number transformed into a relative position indicator).

- *Index Sequential.* A combination of random and sequential storage in which a hierarchy of indices points to the portion of the file in which the record is located. Index sequential organization can be an efficient approach to storing data which requires a considerable amount of both random and sequential processing.

Package, Packaged Software, Packaged System. Primary software or a set of application programs that can be used in more than one installation without substantial modification of program code. This contrasts with custom systems developed exclusively and specifically for a single organization. Packages are usually acquired from hardware or commercial software vendors and are table driven, that is, make extensive use of tables and files that allow specialization to a specific environment without the need for extensive program changes.

Partitioned Data Base. A data base created in the form of nonredundant partitions connected to different processors. For example, an inventory data base may be partitioned into several pieces attached to minicomputers at different warehouses. Partitioned data bases are used in distributed processing.

Personal Computing. Computing activities performed by individuals in their own homes on their own computers. The advent of inexpensive home minicomputers has made personal computing by both hobbyists and professionals a fast-growing trend. Personal computing applications address tasks such as the monitoring of personal finances. However, they are also frequently used for recreation purposes, such as computer games.

Primary Software. Computer programs used to support the development, operation, and maintenance of application systems. Primary software includes operating systems, compilers, assemblers, sorts, and other utilities, as well as development aids, such as interactive programming software.

Procedure. A series of operations performed in a regular sequence to accomplish a stated purpose. Procedures may be manual or computerized. The latter are often referred to as "procs."

Program. An ordered series of instructions written in a programming language. If translated into object code, these instructions are potentially executable by the computer.

Program Evaluation and Review Technique (PERT). A project management planning and analysis tool that uses a graphic display (network) to show relationships between tasks that must be performed to accomplish an objective. It is virtually identical to CPM except that a statistical treatment of uncertainty in activity performance times is factored into PERT calculations.

Program Library. Computer programs in source or object form that are stored on machine readable media.

Program Testing. See *Unit Testing*.

Program View. The information a computer program under the control of a DBMS is given about the data base it accesses. Considerations of security often limit the information a program is allowed to process. For example, personnel system programs may be locked out of payroll information stored on the data base.

Pseudo Code. A shorthand form of program logic notation used by programmers as a preliminary step to program coding. Pseudo code is frequently used in a structured programming environment to develop major logic flows.

Quality Assurance (QA), Quality Control (QC). The process of ensuring that a computer program or system reflects the intention of its designers and can be successfully run in a production environment. QA also refers to checking computer outputs for correctness prior to delivery to end users.

Quality Control (QC). See *Quality Assurance*.

Real Time. The concept of returning the results of a computer process to a user quickly enough to take action. For example, the ability to update a customer file with orders and payments as they occur enables customer service personnel to accurately advise customers on their outstanding line of credit, even if the last order was placed only a few minutes before the inquiry. This is in contrast to a batch system in which the master file is updated only once a day and may, therefore, be an average of 12 hours behind actual orders and payments.

Replicated Data Base. A distributed data base that is created by copying all or part of a master data base and placing each copy at a different location within the distributed system. Local copies of the DB may then be used for inquiry and reporting purposes while file updates are restricted to the central version. Replicated data bases can also be used in multiple CPU, nondistributed systems.

Response Time. The time lapse between entry into and receipt of data from a computer system. Generally refers to the wait a terminal user experiences.

Schema. A complete description of all data elements, fields, records, and other components of a data base. This includes names, attribute, and relationship information.

Software. Generic term used to describe all computer programs. However, it most commonly refers to primary software. See also *Primary Software*.

Software Programming. See *System Programming*.

Source Code. Program code that appears in the computer language the programmer used to write the program. Source code is not executable by the computer. It must be translated into object code by the appropriate assembler or compiler.

Source Document. Document used to record information that will be keyed into a terminal, keypunch, or other device for keying purposes. Source documents are usually formatted to reflect keying sequence and are designed to encourage accurate, legible recording of each information field.

Standards. The rules under which analysts, programmers, computer operators, and other EDP personnel work. Standards usually cover, but are not necessarily limited to, documentation requirements, technical rules, operations procedures, systems development steps and deliverables, and user/EDP relationships.

Subroutine. A single-function computer program that performs a series of calculations or a task commonly needed throughout an installation. Subroutines are always used in conjunction with regular multi-function programs, are called by those programs at execution time, but are assembled or compiled apart from those programs. An example of a subroutine is a program that calculates future dates based on a start date plus a desired number of days.

Subschema. The description of a data base provided to an application program. This enables the program to access appropriate data base information and serves as a linkage to the DBMS. See also *Program View*.

SYSGEN Listing. A listing that is produced as a result of specializing operating system parameters to a specific installation. It reflects information about the devices, features, space allocations, and processing priorities defined to the operating system.

System. A collection of logically related hardware components and/or computer programs designed to fulfill a set of related functions. A system also includes the manual methods and procedures needed to support computer processing.

Systems Programming. Installation, update, and generation of operating systems and other software. Also includes the maintenance of primary software and the development of original code for same. This is usually done in a low-level language and frequently requires extensive knowledge of computer hardware components and primary software internals.

System Testing. The process of testing a set of components, usually computer programs, to ensure that they work correctly together. The key aspect of system testing lies in validating that the logic that controls the flow of applications data and system parameters from program to program has been properly designed and correctly programmed. System testing takes place after the completion of unit testing.

Tabulating (Tab) Equipment. See *EAM Equipment*.

Teleprocessing (T/P). Describes computer programs, hardware components, and systems utilizing technology that allows transmission of data between components via telephone lines.

Terminal. An input or output device located apart from a computer. This is usually a telecommunications device that enables a person to transmit data to and/or receive data from a computer system. Commonly used terminals are teletypewriters and cathode ray tubes (CRTs).

Theory X. The theory of management that expresses an essentially pessimistic view of people's attitudes toward work. It postulates that people will not work unless forced to, require close supervision, will exercise little creativity on the job, and have very little potential for change or growth.

Theory Y. The theory of management that expresses an essentially optimistic view of work behavior. It postulates that people naturally enjoy work, will, under the right circumstances, be creative and enthusiastic about their jobs, should be given considerable freedom to direct their own labors, and can grow to meet ever greater job challenges.

Transaction. A computer processable recording of an external event of interest to an application system. An example is a withdrawal of an item from inventory. Information about the withdrawal is recorded on the Inventory Transactions file and processed by the Inventory system.

Transaction File. A machine-readable file containing transactions. It is relatively transient and its contents change rapidly. For example, withdrawals of items from inventory may constitute a transaction file that is created each day, processed against the inventory master file, and erased after an appropriate retention period.

Transaction Processing System. An application system designed primarily to produce tangible products, such as payroll checks or customer bills. This is in contrast to systems used primarily for decision-making purposes. See also *Decision Support Systems.*

Transistor. The memory technology commonly used in second and early third generation computers. This technology improved processing speeds, lowered space and cooling requirements, and improved system reliability.

Tuning. The process of improving the performance of application programs, an operating system, or a DBMS. This is commonly done by making program modifications, redesigning files, and changing processing priorities.

Turnkey System. A packaged system that requires little or no modification before it can be used productively. For example, application packages are usually claimed by their vendors to be ready for use after installation-specific data have been provided via files, tables, and JCL.

Unit Record Equipment. Electromechanical devices that process punched cards. These include card readers, sorters, card punches, and keypunch machines.

Unit Testing. The process of testing individual computer programs or program modules without regard to their ability to interface with other programs. Unit testing takes place after program coding is completed and prior to the commencement of system or integration testing. Also called program testing.

User. Generic term referring to the individual or organizational unit that is the primary recipient of data from a computer system. For example, programmers are users of primary software, and the payroll department is the user of the payroll system. See also *End User*.

Utility. A computer program that supports the development or maintenance of application systems. Examples of commonly used utilities are sorts, formatted tape dumps, and file compare routines.

Vacuum Tube. Refers to the memory technology commonly used in the first generation of commercially available computers. This technology was characterized by the use of vacuum tubes for core storage, slow internal processing speeds, extensive space and cooling requirements, and relatively low hardware reliability.

VDT (Visual Display Terminal). A terminal resembling a television screen with a keyboard. VDTs are used to enter information into a computer and to perform on-line file inquiries.

Very Large Scale Integration (VLSI). See *Large Scale Integration (LSI)*.

Word Processing. The most commonly used office automation technology. It usually consists of a minicomputer with text processing capabilities that enables secretaries to produce, store, and modify documents. It may also include the ability to route documentation to printers at remote locations.

Zero Fill. The process of placing zeros in the unused left or right portion of a numeric field. Can also be used to fill out an entire numeric field if, for example, a default value of zeros has been specified.

ACRONYM CROSS REFERENCE

CP	Critical Path
CPM	Critical Path Method
CPU	Central Processing Unit
CRT	Cathode Ray Tube
DASD	Direct Access Device
DB	Data Base
DBMS	Data Base Management System
DDP	Distributed Data Processing
EAM	Electronic Accounting Machine
EDP	Electronic Data Processing
I/O	Input/Output
JCL	Job Control Language
LSI	Large Scale Integration
MICR	Magnetic Information Character Recognition
MIS	Management Information System
OA	Office Automation
QA	Quality Assurance
QC	Quality Control
T/P	Teleprocessing
VDT	Visual Display Terminal
VLSI	Very Large Scale Integration
WP	Word Processing

Index